The Needs of
Counsellors and Psychotherapists

Edited by
Ian Horton with Ved Varma

SAGE Publications
London • Thousand Oaks • New Delhi

Editorial arrangement © Ian Horton and Ved Varma, 1997
Chapter 1 © Ian Horton, 1997
Chapter 2 © Colin Feltham, 1997
Chapter 3 © Simon du Plock, 1997
Chapter 4 © Hazel Johns, 1997
Chapter 5 © Zack Eleftheriadou, 1997
Chapter 6 © Joyce Cramond, 1997
Chapter 7 © Alan Lidmila, 1997
Chapter 8 © Sue Wheeler, 1997
Chapter 9 © Michael Carroll, 1997
Chapter 10 © John McLeod, 1997
Chapter 11 © John Mellor-Clark and Michael Barkham, 1997
Chapter 12 © Rowan Bayne, 1997
Chapter 13 © Brian Thorne, 1997
Chapter 14 © Judith Baron, 1997
Chapter 15 © Cassie Cooper, 1997

First published 1997

SAGE Publications Ltd
6 Bonhill Street
London EC2A 4PU

SAGE Publications Inc.
2455 Teller Road
Thousand Oaks, California 91320

SAGE Publications India Pvt Ltd
32, M-Block Market
Greater Kailash – I
New Delhi 110 048

British Library Cataloguing in Publication data

A catalogue record for this book is available
from the British Library.

ISBN 0 7619 5298 5
ISBN 0 7619 5299 3 (pbk)

Library of Congress catalog card number 97–069230

Typeset by Mayhew Typesetting, Rhayader, Powys
Printed in Great Britain by The Cromwell Press Ltd,
Broughton Gifford, Melksham, Wiltshire

Contents

Editors and Contributors

The editors

Ian Horton is a Principal Lecturer in Counselling and Psychotherapy and Course Director of the Diploma/MA in Therapeutic Counselling/Psychotherapy at the University of East London. He is a UKRC Registered Independent Counsellor and a Fellow of BAC.

Ved Varma, PhD is now retired. He worked as an educational psychologist at the Tavistock Clinic, London, and in Richmond-upon-Thames and Brent.

The contributors

Judith Baron is Chief Executive of the British Association for Counselling. She is a Fellow of BAC.

Rowan Bayne, PhD is Senior Lecturer in Counselling and Psychology at the University of East London.

Michael Barkham, PhD is Senior Lecturer in Clinical Psychology, Deputy Director of the Psychological Therapies Research Centre at the University of Leeds and Honorary Consultant Clinical Psychologist with Leeds Community Mental Health Teaching Trust. He is Chair of the Standing Advisory Committee on Quality (Division of Clinical Psychology BPS).

Michael Carroll, PhD is Director of Counselling and Counsellor Training for Right Cavendish, London. He is a Chartered Counselling Psychologist and a Fellow of BAC.

Cassie Cooper is former Head of the Counselling and Advisory Service at the University of Westminster (Harrow Campus). She is Editor of the Newsletter of the Psychotherapy Section of the British Psychological Society. She is a Fellow of BAC and a UKCP Registered Psychotherapist.

Joyce Cramond was until recently Course Leader of the BSc (Hons) Therapeutic Counselling at Leeds Metropolitan University. She is now a Principal Clinical Psychologist at St. James's University Hospital, Leeds.

Emmy van Deurzen is professor in psychotherapy at Schiller International University and Director of the New School of Psychotherapy and Counselling, London. An honorary lecturer at Sheffield University, she is a past chair of UKCP, external relations officer to the European Association of Psychotherapy and founder of the Society for Existential Analysis.

Simon du Plock is Head of MA Programmes at the Regent's College School of Psychotherapy and Counselling, London. He is editor of the *Universities Psychotherapy Association Review* and co-editor of the *Journal of the Society for Existential Analysis*. He is a UKCP Registered Psychotherapist and Chartered Counselling Psychologist and was a founder member of Psychotherapists and Counsellors for Social Responsibility.

Zack Eleftheriadou is co-ordinator of Child and Family referrals at the Inter-Cultural Therapy Centre, Nafsiyat, and co-ordinator of the Cross-Cultural Counselling and Psychotherapy Certificate at the Regent's College School of Counselling and Psychotherapy. She is ex-chair of BAC Race and Cultural Education in Counselling Division, a Chartered Psychologist and UKCP Registered Psychotherapist.

Colin Feltham is a Senior Lecturer in Counselling and Head of the Counselling Development Unit at Sheffield Hallam University. He is an Accredited Counsellor and Fellow of BAC.

Hazel Johns is Senior Lecturer and Staff Tutor in Counselling and Applied Psychology and Head of the Counselling Education and Training Unit at the University of Bristol.

Alan Lidmila, PhD is a Lecturer in Psychotherapy on the MA in Psychoanalytic Psychotherapy at the Centre for Psychotherapeutic Studies, University of Sheffield. He is a member of the Universities Psychotherapy Association training sub-committee and was actively involved in UKCP 1987–96. He is a UKCP Registered Psychotherapist.

John McLeod, PhD is Professor of Counselling Studies and Head of the Department of Applied Social Studies at the University of Keele.

John Mellor-Clark is Evaluation Manager at the Psychological Therapies Research Centre, University of Leeds.

Brian Thorne is Professor and Director of Counselling at the University of East Anglia, Norwich and a Founder Member of the Norwich Centre. He is a UKRC Registered Independent Counsellor and Fellow of BAC and the College of Preceptors.

Sue Wheeler is a Senior Lecturer in Counselling and Course Leader of the Diploma/MA in Psychodynamic Counselling at the University of Birmingham. She is Co-Chair of the BAC Scheme for the Accreditation of Counsellor Training courses, a UKCP Registered Psychotherapist and BAC Accredited Counsellor.

Foreword

Emmy van Deurzen

Do counsellors and psychotherapists have needs? It seems a rather shocking suggestion. Are counsellors and psychotherapists not supposed to be above the satisfaction of personal needs? Are they not superhuman, giving generously, from unlimited resources to those who are in need?

Fortunately such idealized fantasies about counsellors and psychotherapists have long been corrected and have been replaced by realistic professional standards for training and practice. There is much reference in this book to those standards and the professional bodies that uphold them. This book could not have been written before this sanitization of the profession had been carried out. The editors should be congratulated on producing this book at this point when it has become so urgent to ask some fundamental questions that are not taken care of by professionalization.

The book takes us well beyond the fundamentals of standards and ethical codes. Some of its best chapters discuss the complex matters of social, cultural, intellectual and personal needs that have to be addressed in order to deal with clients competently.

Although some of the authors still hesitate to address the more personal needs of the counsellor and psychotherapist, the book will stimulate individual practitioners to wonder about their own multifarious needs. There is much up-to-date information in these pages, and embedded in it are numerous challenges to those who work in this field.

Behind all of these important matters there is one particularly pertinent question of needs that must be considered. It is one that is referred to in several chapters of the book and which is usually dealt with by providing trainees with an experience of personal psychotherapy or training analysis: the crucial matter of personal development and individual needs. The interplay between the personal and the professional is one of the most disturbing though also one of the most determining factors of success in this field. A striking piece of learning in my own career and in that of many of my supervisees and trainees has been that my work as a professional is constantly informed and limited by personal life experiences.

I remember with pangs of guilt and shame at my own limitations, how I had to come to terms with the realization that I was unfit to work with male clients during a period of my life when I was young and single and had personal needs for male attention and affection that were not satisfied in my private life and that would inevitably interfere with my professional work. Nowadays there are other needs of which clients may remind me: clients' stories of foreign holidays or other forms of leisure may trigger my own desire for such experiences. Clients' discoveries of new strengths or their struggles with hidden aspects of their own nature may inspire my own desire to take seriously some unheeded need to confront forgotten elements of existence.

Being a counsellor or a psychotherapist, in this sense, is about being eminently human and allowing ourselves to be reflective about our human needs, so as to become articulate about them as well as using them as a guide to our own actions. This should also allow us to remain or become increasingly self-critical and achieve a new humility about our personal ability to understand the complexities of life with which our clients are struggling.

Seeing our own needs reflected in our clients' dilemmas and conflicts should keep us alert and enhance our capacity for a healthy amount of doubt and self-doubt. Perhaps this constant reminder of our own and other people's needs through our daily confrontations with clients' preoccupations is one of the most valuable assets of being a psycho-therapist or counsellor.

If we can recognize this we may find ourselves able to conclude that in the final analysis the greatest need of counsellors and psychothera-pists is for our clients. Without them we would not just be out of a job, we would also miss out on an essential source of rejuvenation and self-improvement. It is well worth reflecting on how this in fact implies that we thrive on and need the distress of human life.

Sheffield
April 1997

Acknowledgements

I would like to thank Ved Varma for inviting me to edit this book with him. The book was his idea.

I see this book as the product of the collective efforts of the people who have written the chapters. I am delighted to have been able to work with them. I would like to thank the contributing authors and especially Emmy van Deurzen for kindly agreeing to write the Foreword.

I am most grateful to Susan Worsey, Commissioning Editor at Sage, for her warmth, encouragement and guidance and to my colleague, Rowan Bayne, for his advice and ever present support.

Once again I relied very heavily on Susamma Ajith. I appreciate her skill with wordprocessing and would like to thank her for her patience and calmness at such a busy time in the UEL Psychology Department office.

Ian Horton

1

The Needs of Counsellors and Psychotherapists

Ian Horton

Over the last decade public interest in counselling and psychotherapy has mushroomed. An increasing number of people train and work as counsellors or psychotherapists. The demand for their services continues to grow with more and more people turning to counsellors or psychotherapists to help them cope better with psychological problems and to live a more fulfilling life. However, although numerous books have been published on almost every aspect of counselling and psychotherapy, surprisingly little has been written about the needs of counsellors and psychotherapists themselves.

This book is about the people who offer psychotherapeutic services. It addresses the emotional, intellectual, behavioural, physical, social and professional needs of counsellors and psychotherapists. The aim is to identify and discuss what practitioners need in order to provide an effective service. It examines what they need not only to survive but thrive in what can be a deeply rewarding role, yet one that can also be personally and professionally isolating, frustrating and emotionally draining.

This book is written for anyone with an interest in psychological counselling and therapy: consumers or clients, employers of those who deliver the service, but more particularly, for anyone who works or aspires to work as a counsellor or psychotherapist. It seeks not only to reflect current knowledge and practice but also to influence trends and developments in the field.

This opening chapter will start by examining the issues around the meaning of the words used in the title of the book. The first issue concerns the ambiguous nature of the concept of needs and the second issue, possibly more contentious, is about the fact that the book seeks to address the needs of both counsellors and psychotherapists. The chapter will then go on to outline the rationale and structure of the book before discussing the need for ongoing professional development, which is implied but not explicitly addressed elsewhere in the book. The chapter will also present a general theory of the nature of professional work that can be applied to counselling and psychotherapy. It concludes by reflecting briefly on the need for counsellors and psychotherapists to become aware that it is possible to view the whole field of counselling and psychotherapy as having reached a 'critical state' that may fore-shadow decline or herald an exciting and more unified future. This theme re-emerges in various chapters throughout the book.

Meaning

It is tempting to skirt over the title of the book and assume that the words have an everyday meaning that will not be questioned. Perhaps I am raising an issue where none exists? Magee (1982: 49) discusses Popper's view that it is not necessary to define our terms before we can have a useful discussion. Defining terms can obscure clear thinking and lead to endless debate about the words themselves instead of about matters of substance. Yet counselling and psychotherapy, both for the client and therapist, is an individual and personal matter. No therapist and no theory or system has the 'right answer' to understanding human beings, nor the best way to help them with psychological problems. The meaning of words does matter. The problem of language and the meaning of concepts confounds understanding and often inhibits dialogue between adherents of the many and diverse psychotherapeutic approaches. Norcross and Grencavage (1990: 17) suggest that approach specific lan-guage 'encourages clinicians to wrap themselves in semantic cocoons from which they cannot escape and which others cannot penetrate'. I believe that any book which asserts that it is possible to discuss the generic needs of counselling and psychotherapy practitioners should at least make some attempt to identify the assumptions that underpin what it is trying to communicate. So at the risk of introducing issues that some readers may regard as irrelevant, I will examine briefly the concept of need and the decision to bring together the needs of both counsellors and psychotherapists.

Concept of need

The concept of need has been widely used in psychology yet it remains vague and ambiguous. The *Dictionary of Psychology* (Reber, 1985) has twenty-one entries related to the concept. Psychologists believe that some needs are instinctual and that some are learned. This raises a question about which needs are acquired and which are inherent. It seems apparent that what have been referred to as higher order needs (Maslow, 1987) such as achievement, cognitive and self-actualization needs are acquired, but some psychologists (for example, Salancik and Pfeffer, 1977) argue that even such basic needs as food, sex and safety may be in part socially conditioned. So where needs originate, how they develop and even what they mean or how they can be defined in a way that permits measurement remains an unanswered question, at least with any consensus.

Salancik and Pfeffer (1977) examine a need satisfaction model that has been used to understand job satisfaction and how people feel about their work. The model asserts that people have basic, relatively stable and identifiable attributes, including needs. It also posits that jobs have stable, identifiable sets of characteristics and that people will derive satisfaction from a job in which their individual needs are compatible with the characteristics of the job. This assumes a causal relationship in which people's attitudes and motivation towards a job are a result of the degree to which their needs are met by the characteristics of the job. However, Salancik and Pfeffer (1977) argue that the concept of need is defined inadequately and that this does not give people much credit for adaptability in the pursuit of job satisfaction. Furthermore, they suggest it is possible that job characteristics are social constructed realities and that people who like their work, for whatever reason, may attribute positive characteristics to their jobs as a consequence. Yet the concept of needs remains seductive. It offers a simple and easily expressed view of human behaviour. Perhaps the fact that the concept is ambiguous permits its use as an almost universal explanation of behaviour – although lacking any real scientific rigour. It does not seem possible to produce a systematic analysis of the needs of counsellors and psycho-therapists based on some form of empirical research that takes account of individual differences and the temporal and developmental nature of individual needs.

The needs discussed in this book represent the collective experience of leading academics, researchers and clinicians – in effect the needs are 'postulated by pundits' as Bradshaw (1972: 641) succinctly defined one valid measure of needs used by administrators and researchers in the context of social need. Bradshaw's taxonomy of (social) needs may provide a useful framework for defining the needs of counsellors and psychotherapists. It has four separate yet interrelated definitions which are adapted here.

1 *Normative need*. This is what the professional or expert counsellor or psychotherapist regards as the desirable or necessary standard. This is the category of need Bradshaw defines as 'postulated by pundits'. Obviously there can be no one consensual definition of normative need. In the field of counselling and psychotherapy there exist different sets of standards laid down by experts according to their professional body affiliation and espoused theoretical orientation. Nevertheless a close examination of, for example, the training requirements of BAC and UKCP reveals a remarkably high degree of common ground on what constitutes essential training needs. Normative standards also change as a result of developments in knowledge, research findings and the changing values of society. Such changes are illustrated in this book by

the inclusion of chapters on social responsibility, cultural differences, evaluating effectiveness, research and collaboration with colleagues. It is not so many years ago that these normative needs would not have been acknowledged.

2   *Felt need.* Bradshaw (1972: 642) regards this as an important component of any definition of need. Felt needs are what individuals think they want, but as Bradshaw points out, felt needs are 'limited by individual perception' and by subjective experience and represent an inadequate measure of 'real need'. Trainee therapists (and more experienced therapists) may be reluctant to expose what may feel like personal weaknesses or a lack of skill or knowledge. Other felt needs may be inappropriate in the context of the therapeutic relationship such as the need for friendship, sexual gratification or the need to feel important and significant to clients. Felt needs are not always expressed or openly discussed even in training or in supervision.

3   *Expressed need.* This is a felt need which is expressed. In this sense it is the easiest measure of need to obtain but not necessarily the most adequate. Trainee therapists may sometimes articulate their need to understand their clients and need to feel like an expert in how to help their clients. They often find it hard to tolerate ambiguity and not knowing and not being told by their supervisor or trainer what to do next with their clients.

4   *Comparative needs.* This measure of need is derived from studying the characteristics of good counselling and psychotherapy practice. It can apply to knowledge and skills, service provision, professional development and training. It can be seen as an attempt to standardize; obvious examples are the training requirements and codes of ethics and practice laid down by the various professional bodies.

These four definitions of need overlap. It may be possible to identify some core needs which are covered by all four definitions – for example, clinical supervision and some form of theoretical base in training. However, other needs may be normative and comparative but not necessarily felt – an example might be the need for personal therapy. Trainee therapists are usually required to have personal therapy, but sometimes feel they have nothing much to talk about. Other needs may be accepted by some experts and are felt by some individuals, but there is no demand, as well as, and possibly because of, the absence of good practice, for example, at least until recently, the need to be aware of social responsibility. Numerous other permutations of the four definitions of need exist. Despite the limitations of each definition, taken together they provide a potentially useful framework for assessing the needs of counsellors and psychotherapists. However, there remains a difficult decision about what categories of need should be given priority in any given situation.

The other contentious issue in the title relates to the use of both words, counselling and psychotherapy.

Counselling and psychotherapy

A comparison of functions between counselling and psychotherapy reveals much common ground (Bond, 1996: 52). Over ten years ago in the introduction to a book entitled *Theories of Counselling and Psychotherapy*, Patterson concluded: 'There are no essential differences between counselling and psychotherapy in the nature of the relationship, in the process, in the methods or techniques, in the goals or outcomes (broadly conceived), or even in the kinds of clients involved' (1986: xiv).

Much has been written and debated about the seemingly intractable problem of differentiating between counselling and psychotherapy and the often implied if not explicit claims for the superiority of one approach over others. In 1992 Thorne explores 'why in the face of the apparent hopelessness of the quest for differences the search nonetheless continues'. He goes on to ponder whether 'counsellors and psychotherapists are often ruthless rivals intent on survival and the acquisition of economic, professional and ideational power or advantage' (1992: 247). Thorne appeals for an urgent response to the need for a united therapeutic profession. (This issue is explored further in Chapter 2 on the nature of counselling and psychotherapy and in Chapter 13 on the need for collaboration.) However, a counselling and psychotherapy dichotomy presents barely half the picture and disguises the fact that the differences within psychotherapy about what is and what is not psychotherapy are at least as great and 'perhaps more hostile and intense' than the possible differences between counselling and psychotherapy (Inniss and Bell, 1996). Bloch recalls a striking memory of his own introduction to psychotherapy, 'how bewildering it all seemed, no one could define it, controversy raged over the question of its effectiveness and different schools engaged in constant warfare with one another' (1982: 1). Future generations of trainee counsellors and psychotherapists may still have to confront a similar experience.

Within psychotherapy, the differentiation between psychotherapy and psychoanalysis in particular remains not just an issue concerning scientific theory and technical practice, but has even more to do with what Hinshelwood describes as the 'unseemly matters of prestige, privilege and money' (1988: 147). If we believe the overwhelming research evidence that fails to indicate any general superiority of one approach over another (Bergin and Garfield, 1994) then one logical conclusion may be that the essence of this debate is more about professional status, levels of remuneration and competition for work than about any real differences either within or between counselling and psychotherapy (Bond, 1996: 55). This issue is addressed specifically in Chapter 2 on What is Counselling and Psychotherapy but inevitably re-emerges elsewhere throughout the book.

On a more positive note, in 1996 a joint Lead Body group of counsellors and psychotherapists started working together to formulate counselling and psychotherapy competencies. The focus was on commonalities and the Lead Body report concluded that the issues of differentiation were largely around various modalities and contexts. It was suggested that the notion of level of complexity may be at the heart of the distinction debate – but again confirmed that this was as much inside psychotherapy as between counselling and psychotherapy.

The intention here is to acknowledge the existence of a debate which is likely to go on into the next millennium and is doubtless further entrenched by the existence of two quite separate professional bodies determined to establish separate procedures for registration or accreditation and standards for training and good practice.

Professional bodies

One obvious difference between counselling and psychotherapy is professional affiliation and allegiances. In Britain, the Standing Council for the Advancement of Counselling (SCAC) was formed in 1970 and became the British Association for Counselling (BAC) in 1977. BAC was responsible for setting up the Rugby Conference for Psychotherapy in 1980. This became the United Kingdom Standing Conference for Psychotherapy (UKSCP) and was established as a formal organization in 1989, becoming the UK Council for Psychotherapy in 1993.

BAC is a large umbrella organization that serves the very diverse range of interests and theoretical orientations of its members. Individuals and organizations can apply for membership. There are several grades of BAC membership according to individual experience and qualifications. BAC fellowships were introduced in 1996. BAC members can also apply to join one or more of the divisions representing different areas of counselling: pastoral care, student counselling, work, education, medical settings, personal/sexual/relationship/family and race and cultural education. The BAC Management Committee delegates specific responsibilities to sub-committees for accreditation, disability, publications and AVA, professional issues, research, standards and ethics and complaints. It has separate and well-established schemes for the accreditation of individual counsellors, supervisors, trainers and counsellor training courses as well as formal procedures for dealing with complaints against members. BAC is responsible for the management of the UK Register of Counsellors and publishes a quarterly journal.

The UKCP has a different federal structure in which similar kinds of psychotherapy are grouped together in sections. The sections are largely independent of the Council. Only organizations can apply for membership of UKCP, initially to the Council, then to the appropriate section. UKCP operates a national register of psychotherapists. Both BAC and UKCP are concerned to respond to the felt and often expressed needs of counsellors and psychotherapists for professional status and recognition.

Many practitioners are both members of BAC and through their training organization registered with UKCP.

Structure of this book

Fourteen authors representing a wide range of theoretical orientations and professional affiliations have each been invited to discuss a specific area of need. The areas of need have either been identified as important by the author, often felt and sometimes expressed as critical areas of need by trainees and experienced practitioners or have evolved as part of established good practice. The book seeks to address the needs of practitioners in a rapidly changing context. The authors present not only a traditional and well-established analysis of practitioner needs, but by including such topics as collaboration with colleagues, evaluating effectiveness, social and spiritual responsibility, reading, writing and research, they seek to influence attitudes and practice by reinforcing perceptible trends and new directions.

The first need to be addressed concerns the self and role differentiation of counsellors and psychotherapists. In Chapter 2, Colin Feltham discusses some of the problems and complexities in attempting to identify the similarities and differences between counselling and psychotherapy and related disciplines. He argues that counsellors and psychotherapists need to ask some fundamental questions about the nature of what they do. The remaining chapters are written on the premise that it is either not possible or not useful to distinguish in general terms between counselling and psychotherapy – although specific professional body related differences are examined briefly. The relationship between the various areas of need is complex and seems to defy any clear rationale for a structure that would hold together all the chapter topics in a logical sequence. The notional developmental sequence of the present structure has inevitably something of an arbitrary appearance that does not imply importance or priority of needs.

In Chapter 3 on social responsibility, Simon Du Plock extends the scope of the role definition of counsellors and psychotherapists and argues that they need to consider the social context of their clients and not isolate themselves in the therapy room. Plock challenges much conventional wisdom that seems to neglect this area of need.

Historically, self-development, usually in the form of personal therapy, is the first form of learning for most counsellors and psychotherapists. In Chapter 4, Hazel Johns presents the need for self-development as an integral part of a 'lifelong curriculum' for competent and ethical practice. She explores the relationship between self-development, personal learning and cultural differences. Psychological therapy is one element of self-development, but it is less accessible for some minority groups who may often experience great difficulty in finding therapists with adequate cultural understanding (NHS, 1996: 96). Counsellors and psychotherapists need to be aware of the impact of social and cultural factors from three perspectives, namely, human development, the therapeutic relationship between therapist and client, and the values and assumptions of counselling and psychotherapy generally (Dryden et al., 1995). The increasingly felt and expressed need for culturally skilled counsellors is attributable, in part, to the growing political and social presence of diverse cultural groups in Britain (Ponterotto et al., 1996). These issues are explored by Zack Eleftheriadou in Chapter 5.

Although professional training necessarily brings together many of the areas of need developed fully in other chapters, historically, the need for learning about theory comes before the more recent 'comparative need' for systematic and in-depth professional training and this is reflected in the order of these chapters. In Chapter 6, Joyce Cramond examines the nature and purpose of theory before presenting an overview of the major theoretical perspectives and challenging adherence to single theories. Theory is a key element of practitioner training. Since the early 1990s professional bodies have developed training standards and criteria for course accreditation. Alan Lidmila describes the emergence of systematic professional training as 'the public expression of practitioner needs'. In Chapter 7 he explores the politics, nature and purpose of professional training standards and the concomitant wave of professionalism. For a straightforward description of the established components of counsellor training, readers could consult Dryden et al. (1995). The theme of training standards is developed in Chapter 8. Sue Wheeler examines the meaning of competence and what is needed to make 'a good counsellor or psychotherapist'. Supervision is a core element of both professional training and ongoing competence to practice. In Chapter 9, Michael Carroll traces the history and upsurge of interest in the theory and practice of supervision. He presents clearly the case for supervision as a 'necessity rather than a luxury'.

In Chapter 10, John McLeod examines the important and often neglected and unacknowledged contribution of reading, writing and research to developing a professional identity, but he highlights the differences between the spoken and written word and warns of the potential dangers of becoming too immersed in these activities. Trainee counsellors and psychotherapists read and write as part of their assessed course work, yet few if any training courses encourage their trainees to see reading, writing and conducting research as an integral part of professional practice after training. Only the BPS requires trainees to become active researchers. Although BAC and UKCP have research groups, both professional bodies may need to reflect on whether their training standards do enough to encourage practitioners to become active researchers and conversely for the researcher, typically based in academic institutions, to maintain a counselling or psychotherapy practice.

The NHS review of psychotherapy services in England (1996: 100) states that 'all psychotherapists should audit their work'. It argues that 'the provision of psychotherapy services should be driven by empirical evidence' and that there should be a clear commitment to the evaluation of whether clients' needs will be met by a particular counselling or psychotherapy service. The hard reality of the future is that resource allocation may well depend increasingly on the results of evaluation. Evaluating effectiveness is the subject of Chapter 11. John Mellor-Clark and Michael Barkham examine why individual practitioners need to evaluate their effectiveness, what problems they might anticipate in attempting to do so, how these problems might be overcome and what benefits practitioners may gain for themselves. Perhaps the knowledge and skills necessary to evaluate effectiveness need to be added to the training criteria and requirements for BAC and UKCP accredited courses.

In Chapter 12 Rowan Bayne discusses some of the potential perils facing counsellors and psychotherapists who spend so much of their working life responding to the mental pain and distress of others. He takes a clear and pragmatic look at some of the strategies that may help counsellors and psychotherapists to 'not only survive but to survive well'. The relationship between psychological type and stress is examined. Possibly one way to cope more effectively with the inevitable stress of working as a counsellor or psychotherapist is to 'develop a discipline which pays due regard to the spiritual dimension' of what they do. Brian Thorne explores the need for spiritual responsibility in what he describes as an essentially secular profession (Chapter 13). Counsellors and psychotherapists need to believe in themselves, in their clients and in what they are doing.

While a minority of practitioners, especially within BAC, continue to resist the seemingly unstoppable wave of 'professionalization' which they see as 'fostering restrictive practice, stifling initiative and motivated by money, status seeking and bargaining power' (Baron, 1996: 23) the majority of practitioners express the need for formal professional recognition.

Judith Baron explores the issues of professional status and recognition in Chapter 14. However, one of the possible consequences of all the efforts to achieve greater professional status through the patronage of the separate professional bodies is that the need for rapprochement between them becomes even more critical. In the final chapter Cassie Cooper argues that if the profession is to have any chance of fending off 'its more articulate and mature critics in an increasingly hostile press and have any chance of maintaining the prestige of the talking therapies then inter school and inter professional body collaboration' is imperative. She develops the problems and issues introduced by Colin Feltham in Chapter 2 and while she celebrates the 'richness of possibilities for collaboration', she also warns that counsellors and psychotherapists 'stand in danger of becoming anachronisms and facing ultimate extinction if they continue to persist in making a mockery of what they allegedly stand for'. For the profession to develop, counsellors and psychothera-pists need to recognize first the need for collaboration and then find ways of achieving it.

The next section of this chapter moves from the development of the profession to the professional development of individual practitioners.

Professional development

Professional development is not complete at the end of training as a counsellor or psychotherapist. Experienced practitioners recognize the need for ongoing professional development throughout their working life and the need to establish healthy patterns of personal and pro-fessional self-care early in their career. In this way they learn to deal constructively with the inevitable stress of psychotherapeutic work and prevent professional burn-out.

Dooley (1994: 787) suggests that a 'profession' needs to have clear standards of conduct by which the public are protected. In 1997 there is still no statutory regulation of who can offer and provide psychother-apeutic services. Membership of one or both of the two main pro-fessional bodies (BAC and UKCP) has become an important aspect of professional development and practice insofar as it implies working within the prescribed ethical codes and provides the opportunity to work towards accredited or registered status. While this voluntary regulation serves to protect the needs and interest of clients and provide lines of practitioner accountability and related complaints procedures to deal with alleged malpractice, it also serves to protect the interests and entitlements of practitioners (Bond, 1993: 36). Winter and Maisch (1996: 44) corroborates this when he suggests that 'many would argue that professional work is defined by its involvement with ethical issues, just as much as by its specialist knowledge'. Counsellors and psychothera-pists need codes of ethics and practice to provide a framework within which they can monitor and regulate their own practice and to help them ensure that they are working within established standards of good practice. Ethical codes cover typically such aspects of professional prac-tice as: client safety and client autonomy, legal liability, insurance, con-tracting, competence to practice, self-care, confidentiality, supervision, responsibility to clients, colleagues and the wider community, adver-tising, research and so on. These codes also provide a framework for ethical decision-making and guidelines for resolving conflicts between ethical priorities and conflicts of interests. However, Bond points out that 'most counsellors [and psychotherapists] are providing services which are not established on a statutory basis and are therefore covered only by

Table 1.1   *Summary of approaches to possible development and diversification of professional activity*

Arenas	Individuals	Groups	Organization
Aims	Remedial	Developmental	Educational and preventative
Approaches	Direct service to clients	Training, supervision and consultation	Research, writing and/or production of audio, video and/or printed materials
Level	Voluntary	Paid part-time or sessional work	Full-time and salaried
Setting	Training organization	Agency or employer	Private practice

general principles of law which have been developed without explicit consideration of counselling' (1993: 38).

Counsellors and psychotherapists need to explore further the legal basis and ramifications of their professional practice and should be able to look to their professional bodies for guidance on these matters.

Membership of BAC or UKCP brings further professional benefits including the opportunity to attend the annual conferences, gain support through informal networking, joining one of the local groups or specialist divisions and for counsellors through BAC to receive the journal and keep up to date with changes and developments within the field both in Britain and Europe.

Few counsellors and psychotherapists continue to see clients or patients one after the other each day, week after week, year after year throughout their professional career. Experienced practitioners often feel that they need (or want) to develop their work through a diversification of activity. Ivey et al. (1987: 336) use a simplified version of Morrill et al.'s (1980) model to describe the possible range of psychotherapeutic activities. The original model has three dimensions and is extended in Table 1.1 to include 'level' and 'settings'. It is presented as a summary of approaches to the possible development and diversification of professional activity.

Most practitioners start work by offering a direct service to individual clients. The work tends to be remedial or developmental. At some point practitioners may want to shift the arena into working with couples, families or specialists groups or even into working with organizations as their 'client'. They may also be interested in moving from remedial into more psychoeducational activities. These activities may involve social skills, relaxation and assertiveness training. A typical path for professional development to take is from voluntary work, usually part-time or sessional to full-time paid employment. Perhaps the most exciting and rewarding professional development for many counsellors and psychotherapists is to move into working as a trainer, clinical supervisor or consultant. It is fairly widespread practice for counsellors and psychotherapists to continue their work with clients while also offering clinical supervision to other practitioners and trainees.

Most professional bodies also require trainers to be active practitioners (BAC, 1996). Since the early 1990s opportunities for research, writing articles and books and producing other audiovisual or printed material have increased enormously. Additionally, the mid-1990s have seen an increasing demand for quality assurance and accountability. I imagine that in the future few counsellors or psychotherapists will escape the need to evaluate the efficacy of their work. This may become very much a part of professional development.

Reflective practitioner

Probably more than in almost any other career training, counselling and psychotherapy tend to involve trainees in their own monitoring and assessment. Indeed their long-term professional development will depend on their ability to reflect upon their practice and identify their own continuing development needs.

The term 'reflective practitioner' is most closely associated with the work of Schon (1983). It refers to the various forms of reflection which need to occur within the person and as an integral part of professional practice. Counsellors and psychotherapists need to learn from their practice experience through self-monitoring, clinical supervision or consultation and personal therapy. In this way professional development through the accumulation of concrete experience is achieved by what Winter and Maisch (1996: 48) describe as a 'cyclical movement in which practice and reflection both develop by mutually informing one another'.

Professional practice

According to Windt et al. (1991) someone with professional status has authority, social importance, commitment, autonomy, self-regulation and expertise. But what is the nature of this expertise? The current project aimed at developing NVQs (National Vocational Qualifications) for counselling and psychotherapy is a specific competencies based model derived from a functional analysis of a practitioner's role (Inniss and Bell, 1996). Winter and Maisch (1996) reinforce the critical attitudes of many practitioners and academics when they suggest that the 'essential quality of performance within a role cannot be expressed in a list of detailed specifications which are simply added together to indicate the required overall accomplishment' (1996: 39). The work of counsellors and psychotherapists is shaped by a complex combination of often contradictory values, motives, feelings, understandings, theoretical models, skills and responsibilities.

Winter and Maisch (1996) propose a general model of professional work which provides a framework for defining criteria for professional practice. Although the model was originally developed to inform the formulation and assessment of social work competencies, it applies equally to any of the 'helping professions', including counsellors and psychotherapists. The model has four dimensions of professional competence and practice: values, enshrined for therapists in professional body codes of ethics and practice; an emotional dimension, inherent in the client/therapist relationship; professional knowledge, or the theoretical models that underpin counselling and psychotherapy; and reflection on practice as a learning process. The model contains ten propositions which represent a summary of the professional competence needs of counsellors and psychotherapists:

1   The nature of professional work is that situations are unique and knowledge of those situations is therefore never complete. Good practice, therefore, for professional workers, is practice whereby knowledge is developed through the forms of reflection which practice itself requires.

2   It follows that, for professional workers, a given state of reflective understanding will be transformed by further experience of practice, and that (by the same token) future practice will be transformed by the reflection which arises from practice.

3   Professional work involves commitment to a specific set of moral purposes, and professional workers will recognize the inevitably complex and serious responsibilities which arise when attempting to apply ethical principles to particular situations.

4   The responsibility for equitable practice which characterizes the professional role commits professional workers to the comprehensive, consistent, conscious, and effective implementation of 'anti-oppressive' non-discriminatory principles and practices.

5   Authoritative involvement in the problem areas of clients' lives inevitably creates a complex emotional dimension to professional work, and professional workers therefore recognize that the role involves understanding and managing the emotional dimension of professional relationships.

6   Consequently, professional workers recognize that the understanding of others on which their interpersonal effectiveness depends is inseparable from self-knowledge, and consequently entails a sustained process of self-evaluation.

7   The incompleteness of professional knowledge (see 1 and 2 above) implies that the authoritative basis of judgements will always remain open to question. Hence, for professional workers, relationships

with others will necessarily be collaborative rather than simply hierarchical.

8   Professional workers will be aware of available codified knowledge, for example, concerning legal provisions, organizational procedures, resources, and research findings, but they will recognize that the relevance of this knowledge for particular situations always depends on their own selection and interpretation.

9   Professional workers will have at their command a grasp of the relationships (similarities and contrasts) between a wide range of situations (different clients, different legal frameworks, and different practice settings).

10   The process of analytical understanding which professional workers will bring to their practice involves:

  (a)   creative translation of meanings between contexts (see 9, above);
  (b)   synthesis of varied elements into a unified overall pattern;
  (c)   relating a situation to its context (institutional, legal, and political);
  (d)   understanding a situation in terms of its tensions and contradictions;
  (e)   understanding a situation in terms of its inherent processes of change. (Winter and Maisch, 1996: 49; reprinted here with permission from Falmer Press)

Winter and Maisch (1996: 49) explain that the ten propositions are intended to form interdependent elements of a unified process which links professional practice, knowledge, understanding, skills, commitments and self-knowledge. It provides a framework for professional development through ongoing reflection on practice. In this sense, working as a professional counsellor or psychotherapist is defined as a learning process.

Conclusion: into the next millennium

> What does it say about a society when one of its main growth industries is that of counselling and psychotherapy? What does it say about a culture when people need to turn to experts in order to learn how to manage their day-to-day lives and their ordinary human relationships? (van Deurzen, 1996: vii)

There seems little doubt that the societal attitudes and the economy of the 1990s supported the booming growth of counselling and psychotherapy. But where will it all stop? Surely the demand from people who want to train as counsellors or psychotherapists and the demand from people who want to benefit from counselling and psychotherapy will reach saturation point? The expanding bubble will burst. Matthews (1996: 19) refers to what physicists call 'self-organising critical phenomena', that is, things that build up and up until they reach a 'critical state' and suddenly rearrange themselves, or self-organize into a more stable state. He suggests that this phenomenon has been widely used to describe such things as share prices that continue to rise up and up, and then collapse and threaten the economy, or to depict the effects of global warming in which the Earth's atmosphere may get hotter and hotter before 'flipping' to create significant changes in weather patterns. Matthews uses the analogy of children playing with piles of salt on the dining table, seeing how big a heap can be made before it collapses back down again.

The phenomenal build-up of demand for counselling and psycho-therapy may be regulated by market forces and by the growing insistence from managers, employers and accountants for quality assurance and accountability. Consumer interest may decline if clients become dis-illusioned with the promise that counselling and psychotherapy seems to offer. But the build-up exists within counselling and psychotherapy too: the frequent introduction of new and different theoretical models; inter-school sibling rivalry; attempts by groups and the increasing number of professional bodies staking claims of ownership to different sectors of the profession and seizing the initiative to insist on standards of training and practice each more rigorous than those of rival bodies; each trying to outdo the other in an attempt to establish not only a superior and idealized version of the professional person, but to establish the needs of an aspiring sector of the profession.

Van Deurzen (1996: xii) warns that practitioners 'are too busy per-fecting and packaging their products, and clients too preoccupied con-suming them, to wonder about the justification for all this effort'. The danger is that in working in the relative isolation of their own patch, individuals or groups of counsellors and psychotherapists may fail to see what may be happening both within what remains a divided pro-fession and outside to changes in societal attitudes towards it. Matthews (1996) says that in salt piles you get lots of small slips before the one big avalanche that brings down the whole heap. However, it is impossible to predict just which additional grain of salt will cause that to happen. In the field of counselling and psychotherapy the only thing we can be sure about is that we cannot predict accurately what will happen to the 1990s boom. As I write this I am aware that I am coming to the end of my career in counselling and psychotherapy. Part of me knows that I can deal with any 'critical state' in me by retiring. Yet I am also con-cerned that all those people about to embark on their training as counsellors or psychotherapists will eventually be able to enter a stable and unified profession that can celebrate and work with differences in a shared vision of the future.

Therapy is now not only widely accepted by society but actively sought by people with mental health problems. The review of strategic policy for NHS psychotherapy services (NHS, 1996) recommended that talking treatments should be one of the options offered first to someone in mental distress. The challenge for counsellors and psychotherapists is to ensure that the profession develops in such a way that it is able to continue to provide a human and thoughtful response to the needs of those who want to benefit from it.

Note

Throughout this book authors will use such terms as counsellor, therapist, psychotherapist and practitioner interchangeably.

References

BAC (1996) *Recognition of Counsellor Training Courses*. Rugby: British Association for Counselling.

Baron, J. (1996) The emergence of counselling as a profession, in R. Bayne, I. Horton and J. Bimrose (eds), *New Directions in Counselling*. London: Routledge.

Bayne, R., Horton, I., Merry, T. and Noyes, E. (1994) *The Counsellor's Handbook*. London: Chapman Hall.

Bergin, A.E. and Garfield, S. (eds) (1994) *Handbook of Psychotherapy and Behaviour Change*, 4th edn. New York: John Wiley.

Bloch, S. (1982) *What is Psychotherapy?* Oxford: Oxford University Press.

Bond, T. (1993) *Standards and Ethics for Counselling in Action*. London: Sage.

Bond, T. (1996) Future developments in ethical standards in counselling, in R. Bayne, I. Horton and J. Bimrose (eds), *New Directions in Counselling*. London: Routledge.

Bradshaw, J. (1972) The concept of social need, *New Society*, 30 March: 640–3.

Dooley, C. (1994) Professional issues in the 1990s and beyond, in S.J.E. Lindsay and G.E. Powell (eds), *Handbook of Clinical Adult Psychology*. London: Routledge.

Dryden, W., Horton, I. and Mearns, D. (1995) *Issues in Professional Counsellor Training*. London: Cassell.

Hinshelwood, B. (1988) Editorial, *B.J. of Psychotherapy*, 5 (2), Winter.

Inniss, S. and Bell, D. (1996) *Final Project Report for Therapeutic Counselling, Couple Counselling and Psychotherapy Competencies* (Report 39, May). Welwyn: The Advice, Guidance, Counselling and Psychotherapy Lead Body.

Ivey, A.E., Ivey, M.B. and Simek-Downing, L. (1987) *Counselling and Psychotherapy: Integrating Skills, Theory and Practice*, 2nd edn. Englewood Cliffs, NJ: Prentice-Hall.

Magee, B. (1982) *Popper*. London: Fontana.

Maslow, A.H. (1987) *Motivation and Personality*, 3rd edn. New York: Harper & Row.

Matthews, R. (1996) Earthquakes: There's a grim warning in that pile of salt, *Sunday Telegraph*, 24 November: 19.

Morrill, W., Hurst, J. and Oetting, E. (1980) *Dimensions of Intervention for Student Development*. New York: Wiley.

NHS (1996) *NHS Psychotherapy Services in England. Review of Strategic Policy*. Wetherby: Department of Health.

Norcross, J.C. and Grencavage, L.M. (1990) Eclecticism and integration in counselling and psychotherapy: major themes and obstacles, in W. Dryden and J.C. Norcross (eds), *Eclecticism and Integration in Counselling and Psychotherapy*. Loughton: Gale Centre.

Patterson, C.H. (1986) *Theories of Counselling and Psychotherapy*. New York: Harper & Row.

Ponterotto, J.G., Casas, J.M., Suzuki, L.A. and Alexander, C.M. (eds) (1996) *Handbook of Multicultural Counselling*. London: Sage.

Reber, A.S. (1985) *Dictionary of Psychology*. Harmondsworth: Penguin.

Salancik, G.R. and Pfeffer, J. (1977) An examination of need-satisfaction models of job attitudes, *Administrative Science Quarterly*, 22: 427–56.

Schon, D. (1983) *The Reflective Practitioner*. New York: Basic Books.

Thorne, B. (1992) Psychotherapy and counselling: The quest for differences. Counselling, *BAC Journal*, 2 (4): 244–8. Rugby: British Association for Counselling.

Windt, P.Y., Appleby, P.C., Franers, L.P. and Landesman, B.M. (1991) *Ethical Issues in Professions*. Englewood Cliffs, NJ: Prentice-Hall.

Winter, R. and Maisch, M. (1996) *Professional Competence and Higher Education: The ASSET Programme*. London: Falmer Press.

van Deurzen, E. (1996) Foreword, in A. Howard, *Challenges to Counselling and Psychotherapy*. Hampshire: Macmillan.

2

Counselling and Psychotherapy: Differentiation or Unification

Colin Feltham

While there is a need in every field to make some assumptions, to avoid the paralysis of analysis and the labouring of the obvious, there is always the parallel need to wrestle with fundamentals. Every reader of this book is sure to have some understanding of what is meant by counselling, psychotherapy and related actvities but this is always a personal and probably evolving understanding, depending on experience, training, circumstances and preferences. All practitioners, no matter how experienced, need to reflect on where they stand within the therapeutic enterprise, on how they describe their work to clients, and on what they can and cannot deliver. Arguably, counselling and psychotherapy cannot be understood at all outside the context of the theories, institutions and traditions which represent them. Since this is a rapidly changing field, practitioners are wise to keep abreast of professional developments and also to anticipate creatively in which areas theory and practice need to expand.

I intend to present within this chapter, first, reasonably uncontentious, necessarily succinct outlines of what counselling, psychotherapy and related disciplines are commonly considered to be; second, some suggestions as to how these outlines may be problematic; and, third, the proposition that the need to ask fundamental questions about the nature of counselling and psychotherapy is of paramount importance. Hopefully this will generate a degree of constructive friction when read alongside other chapters in this book. Perhaps there are official, orthodox views and definitions at one end of a spectrum, and dissenting, even destructive views at the other. I suspect that most counsellors' views will reflect nuances within the intermediate range.

What is counselling?

Originally, counsel referred to advice or consultation but counselling has recently come to be understood as a disciplined form of helping, facilitative but non-advisory activity. People are unlikely to be given straightforward advice by counsellors, even when their personal problems are characterized by a need to make decisions. When a client asks whether she should have an abortion, change her career or leave her husband, for example, a counsellor will typically avoid telling her what to do, will probably avoid disclosing his own opinion and will encourage the client to explore her own options and resistances sufficiently well to make her own decision. In this picture, counselling is non-directive and based on the humanistic belief that people are self-determining, that it is better that they should enlarge their capacity for self-determination and that counsellors should not short-circuit this autonomous process. Counselling is, then, a kind of personal nurturing, challenging, encouraging and (more often than not) one-to-one consultancy provided within a protected, reflective space.

We cannot proceed very far without seeking to differentiate between counselling and similar activities. Many of these issues are fully debated in Feltham (1995). Is counselling identical or almost identical to coaching, mentoring, spiritual care, casework, guidance, befriending, self-analysis and co-counselling, for example? The position of the British Association for Counselling (BAC) is that it is not, overlaps notwithstanding. Counselling aims to facilitate the client's autonomy in relation to a variety of issues in a confidential setting, within a contractual, non-judgemental relationship protected by a professional code of ethics, underpinned by recognized training, supervision and, increasingly, professional accreditation and registration. It is not a casual matter. Anyone may use certain counselling skills in everyday life and work situations but counselling per se is a formal undertaking. Counselling may deal with crises and specific life events but is equally applicable to ongoing, developmental, personality transforming objectives as well as having psychoeducational aspects.

The body of knowledge upon which counselling practice rests often appears to be more or less identical with that of psychotherapy. In other words, trainee counsellors study psychotherapeutic texts on a wide variety of clinical and personality, developmental and personal change theories. Thus, person-centred, psychodynamic, cognitive-behavioural and the dozens of other theoretical approaches and brand names associated with psychotherapy are also associated with counselling. Counselling is not, however, necessarily exclusively dependent upon the study and mastery of strictly psychological or psychotherapeutic principles but might potentially draw upon many academic disciplines, such as anthropology, theology, sociology and philosophy (Thorne and Dryden, 1993). In this potential catholicity, such training might partly resemble that of priests, social workers and youth and community workers.

Unlike psychoanalytic psychotherapy, counselling has always tended to emphasize the role of interpersonal microskills in training and practice, a tradition stemming from an empirical research and practice base associated with Rogers, Carkhuff, Truax, Gilmore, Ivey, Egan, Nelson-Jones and others. It is also worthy of note that counselling theory, stemming from the early part of the 1900s, is heavily American, whereas (psychoanalytic and existentialist) psychotherapy is of course of mid-European origin. This difference may explain a tendency for much counselling, personal growth work and lifeskills training to be pragmatically and positively toned, extroverted and future oriented, compared with psychotherapy that is typically oriented towards introversion, the past, problems, and psychopathology. Historically, counselling has frequently been located within voluntary and educational organizations and has moved from amateur towards professional status, while much psychotherapy has developed in private practice and has wavered between a medical and lay identity.

Provisionally we may say that counselling is often understood to be concerned with people's everyday problems and hassles, with taxing personal crises, decisional dilemmas and transient, moderate depressions, anxieties and psychological obstacles to normal and relatively happy functioning. For some counselling practitioners, concepts of psychopathology and psychodiagnosis are anathema, and any presenting problem may be considered for counselling when the client is self-referred. Phenomenologically, counselling is characterized by one person formally or contractually taking the role of listener/facilitator being available and the other voluntarily taking the role of client/counsellee/ the one who needs help or who seeks something.

What is psychotherapy?

Psychotherapy, originally understood as a less intense form of psychoanalysis, has a longer lineage than counselling, being at least 100 years old. Ehrenwald (1976) traces the origins back to ancient Assyria and includes magic and religion in his survey, but I am referring here to modern clinical psychotherapy. The term is still often understood to refer properly to psychoanalytically oriented psychotherapy, but in fact the United Kingdom Council for Psychotherapy (UKCP), the most influential such body in Britain, accommodates and recognizes a wide range of theoretical and clinical orientations including psychoanalytic, Jungian, humanistic and integrative, behavioural and cognitive, experiential constructivist, hypnotherapy, as well as family, marital, sexual and child psychotherapy. BAC is known as a friend of the council and no purely counselling institution is a member organization. Similarly, the British Psychological Society (BPS) and the Royal College of Psychiatrists are 'special members', not mainstream members of the UKCP. Member organizations of UKCP are a mixture of independent and academic training bodies.

It is significant that the British Confederation of Psychotherapists (BCP), formed as a breakaway group from the original UKSCP, is comprised of ten, more purist, longstanding psychoanalytically oriented organizations who demand among other things that trainees undergo their own extensive training analysis (at least three times a week for a minimum of four years). BCP is necessarily a modestly sized, specialist group of 'senior institutions' parallel with, but without the extensive influence of, bodies such as BAC, UKCP or BPS.

At the other extreme, another small group known as the Independent Practitioners' Network (IPN), has broken away from BAC and UKCP due to disaffection with increasing moves towards registration and other forms of bureaucracy and external loci of control associated with pro-fessionalization. Largely humanistic in orientation, IPN members seek to establish self-monitoring practitioner cells, each responsible for quality, accountability and supervision. Mowbray (1995) captures much of the thinking associated with the formation of this group.

Implicit in this brief summary of major professional or practitioner groupings is the question: who has the right to define and to have proprietorial rights over psychotherapy and the talking/psychological therapies? Noticeable too is a mirroring of politics, with liberal and conservative tendencies forming themselves.

Psychotherapy is, like counselling, a form of talking treatment based on principles derived from the work of Freud, Jung, Perls, Berne, Klein and many others. It is sometimes said that the singular form, 'psycho-therapy', is inaccurate since there are possibly around 400 different psychotherapies and these may be delivered in a variety of formats (individuals, couples, families, etc. – see Bloch, 1986). Jerome Frank gives the following definition:

> The attempt of one person to relieve another's psychological distress and disability by psychological means. These are typically words, but include other communicative or symbolic behaviours, ranging from laying a reass-uring hand on someone's shoulder to elaborate exercises aimed at combatting noxious emotions and promoting inner tranquility. (1986: 1)

Frank goes on to qualify this description which, after all, is not distinct from the help offered informally by many people, by saying that formal psychotherapy is always delivered by those with specific training and specifically sanctioned by society. In addition, psychotherapists always practise on the basis of an articulated theory which claims to explain sources of distress and appropriate methods of alleviating it. Since there are hundreds of different explanations and methods it is not possible within this chapter to go into this territory. Suffice it to say here that psychotherapy and counselling both address themselves to a wide variety of forms of human distress, by means of disciplined listening and responding, underpinned by explanatory theories (Feltham and Dryden, 1993; Feltham, 1995).

It is sometimes argued that psychotherapy works at a deeper level than counselling since it always involves transference dynamics. It is also said that psychotherapy takes longer and effects change in clients (often known as patients) that is more profound and enduring, and that surpasses mere symptom relief or crisis intervention (Clarkson, 1994). Certainly it is the case that psychotherapy trainees often spend four, five or more years in training and usually have extensive periods of their own personal therapy as part of their training. Counselling training currently is often only two years in length, and personal therapy is not always mandatory (although some mandatory personal growth work is becoming the norm).

In reality, however, the picture is much more complex than this, as argued in Feltham (1995) and James and Palmer (1996). Counsellors are obliged to have career-long clinical supervision while, at the time of writing, psychotherapists, clinical psychologists and others are not. Behavioural psychotherapy, to make another comparison, usually involves no work with the (Freudian) Unconscious, does not necessarily take very long or aim at more than symptomatic relief. In addition, some training courses in psychotherapy are only two or three years in length, and some include counselling in the title of the award, making no apparent distinction between the two activities. Increasingly, courses are adopting titles such as 'therapeutic counselling', a term which is also used by the Advice, Guidance, Counselling and Psychotherapy Lead Body (AGC&PLB) to underline the difference between this kind of counselling and, for example, debt counselling, which is actually information and advice giving.

At a theoretical level, the differences between counselling and psychotherapy have often been debated in the pages of the journal *Counselling* in the last few years, but without resolution. Those representing the more psychoanalytic end of the debate (for example, Naylor-Smith, 1994) maintain that there are important differences, while others consider it imperative to insist that counselling and psychotherapy are indivisible (Thorne, 1992). At the publicity and consumer level, however, any differences surely must be addressed. It is quite typical, in my experience, for some clients or potential clients to be advised that in certain instances their concerns appear to need sustained attention over a lengthy period, perhaps by a practitioner specially trained (in psychotherapy) to understand and deal with deep, longstanding, complex psychological phenomena. All clinical practitioners need to make such judgements at times and to prepare for them by weighing up the kinds of arguments gathered in this chapter.

By contrast, counselling is sometimes described as situation specific and relatively short-term. The fact that much counselling is delivered in agencies whose client group is specified (for example, students, employees, people in troubled relationships, victims of abuse or violence, people with AIDS, etc.) and is sometimes time limited, supports this view of an important difference between counselling and psychotherapy. However, often all that is actually conveyed to clients, most of whom probably are not concerned with semantics or professional turf wars, is that they may need shorter or longer term help. (See Feltham (1997a) and Shipton and Smith (in press) for respective arguments about short-term and long-term client needs.) I should add a caveat to this. Since the term 'psychotherapy' with its Greek etymology and medical flavour, tends to convey a sense of expert treatment, some clients are overly impressed or frightened by the term in relation to counselling, which often conveys by comparison a more egalitarian and informal, or less expert process. Dryden (1996a) argues that practitioners who possess multiple (counselling, psychotherapy and applied psychology) qualifications may highlight whichever of these seems most congenial to particular clients.

Class is a significant but overlooked issue in this debate too. Long-term, psychoanalytic therapy is mainly available in private practice. Even those NHS clinics offering such relatively long-term treatment often take in practice the more articulate and/or moderately disturbed, psychologically minded clients who are by definition usually middle class (Holmes and Lindley, 1989). Individuals with disposable income who wish to spend time and money on non-specific, psychological self-exploration are quite likely to consult psychoanalytic and humanistic psychotherapists in private practice. This picture may be changing slightly, but the trend towards funding for time-limited therapy or counselling will possibly reconfirm class variables.

Certain forms of radical, purportedly life-transforming psychotherapy, such as primal therapy, are usually available only from independent practitioners (whether individuals or group practices) at considerable overall cost. They are likely to appeal to informed, middle-class, relatively young people whose income and/or lifestyle allows for such self-explorations, which in many ways – especially in humanistic, existential and transpersonal therapy – resemble spiritual or existential quests for meaning and new lifestyles. Those suffering from acute distress, who know little about psychotherapy and have few resources but many pressing, everyday worries about money, work and family stresses, almost inevitably receive counselling, clinical psychology or (non-radical) psychotherapy via a GP referral or voluntary agency (Ollerton, 1995).

What is counselling psychology?

Historically, counselling has arisen in diverse agency settings and its training has been conducted in, and reflected the orientation of, departments of education, social work and pastoral studies as well as psychology. In 1982, BPS established its Counselling Psychology Section in recognition of growing interest in counselling among its members. In 1992 a Diploma in Counselling Psychology was launched and in 1994 a

Division of Counselling Psychology. While counselling psychology obviously has a vast amount in common with counselling, Woolfe (1996) suggests that the former adds a scientific, evaluative base to a valuably humanistic field. Counselling psychology, which is self-evidently a new product, can only be practised by those with a formal training in psychology, and it aims to be useful not only to individual clients but also to organizations. Counselling psychologists must be familiar with research methodology and should partly base their practice on research. In this, it is said, they will be differentiated from counsellors who practise without any scientific underpinnings.

Is there something that counselling psychologists can do that counsellors cannot, or are there areas of practice in which the former can outperform the latter? The answers are not currently clear and critiques of the applied psychologies would suggest that differences may relate more to professional anxieties and territorial defences than to clinical realities (Pilgrim and Treacher, 1992; James and Palmer, 1996). Readers who are not counselling psychologists may wish to ask themselves: do I use, do I need, or to what extent do I need, psychology in my work? Is psychology (or exactly which aspects of psychology are) fruitful for counselling practice, or even perhaps detrimental (Deurzen-Smith, 1993)? Questions surrounding the tension between the humanistic values of counselling and the scientific pull of psychology have been addressed by Strawbridge (1996).

Health psychology, another emerging field, refers to the work of applied psychologists in academic research units and health authorities, relating to attitudes towards health, communication with patients, and service evaluation. There is a growing literature supporting the value of counselling and counselling skills in health settings which may enhance health awareness, medical treatment and, for example, the management of chronic illness and pain.

What is clinical psychology?

British clinical psychology dates from the 1950s and, unlike counselling and psychotherapy, began as a statutory endeavour. Clinical psychologists are members of BPS and must have completed a first psychology degree (or equivalent), plus additional clinical training, leading to chartered status (comparable with registration for counsellors and psychotherapists). Historically, the training of clinical psychologists has evolved from behaviour therapy to psychometrics, psychodynamic therapy, eclecticism, and what Pilgrim and Treacher (1992) refer to as managerialism. Due to its origins, clinical psychology tends to have strong roots in the study of research methodology, psychopathology, clinical assessment and case management traditions. This model of the scientist-practitioner is still advocated, although often criticized by many counsellors and psychotherapists for dwelling unjustifiably and inappropriately on mechanistic theory and technique and minimizing the importance of the therapeutic relationship.

Clinical psychologists may work in hospital or community settings (for example, in community mental health teams) or privately. As members of a statutory profession, they enjoy the benefits of an established salary scale and employment prospects, unlike most counsellors or psychotherapists. Clinical psychologists frequently describe their clinical work as psychotherapy, although they do not necessarily partake of their own therapy in training. They may work with clients with problems of depression, anxiety, phobias, eating disorders, sexual problems, learning difficulties, head injuries, strokes and clinically significant problems of ageing. Some of their work, for example, rehabilitation of people who have sustained brain damage following an accident, may be highly specialized. The extent to which clinical psychology differs in general from counselling psychology (and from psychotherapy and counselling), is debated interestingly but still inconclusively in James and Palmer (1996).

What is psychoanalysis?

Psychoanalysis is the name given by Freud to the tradition he founded, a discipline of clinical practice and theory stemming from the turn of the twentieth century. Psychoanalysis rapidly travelled from Europe to Britain and the USA around the turn of the century. The Tavistock Clinic was founded in London in 1920, the London Clinic of Psycho-Analysis in 1926, and further significant institutional expansions occurred around the 1950s. Psychoanalysts are represented as a professional group by both the UKCP and BCP. The British Psycho-analytical Society is the only UK organization authorized by the International Psychoanalytical Association to train and qualify psychoanalysts. Properly speaking, psychoanalysis is the term reserved for Freudians and others who have remained loyal, or relatively loyal, to that tradition, such as Kleinians, with Jungians historically known as analytical psychologists and Adlerians as individual psychologists. In practice, however, the term 'analyst' is used by Jungians and other groups.

More confusing are the differences between psychoanalysis, psychoanalytic psychotherapy, depth psychology, dynamic psychiatry, dynamic short-term therapy, psychodynamic counselling and other variations. All such terms assume the existence of the unconscious, that mental function whereby much of our experience from babyhood and infancy onwards is repressed, forgotten, symbolized and processed conflictually, appearing in disguised form in dreams, acting out, slips of the tongue, jokes and other ways, including, in the therapy setting, free association. Classical psychoanalysis is sometimes distinguished from psychoanalytic psychotherapy by reference to the former's use of the couch, free association and daily sessions (Solomon, 1992).

Psychoanalysis is regarded as an intensive treatment, requiring commitment from the patient, or analysand, of up to five fifty-minute sessions each week, for several years. The patient will disclose his or her thoughts, feelings and associations, however seemingly absurd or unrelated, as freely as possible. These will include feelings, positive and negative, about the analyst, many of which will be regarded as transference, or unconscious messages based on meaningful figures from the patient's past. The analyst, having spent many years in personal analysis and training (five times a week for at least four years), learns to discriminate between real, appropriate responses, and unconsciously charged material. She or he interprets this with skilled timing and, in the passage of time, the patient's unconscious conflicts are worked through until a healthy degree of resolution is achieved. Psychoanalysis is, then, extremely time-consuming, labour intensive, expensive and relatively inaccessible, and its outcome record has frequently been criticized (Andrews, 1991).

Questions to be considered within our context here are: what place does psychoanalysis have in the understanding and treatment of mental health problems? How feasible is it to offer undiluted psychoanalysis to more than a minority of people who are affluent enough to gain access to it (or fortunate enough to be seen for low fees at the London Clinic of Psycho-Analysis)? Are there clients for whom only psychoanalysis will supply an enduring remedy? Exactly what is the relationship between intensive, long-term psychoanalysis (the so-called 'Rolls-Royce of therapies') and briefer forms of psychodynamic counselling? Inescapably, too, we must ask whether or not psychoanalytic methods have been outperformed by the newer cognitive-behavioural therapies (Andrews, 1991).

What is psychiatry?

Psychiatry is the practice and profession, based on medical training, which addresses serious mental health problems or 'disorders of the mind' such as clinical depression and anxiety, manic-depressive illness, schizophrenia and dementia. Psychiatrists, members of the Royal College of Psychiatrists, may also deal with addictions, epilepsy, mental handicap and certain forms of criminal behaviour, among other things. They have the power authoritatively to assess mental states, prescribe medications, advise or order electroconvulsive therapy, and to detain people under the Mental Health Act (1983). Psychiatrists and psychiatric nurses often have responsibility for observing patients in hospital who have made suicide attempts or have mutilated themselves, for example. Psychiatrists may also practise psychotherapy, group therapy and other forms of talking therapy.

Briefly, some of the main professionals in or associated with psychiatry are described. Psychiatric nurses working on hospital wards observe patients, monitor their progress or deterioration, may advise on discharge, oversee the taking of medication, run groups and other therapeutic programmes, provide support and general assistance. Community psychiatric nurses (CPNs) play a similar role, but in community settings or clients' homes, sometimes offering counselling or other therapeutic programmes. (Some GPs regard CPNs as counsellors, and I have known people to be sometimes inappropriately referred to a CPN with very limited time when they had clearly sought regular counselling sessions.) Occupational therapists (OTs) provide support of a rehabilitative nature, as well as social skills and lifeskills training and sometimes counselling. Psychiatric social workers (PSWs) are social workers specializing in the care and support of clients with mental health problems. Some of these are Approved Social Workers (ASWs) whose role is often to exercise judgement in assessing a need for, and facilitating hospital treatment. Counselling skills will be used by all these groups, some of whom may have had counselling training.

What counsellors need to consider here is the boundary between counselling and psychiatry. Put differently, we need to know when our competency is challenged by clients whose mental state is disturbed beyond our capacity to help or safely contain them. Although it is an ethical requirement for counsellors to take appropriate steps when certain clients present in or enter such states (BAC, 1992), historically there has been much disagreement about where (if anywhere) to draw the line between normality, unhappy and neurotic behaviour, and disturbed behaviour requiring psychiatric assessment and treatment, or socio-political analysis (Parker et al., 1995).

The radical psychiatry or anti-psychiatry of Laing, Cooper, Esterson and others suggested almost evangelically at one point that psychotic states could be contained and converted by suitably understanding and committed psychotherapists. Thomas Szasz has consistently challenged the very concept of mental illness. The International Symposium for the Psychotherapy of Schizophrenia challenges the exclusively biomedical view of schizophrenia. The over-prescribing of tranquillizers and indifference to side effects of psychiatric medication displayed by some psychiatrists has been successfully challenged by counsellors, psychotherapists and many in the self-help movement. Government policy of care in the community has probably led to a greater number of people suffering from serious mental health problems presenting or finding themselves before counsellors, social workers and probation officers. Some people have sought to avoid the stigmatizing tendency of psychiatry by turning to self-referred, drug-free, nonjudgemental and confidential counselling. In all the above ways, the balance has probably shifted from passive dependence on or awe of psychiatry towards a demand for counselling and psychotherapy. There are also signs that much traditional psychiatry may mellow under the growing influence of certain evolutionary and psychotherapeutic theories (Stevens and Price, 1996).

Conversely, concern about the possible failure of counsellors and psychotherapists to recognize severe mental health problems and properly to refer such cases to psychiatric services, usually via general practitioners, has been expressed (Persaud, 1996). In the light of this, it seems increasingly necessary for counsellors in their initial training, continuing professional development and daily practice, to be informed about any contraindications for counselling in this area (Daines et al., 1997; Palmer and McMahon, 1997). This obviously does not mean that counselling has no role in primary care, in helping clients to withdraw from prescribed drugs (Hammersley, 1995) and from sometimes offering their skills alongside psychopharmacology and other psychiatric inputs. It may mean that counsellors still need to explain better to psychiatrists and doctors when clients may benefit more from counselling or psychotherapy than from physical or hospital-based treatments. I have stressed the importance of counsellors recognizing the limits of their competency and knowing when to refer to other professionals. It is, on the other hand, also interesting and encouraging to note the positive contributions that counsellors are making in diverse domains traditionally dominated by, for example, medical staff (Sanders, 1996) and human resource staff (Feltham, 1997b).

How are the different theoretical models to be understood?

Since it is not possible here to do any more than refer somewhat broadly and illustratively to the three main theoretical allegiances in counselling and psychotherapy, I will confine myself to that task and refer the reader to texts such as Dryden (1996b) for more detail on major schools. In spite of arguments for at least some degree of urgent integration of the 400 or so brand name psychotherapies, it is worth noting that according to the Strasbourg Declaration on Psychotherapy of 1990, 'the multiplicity of psychotherapeutic methods is assured and guaranteed' (EAP, 1996: 40).

Psychoanalytic

Psychoanalysis and its derivatives have been briefly covered above. In the context of asking what are the needs of counsellors, however, I make the following suggestions. Psychodynamic counsellors obviously need a fairly substantial amount of their own therapy, close supervision, (usually) the opportunity to work at some length with clients who are able to benefit from the particular boundaries, relative counsellor neutrality and interpretations associated with this approach. Psycho-dynamic counsellors need to understand, in my view, which clients are suitable for the approach and which are not, since many practitioners have traditionally assumed, for example, that everyone has unconscious conflicts that must be worked with at length. Experience, consumer reports and research would seem to suggest that this is not the case, that many prefer short-term, symptom oriented treatment from a counsellor who is fairly active. A particular difficulty for psychodynamic coun-sellors is presented in the increasing call for counsellors fully to explain their approach and its techniques to clients in the spirit of informed consent (Dryden and Feltham, 1994, 1995). People entering training need to consider whether this is the right approach for their temperament, their envisaged client group and their career aspirations. However, in spite of any reservations, psychodynamic counselling remains one of the most popular approaches with counsellors in Britain.

Humanistic

The humanistic approaches include person-centred counselling, Gestalt therapy, psychodrama, transactional analysis, primal therapy, encoun-ter, transpersonal therapy, and the many varieties of existential and experiential therapy and personal growth work individually and in groups. These approaches are characterized by an interest in the full range of human feelings and experiences from birth to death, and do not assume that only painful and pathological material is pertinent. Humanistic practitioners place greater emphasis on innate goodness, energy and self-actualizing tendencies than do their psychodynamic counterparts. Sessions are more likely to contain overtly expressed strong feelings, movement, touch, and self-disclosure on the part of the counsellor. Not only theoretically but also phenomenologically, humanistic therapy will appeal to practitioners and clients who value human potential, experimentation, flexibility and creativity. The radical end of this approach (for example, primal therapy) is unlikely to be found in office settings such as in student counselling and employee counselling services, since the work can be noisy, frightening and unconventional and may have sometimes powerful, unsettling spiritual and lifestyle outcomes.

Humanistic therapies tend to be rather egalitarian, therefore allowing for greater self-disclosure and authenticity on the part of the counsellor. Adherents tend to be critical of the tendency of psychoanalytic practi-tioners to dwell on what is historical, conflictual and hidden, to be identified and interpreted by an expert. They are also critical of cognitive-behavioural practitioners' tendency to dwell on external factors and isolated problem behaviours, and to espouse a narrow and inauthentic scientific model of therapy. They insist that it is not only the thinking mind but also the body, feelings and soul that need to be taken holistically into the picture.

It is from the humanistic base that transpersonal therapy has grown. Sometimes considered an additional, fourth approach in its own right, the transpersonal has been said to date from the writings of William James on the psychology of religion and to include Jungian and psychosynthesis therapies, meditation, astrology, intrauterine, past lives and near death experiences, and various interpretations of levels of consciousness. Considered weird, unsubstantiated and even dangerous by some, transpersonal therapies are gaining a following, particularly among the so-called New Age community. One possible explanation is that just as psychotherapy generally has in some ways displaced formal religion, so the transpersonal is simply an explicit acknowledgement of the thirst some have for psychospiritual theory, practice and community. Humanistic and transpersonal counselling is less concerned with human deficiency and narrow clinical responses, and more with human potential and its individual and collective actualization. Possibilities of past lives, intrauterine experience, astral travel and reincarnation are not discounted. The problem then is where (and whether) it fits in professionally, and whether it belongs to the psychotherapy scene at all, rather than to an embryonic spiritual revival.

Behavioural and cognitive

Behaviour therapy dates in one (theoretical) sense from the 1920s and experimental psychology, in another (clinically) from about the 1950s, for example, at the Institute of Psychiatry in London. Originally based on relatively simple stimulus–response models of behaviour, this tradition sought to adhere to scientific principles of observation and replication, with the mind or psyche being ruled out of the equation because of its unobservability. This kind of radical behaviourism has very little support now, but many opponents of behaviour therapy anachronistically caricature it as empty and mechanistic. In fact much behaviour therapy resembles and systematizes commonsense principles of child-rearing and adult problem-solving. Behavioural psychotherapy is the term gaining favour now in the UK. Unlike psychoanalysis, it is usually found in NHS settings and not in private practice.

Emphasized in this approach is the need for focusing concretely on the specified problem behaviour and its context, and usually seeking to reduce or eradicate it by either gradual or immediate methods such as systematic desensitization or exposure. This accords with folk psychology and the view that one must put effort into learning new and/or difficult or distasteful tasks and face up to the known, feared situation or object. Lifeskill deficits or weaknesses must be addressed by new learning, for example, by practising exactly how to make eye contact and initiate friendships. Practice, action, determination and courage are perhaps hallmarks of the approach, although the theory and technical language of behaviour therapy can be difficult to grasp. The fact that many people cannot change by willpower alone, or find that a problem that has apparently been overcome returns yet again, casts doubt for some on the claims of behaviour therapy. Nevertheless, there is increasing evidence for its effectiveness in addressing quite clearly defined behavioural problems such as phobias, obsessive-compulsive disorder, post-traumatic stress and sexual dysfunctions, for example.

The cognitive (or thinking) dimension in behaviour therapy has come largely from the disaffection of previously psychoanalytic therapists such as Aaron Beck and Albert Ellis, who founded cognitive therapy (CT) and rational emotive behaviour therapy (REBT) respectively. The observation that prolonged free association, preoccupation with dreams, unconscious conflicts and the transferential relationship often did not yield clinical success led these practitioners to identify various typical, repeated cognitive errors and counterproductively generalized beliefs. Helping clients to make their evaluative and predictive thoughts explicit, challenging these and coaching clients in concerted efforts to practise new behaviours, all form the basis of cognitive-behavioural therapy (CBT). Claims persist that cognitive-behavioural therapy may be more effective in dealing with depression and anxiety than other forms of counselling or medication alone. Claims are now also made that CBT, in particular approaches such as REBT, can be applied not only to crises and transient symptoms but also to enduring personality transformation and personal growth. Although not strictly within the CBT stable, personal construct therapy, transactional analysis and cognitive analytic therapy also dwell on clients' ways of construing and misconstruing their experience.

Debates rage about the merits of each approach, its theoretical elegance, scientific rigour and clinical effectiveness. The need to control the proliferation of models has been repeatedly identified and the integrative and eclectic movement is a response to this concern, consisting of many attempts to combine theories or to focus on appropriate, transtheoretical techniques. Arguably we all need to ask ourselves why we opt for and adhere to a certain approach, how credible and effective each one is and, ultimately, how we can best help our clients regardless of our preferred orientation. Understanding at least some of the traditions of differing approaches and how these help or hinder the development of effective counselling and psychotherapy, can be posited as an essential need (Feltham, 1997c). There is also the constant appearance of new therapies – systemic, narrative-constructivist, solution-focused, neuro-linguistic programming – and resurrection and modification of historic practices such as hypnotherapy, the merits of which practitioners need to assess continually.

Fundamental enquiries about meaning and direction in counselling and psychotherapy

Almost certainly, distressed clients care little for the theoretical and professional debates that practitioners engage in between themselves. They are quite likely to have relatively modest aims and to interpret their experiences of counselling and psychotherapy within much more basic parameters than practitioners (Howe, 1993). Counsellors, however, both individually and as professional groups, need to consider the meanings and directions of their craft for the following reasons.

1   Arguably, counselling exists on the margins of mainstream society, on the fringes of social science, and not too far from a whole host of therapeutic, religious and anomalous activities that are considered by some to be superstitious, spurious, dangerous, cultish quackery. Indeed, I believe that some counselling contains at least some of these undesirable ingredients. Readers may ask themselves how closely and acceptantly they associate counselling with astrology, Scientology, palmistry, reflexology, Christian Science, transcendental meditation, positive thinking, rebirthing, past lives therapy, est, the recovery movement, and so on (Kaminer, 1992). (I am not suggesting that the above methods are of equal status, merit or dubiousness.)

2   Traditionally counsellors have resisted or fought the medical model of understanding and treating psychological (or spiritual or existential) distress. In the process, drug treatments, hospitalization, psychodiagnosis and psychiatric power generally have been eschewed and faith in the innate regenerative and self-actualizing powers of individuals has been promoted. Again, readers may wish to consider where they position themselves in this debate. Can counselling work in tandem with traditional medicine, can it re-educate doctors and psychiatrists, or is it destined to pursue an altogether different path? According to the European Association for Psychotherapy, for example, psychotherapy is an independent scientific discipline. Fascinating reflections are also being made on the possibilities of marriage between psychotherapy and evolutionary science (Stevens and Price, 1996).

3   Much research to date has failed to identify strongly any superiority for particular theoretical approaches, and therefore non-specific or common, relationship factors have been suggested as the truly potent ingredients. Does this mean that counsellors are dispensing, as it were, relationship medicine? If so, is it because relationships in our communities are impoverished? If this is the case, we perhaps need to consider the spiritual and political aspects of counselling. Indeed, organizations such as Psychotherapists and Counsellors for Social Responsibility (PCSR) are doing just that. Our question might then become: what, optimally, could and should counselling and psychotherapy be – perhaps not simply clinical but also socio-political practices (Newman, 1991; McLellan, 1995)? Alternatively, according to some, counselling has

already intruded in medical practice and threatens to become a 'politically correct' statutory requirement (Harris, 1994).

4   If there are over 400 different theoretical models, plus a number of different formats or arenas in which they are delivered, and several competing professions which deliver them, what does this say about the credibility of counselling? Is counselling and psychotherapy a unified field at all? Presumably the term 'integrative', now used so loosely and, I think, so expediently, aims to address this public relations and professional survival problem. Are we all in the same business, equally dedicated to promoting mental health and reducing distress, or are we duplicating efforts and sabotaging our proper mission? The problem of proliferation has been addressed in Feltham (1997c). Some of us may prefer to ask not so much about differentiation in this field, but about the practical and professional need to unify our efforts.

5   If you strip away the packaging, the proliferating theories, professional requirements, related training, supervision, research and publishing industries from what counselling actually looks like and what it actually achieves, what is left? For the most part, it is about two people sitting in a room talking, hopefully bettering modestly the well-being of one of them. It has often been pointed out that theoretical differences are probably minimally in evidence in the counselling room. What actually happens is that well-meaning practitioners use techniques and applied philosophies that after all are not usually dramatically different from common sense, and that they necessarily compromise according to each client's personality, circumstances and abilities. We probably are more therapeutically skilled than the average person in the street, but not necessarily amazingly so, and our work can sometimes be pretty ordinary, clumsy, unpredictable and disappointing for some clients. How can we accurately describe what we do without commercially oriented exaggeration? How can we represent our skills fairly, to instil hope in demoralized clients, without implying that we have, or claiming to have, the answer to everything?

6   A great deal of counselling discourse is just waiting for critics and deconstructionists to tear it apart. This is partly because we are used to writing without evidence, making claims on the basis of faith alone. It may also be attributable to a certain anti-rational, affectively biased tendency. Intellectualization in the context of psychoanalysis is, after all, considered a defence mechanism. It may be that distrust of rational analysis, particularly as authored by non-clinical outsiders such as philosophers and sociologists, has led to counselling developing its own, idiosyncratic form of discourse, likened by some to romantic poetry. It is also a characteristic of psychotherapy that grand systems are built on the inspirations of charismatic founders and not on slowly accumulated and scientifically tested premises and practices. While all this can be justified, we must not be surprised if the language and concepts of counselling begin to receive close critical examination (Silverman, 1996; Erwin, 1997).

Without this critical dimension, I fear we will be developing a kind of 'counselling theology', a discipline based fundamentally on enthusiastic assertion and barricaded subjectivity. Critics usefully force us to ask and explain exactly what are the practices of counselling and psychotherapy, and the theories accompanying them.

7   Respect for the self-determination of the client, embodied in the non-directive, anti-advisory ethos of counselling, can easily escape analysis. Critics have, indeed, referred to an autonomy obsession promoted by counselling and psychotherapy. Likewise, the assumption that counsellors are in their practices morally, religiously, politically and philosophically neutral is widespread. I suggest that we need urgently to re-examine these assumptions. Bimrose (1996) has argued for rigorous attention to be paid to multicultural issues in counsellor training and throughout counselling practice. Objections to the resistance which counsellors have to giving advice and information even when some clients would value it, to including family members in counselling, to discussing their own political, religious and moral views, and to making actual contact with clients' worlds (by, for example, home visits) have been raised by various writers (Newman, 1991; Holdstock, 1993; Lee and Armstrong, 1995; Merry, 1995). Here, we need to ask what counselling and psychotherapy are in a multicultural and postmodern context, and consider whether our very theoretical models might need to change radically.

8   I have previously alluded to the great breadth of psychotherapeutic aims and claims, from support through bereavement to the clinical treatment of obsessive-compulsive disorder; from making a simple career decision to undergoing a total upheaval in relationships and lifestyle; from giving up smoking to recalling and healing childhood sexual abuse and birth trauma; from decision-making about optional cosmetic surgery to curing cancer; from listening to students' homesickness stories to alleviating chronic depression; and from occupational stress management to exploring alternative, higher states of consciousness, past lives and the meaning of life.

Can a single profession or discipline hope realistically to embrace and address all such matters, which traditionally have been the domain of doctors, priests, mystics, philosophers, teachers, family members and friends? Psychotherapeutic systems such as the person-centred approach, psychoanalysis and primal therapy, tend to hold themselves up as explaining all human suffering and having the keys to resolution of them all. We surely need to think rather more rigorously than at present where the lines of our aspirations, competency and accountability are to be drawn. In this process we need to extend our thinking further than that required by bodies determining circumscribed therapeutic competencies, by exposing our work and theorizing to widespread critical scrutiny and analysis. Perhaps paradoxically such scrutiny will add to the knowledge base and status of counselling studies rather than, as often feared, diminishing it.

References

Andrews, G. (1991) The evaluation of psychotherapy. *Current Opinions in Psychiatry*, 4 (3): 379–83.
BAC (1992) *Code of Ethics and Practice for Counselling*. Rugby: British Association for Counselling.
Bimrose, J. (1996) Multiculturalism, in R. Bayne, I. Horton and J. Bimrose (eds), *New Directions in Counselling*. London: Routledge.
Bloch, S. (ed.) (1986) *An Introduction to the Psychotherapies*, 2nd edn. Oxford: Oxford Medical Publications.
Clarkson, P. (1994) The nature and range of psychotherapy, in P. Clarkson and M. Pokorny (eds), *The Handbook of Psychotherapy*. London: Routledge.
Daines, B., Gask, L. and Usherwood, T. (1997) *Medical and Psychiatric Issues for Counsellors*. London: Sage.
Deurzen-Smith, E. van (1993) *Psychology and Counselling*, in W. Dryden (ed.), *Questions and Answers on Counselling in Action*. London: Sage.
Dryden, W. (1996a) A rose by any other name: a personal view on the differences among professional titles, in I. James and S. Palmer (eds), *Professional Therapeutic Titles: Myths and Realities*. Leicester: British Psychological Society.
Dryden, W. (ed.) (1996b) *Handbook of Individual Therapy*, 3rd edn. London: Sage.
Dryden, W. and Feltham, C. (1994) *Developing the Practice of Counselling*. London: Sage.
Dryden, W. and Feltham, C. (1995) *Counselling and Psychotherapy: A Consumer's Guide*. London: Sheldon.
EAP (1996) *Results of the 6th General Meeting of the EAP*. Vienna: European Association for Psychotherapy/Federal Ministry of Health and Consumer Protection.
Ehrenwald, J. (ed.) (1976) *The History of Psychotherapy*. New York: Aronson.
Erwin, E. (1997) *Philosophy and Psychotherapy*. London: Sage.
Feltham, C. (1995) *What is Counselling? The Promise and Problem of the Talking Therapies*. London: Sage.
Feltham, C. (1997a) *Time-Limited Counselling*. London: Sage.
Feltham, C. (ed.) (1997b) *The Gains of Listening: Perspectives on Counselling at Work*. Buckingham: Open University Press.
Feltham, C. (ed.) (1997c) *Which Psychotherapy? Leading Exponents Explain their Differences*. London: Sage.
Feltham, C. and Dryden, W. (1993) *Dictionary of Counselling*. London: Whurr.
Frank, J. (1986) What is psychotherapy?, in S. Bloch (ed.), *An Introduction to the Psychotherapies*. Oxford: Oxford Medical Publications.
Hammersley, D. (1995) *Counselling People on Prescribed Drugs*. London: Sage.
Harris, M. (1994) *Magic in the Surgery: Counselling and the NHS: A Licensed State Friendship Service*. London: Social Affairs Unit.
Holdstock, L. (1993) Can we afford not to revise the person-centred concept of self?, in D. Brazier (ed.), *Beyond Carl Rogers*. London: Constable.
Holmes, J. and Lindley, R. (1989) *The Values of Psychotherapy*. Oxford: Oxford University Press.
Howe, D. (1993) *On Being A Client*. London: Sage.
James, I. and Palmer, S. (eds) (1996) *Professional Therapeutic Titles: Myths and Realities*. Leicester: British Psychological Society.
Kaminer, W. (1992) *I'm Dysfunctional, You're Dysfunctional: The Recovery Movement and Other Self-Help Fashions*. New York: Addison-Wesley.
Lee, C.C. and Armstrong, K.L. (1995) Indigenous models of mental health intervention: lessons from traditional healers, in J.G. Ponterotto, J.M. Casas, L.A. Suzuki and C.M. Alexander (eds), *Handbook of Multicultural Counseling*. Thousand Oaks, CA: Sage.
McLellan, B. (1995) *Beyond Psychoppression: A Feminist Alternative Therapy*. Melbourne: Spinifex Press.

Merry, T. (1995) *Invitation to Person Centred Psychology*. London: Whurr.

Mowbray, R. (1995) *The Case Against Psychotherapy Registration*. London: TransMarginal Press.

Naylor-Smith, A. (1994) Counselling and psychotherapy: is there a difference?, *Counselling*, 5 (4): 284–6.

Newman, F. (1991) *The Myth of Psychology*. New York: Castillo.

Ollerton, D. (1995) Class barriers to psychotherapy and counselling, *Journal of Psychiatric and Mental Health Nursing*, 2: 91–5.

Palmer, S. and McMahon, G. (eds) (1997) *Client Assessment*. London: Sage.

Parker, I., Georgaca, E., Harper, D., McLaughlin, T. and Stowell-Smith, M. (1995) *Deconstructing Psychopathology*. London: Sage.

Persaud, R. (1996) The wisest counsel?, *Counselling*, 7 (3): 199–201.

Pilgrim, D. and Treacher, A. (1992) *Clinical Psychology Observed*. London: Routledge.

Sanders, D. (1996) *Counselling for Psychosomatic Problems*. London: Sage.

Shipton, G. and Smith, E. (in press) *Long-Term Counselling*. London: Sage.

Silverman, D. (1996) *The Discourses of Counselling: HIV Counselling as Social Interaction*. London: Sage.

Solomon, I. (1992) *The Encyclopedia of Evolving Techniques in Dynamic Psychotherapy: The Movement to Multiple Models*. Northvale, NJ: Aronson.

Stevens, A. and Price, J. (1996) *Evolutionary Psychiatry*. London: Routledge.

Strawbridge, S. (1996) Counselling psychology: what's in a name?, in I. James and S. Palmer (eds), *Professional Therapeutic Titles: Myths and Realities*. Leicester: British Psychological Society.

Thorne, B. (1992) Psychotherapy and counselling: the quest for differences, *Counselling*, 3 (4): 244–8.

Thorne, B. and Dryden, W. (eds) (1993) *Counselling: Interdisciplinary Perspectives*. Buckingham: Open University Press.

Woolfe, R. (1996) The nature of counselling psychology, in R. Woolfe and W. Dryden (eds), *Handbook of Counselling Psychology*. London: Sage.

3

Social Responsibility

Simon du Plock

A number of psychologists, sociologists and philosophers has observed that the late twentieth century is a period characterized by an unprecedented degree of change. We live in the most future-oriented society in the history of humanity, but this future is opaque and unamenable to the old ideologies. We all seem to exist in an era of intellectual exhaustion in which the rapidly approaching millennium appears to be more about hopes — symptomatic of which is the plethora of texts marking the end of politics, of science, the family, even history — than it is about beginnings. This situation is unique and palpable in its consequences. The end of the last millennium does not mirror our present experience of being in the vanguard of a history we do not really control anymore. Everything everywhere is in flux, and, with the expansion of instantaneous electronic communication, we now have the technology to know this to be so.

Political life is marked by fragmentation. For good or for ill we have often looked to a nation-state for our sense of identity but now it is often ineffectual, too big to resolve small problems, and too small to control the big problems. If people seek an identity outside their immediate family they are as likely to take it from the multinational company which employs them as they are from the national state which taxes them. We have run up against the limits of industrial expansion and modern civilization does not generate an ethical framework for human life.

Change is nothing new: the late seventeenth and early eighteenth centuries were also times of extraordinary economic change, but the change we see now is far more extensive and profound and is taking place against a backdrop not of the enlightenment, but of an imponderable future. The picture is not entirely dark: therapists are used to working with people who feel they have lost their way and lack a sense of direction of purpose. It is at these times of existential crisis that clients can work most creatively to establish their reason for living. In a society breaking away from the past, therapists have the opportunity to work together with clients toward a new set of ethical standards and goals.

Paradoxically, in a world in which people increasingly feel they do not know who they are or why they do the things they do, therapists are expected to function as though they are certain of their purpose and goals. This is never more true than in 'the world of work', where the majority of adults find themselves for large periods of their life. The very phrase 'world of work' is telling, indicating the extent to which work and the securing of larger and larger incomes has become the *raison d'être* for many people. There are costs here, though, as well as benefits for a small minority on vast salaries and bonuses. Those who are employed are working longer hours while the unemployed are imprisoned in impoverished leisure. The widening gap between the financial status of those in 'management' and the rest of the workforce, and the disproportionately large salaries of top management has led to protest and indicates that a society founded on finance alone is untenable. The business executive, or even the machine operative, who pauses on their treadmill to raise questions about emotional or spiritual well-being are likely to find themselves out of work, downgraded or passed over for promotion. In an anxious world there is a great pressure on the workers to hide their doubts.

This is so often the point where the therapist enters the picture as someone who is willing to be with an individual while they attempt to salvage, or even construct for the first time, their own values against the backdrop of demands and expectations set by their employers, families and associates and, overall, the state. Therapists have noted increasing levels of demand for psychological services. This is a period in our history in which everyone, young and old alike, is beset by stresses which they do not always successfully negotiate. In a situation where long monogamous relationships are rare, where consumerism and poverty are to be found side by side in nearly every street, where we are exhorted to succeed at every stage of our lives, it is the individual who does not show signs of distress who we might think has the greatest difficulty.

In 1994 a study by the UK Office of Population, Census and Surveys provided a snapshot of the nation's health which indicated that one in seven adults – more than six million people – was suffering from depression, anxiety or some other kind of psychological disorder. Close to a quarter of a million people attempt to kill themselves every year in the UK. Of the UK population 2 in 10 (10.6 million) are over retirement age. By the year 2000, 1.2 million will be over the age of 85. An ageing population brings with it increasing rates of mental ill-health, particularly in the over-85 age group. Information from the Mental Health Foundation suggests that 5 per cent of all people over retirement age and 25 per cent of people over 85 currently suffer from clinical dementia; 1.5 million people over 65 are affected by depression. Provision is not keeping pace with the demands made on it – demands which are clearly linked to the type of society in which are we living.

The Jungian analyst, Andrew Samuels, wrote in a recent text linking depth psychology and politics, that:

The tragicomic crisis of our *fin de siècle* civilisation incites us to challenge the boundaries that are conventionally accepted as existing between the external world and the internal worlds, between life and reflection, between extroversion and introversion, between doing and being, between politics and psychology, between the political development of the person and the psychological development of the person, between the fantasies of the political world and the politics of the fantasy world. (1993: 4)

Emmy van Deurzen, a philosopher, therapist and past Chair of the UKCP, has also commented on this society in which we all strive to maintain ourselves in a state in which we can work, relax and love creatively with varying, but increasing difficulty:

A lot of distress is generated by post-modern society, now that humankind has reached a position of potential self-destruction through atomic war or over-population and pollution of the planet. Mass communication increasingly rules our lives, endangering personal relationships whilst little solace is expected from the old structures that used to safeguard human values. People often feel that they have a choice between either becoming commodities themselves as slaves in the production process or focusing so much on achievement in producing more commodities that they will not have time to enjoy the commodities they have accumulated. (1994: 7)

Against this background the rapid expansion of the whole business of therapy and the regularity with which we find therapy and therapists in the newspapers, on television and radio and in the workplace commenting on every aspect of our lives are hardly impressive. This has happened quite simply because the profession, though often misunderstood as being concerned with technical problems about how to cure illness or adjust to abnormality, is, in fact, attuned primarily to the very question which troubles us all – the question of how we live our lives. It is this fundamentally existential concern which permeates both therapy and our *fin de siècle* society.

In these circumstances, and with the demise of organized religion, therapy is the necessary and obvious adjunct of the age. While we enjoy a love–hate relationship with it, it fulfils an important function – that of providing meaning. But many of the therapeutic approaches, far from uniting us in the way religion tended to do, seem to drive us further towards becoming apolitical, atomized consumers. In the past, therapy often denied the evidence daily presented in consulting rooms that particular structural arrangements in our society prevented healthy human development. In recent years many therapists, particularly those broadly aligned with the humanistic approach, have preached the message of individual perfection and self-actualization. This, in fact, is the ultimate form of consumerism in which our object is our 'self', and its perfection. To the extent to which therapists endorse, even actively promote, this isolating unrealistic perspective on the world, they abrogate their responsibility to society to clarify the links between the internal life of the client and events in the external world.

Contemporary commentators can draw on a long line of distinguished practitioners who recognized the intimate relationships between the individual who presents for therapy and the society in which they live and who understood that the insights their clients afforded them constituted a form of social critique requiring social action.

This heritage includes the work of pre-war German psychoanalysts who resettled in North America and Argentina and concerned themselves with the lives of the poor, political prisoners and children; the radical therapists of the 1960s whose work has made it impossible to distinguish rigidly between the mentally ill and the mentally well; and the therapists and analysts, including Anna Freud, who established nurseries and schools embodying insights from psychoanalysis and the Frankfurt School.

Therapy and therapists are by design or default engaged in an activity which has at its heart concern with what it means to be human. What is new is the way in which psychotherapists and counsellors are increasingly and rapidly assimilating this critical tradition and making it their own. Perhaps the most dramatic evidence of the urgency with which they have embraced this new role is the emerging and rapid growth of Psychotherapists and Counsellors for Social Responsibility (PCSR), a campaigning organization which since its establishment in 1995 has recruited 700 members, making it one of the largest special interest groups in the therapy world, an environment which has always since the time of Freud been characterized by its tendency to form groups and counter-groups ad infinitum.

In some respects this growing interest in the personal–political is quite unremarkable, following as it does in the wake of a long tradition which has been present in psychotherapy from the beginning. Freud, certainly, had no doubt of the practical importance of his psychoanalysis:

> to throw light on the origins of our great cultural institutions – on religion, morality, justice, and philosophy. . . our language of the neurotic illnesses of individuals has been of much assistance to our understanding of the great social institutions. (1913: 185–6)

We can go back considerably further into history: Nussbaum (1994) has convincingly argued that the Hellenistic philosophers were engaged, in their pursuit of endomania or the good life, in psychotherapy. These philosophers, whom we might regard as the first psychologists and therapists, were also the first holistic practitioners. They never doubted the impact on the individual of their society and were quick to argue for those changes in social relations which they thought would most readily promote the good life.

Such a critical awareness is growing. In one paper in a recent major compilation on counselling (Palmer et al., 1996) seven leading figures in the field were asked to identify the most significant trend or issue in counselling today. All were concerned either about the social and economic context of counselling, or about the consequence for the nature of counselling itself of its rapid expansion. The two are clearly linked since it is the social and economic context in which we find ourselves that causes, or at least exacerbates, the very problems which it then calls upon us to ease. Therapists have rarely been encouraged to engage in the political activity of making plain these links. They are, rather, encouraged to consider themselves as experts in individual pathology and have been rewarded with the greatest social and professional status when they have done so. If therapists do not make these links they are condemned to treat the individual distress they witness in their consulting rooms as psychopathology. Yet many therapists, probably the majority of them, do make sense of their client's experiences by drawing on their understanding of the internal world. Not to do so, to insist on excluding the external world would be perverse and, in my case, almost impossible.

To attempt to comprehend the world of a stressed executive, a single mother or a redundant shop-floor operative and at the same time to exclude their position in society disempowers both therapist and client. In practice few, if any, therapists do this. What is important, though, is that therapists are clear about the way in which they make links between the internal and external worlds in the consulting room and, further, how they can engage with the political issues which are raised in a pragmatic form while retaining their psychological orientation. What is it that counsellors and psychotherapists are uniquely positioned to offer their clients and society in general in terms of social analysis?

One of the things they are uniquely placed to offer their clients and the wider society is a shift in their own approach to psychological distress. As is so often the case the most potent single action is that which is immediately to hand. As David Smail expresses it:

> Instead of looking inward to detect and eradicate within ourselves the products of 'psychopathology', we need to direct our gaze out into the world to identify the sources of our pain and unhappiness. Instead of burdening ourselves with, in one form or another, the responsibility for symptoms or 'illness', 'neurotic fears', 'unconscious complexes', 'faulty cognitions' and other failures of development and understanding, we would do better to clarify what is wrong with a social world which gives rise to such forms of suffering. (1993: 1)

Is therapy to act as a sticking plaster for society or, worse, a legitimation of the way it is organized, or is it to critique those aspects it deems damaging? If we do wish to offer a critique what can we constructively do? In 1996 PCSR held a conference to address these questions called 'Making a Difference', which asked, given our realization that society impacts on the psychological health of us all, how can therapists make a difference, and what sort of difference do they want to make? Therapists are uniquely well situated to make recommendations about the level and quality of provision of health, education and social services which will provide the optimum conditions for good mental health. When we survey this provision we find that per capita expenditure on many items in these sectors is frozen or cut year on year and spending on social groups with special needs – the elderly, the mentally ill, the chronically ill, the hearing impaired, or children with special learning needs – far from being the exception seems regularly to be specifically targeted for cost cutting.

If the way a society provides for those of its members in great need can be taken as a measure of its humanity we must fear for the psychological well-being not just of these service users who are increasingly viewed as expendable because they constitute a drain on the economic health of the nation, but also for those who formulate policies. There has been a dramatic shift in our system of values over the past two decades: if we persist in viewing each other as profit centres or human resources rather than as fellow citizens we impoverish ourselves in ways, invisible on a financial audit, which weaken us spiritually and emotionally.

Just as the marketplace, with its divisions between purchasers and providers of services, each at odds with the next, is the reduction of the fabric of civil society to 'a war of each against all', so the view of human nature as invariably competitive is a reduction of the fabric of civil society to 'a war of each against all'. The one-dimensional view of human nature as invariably competitive is a reduction and a denial of its richness and complexity. Counsellors and psychotherapists know human nature is not one-dimensional: they recognize that people are greatly affected by the economic systems in which they work or seek to work, the families they are part of, and the education system which shapes them.

Economics

Economics may at first seem a strange thing for psychotherapists and counsellors to concern themselves with. Surely therapists, coming as they do from their work with the emotional life of clients, cannot have anything to say about the hard factual world of finance? How can therapists have the temerity to raise any doubts about this world of costs and benefits? The fact is that there are many things about our present economic system, and our perception of economics, which are troublesome: they fail to deliver benefits proportionate either to need or to effort. One of the hackneyed catchphrases regularly trotted out is the 'level playing field' but we have nothing even approaching a level playing field in terms of access to economic goods in this society. Where benefits are missing to the extent that we talk about an underclass – a concept which a decade ago would have seemed simply shocking – then the costs in human terms are too high. The answer to such a clear-sighted view has been to degrade the language, removing those who suffer most from their status as fellow human beings and in doing so to falsify our balance sheet of humanity. Workers have become human resources to be downsized (rather than sacked); they suffer collateral damage as a result of a closure (it is the company itself which is injured, the employees are strictly incidental) and, should they end up begging on the streets they are to be treated with zero tolerance (intolerance).

What is missing from such a perspective, and what therapists may be able to reintroduce, is an understanding of the impact of economics on the emotional life not just of individuals but of our culture generally: in engaging with this most central of social and political realities therapists are also working towards an 'emotional audit' of economic activity. If they have not produced a coherent emotional audit up to this point it may, in part, be due to their own connection with the economic system. The emergence of counselling and psychotherapy and the forms it adopts are intimately bound up with the economic values of society. The growth of availability of such services over the last half century in Britain and the West generally owes much to the emergence of welfare capitalism. The relationship between psychological values and the capitalist economy is made plain by Richards:

> By and large those practices have developed within the apparatuses of the welfare state, and we might therefore expect that they are deeply implicated in the principle business of those apparatuses, which is the containment and appropriate management of the economic and social tensions generated by the capitalist market. Amongst the main sites of psychological intervention . . . the education and health services: through these vast and socially porous sectors permeate all the conflicts and tensions of society as a whole, along class, gender, ethnicity and party lines; between national and local government; between occupational groups and so on. They are above all scenes of contradiction and of resolution attempted sometimes falteringly and sometimes with a confidence born of traditional authority and/or technological power. This is the modality of power which may be referred to as 'social democracy': a socio-political strategy for moderating market relations . . . through mitigatory provision and conciliatory practice. (1986: 115–16)

While the state is happy to avail itself of the conciliatory functions of therapy it is also vigilant regarding the cost of this function – indeed it often seems that the modern state is aware of little else.

This intimate relationship can have serious deleterious consequences: the wholesale dismantling of much of the welfare state has preoccupied successive governments for nearly as long as welfarism has been in existence. Whatever is deemed too expensive (not cost effective) by the state has been run down and absorbed into the private sector. Therapists are aware of these pressures to be cost effective, to increase throughput, to reduce the number of sessions they provide, to develop briefer and briefer ways of delivering the same service. At the same time they are also pulled in the opposite direction by the need to produce evidence of their effectiveness and a whole literature has been generated apparently indicating that not only can it be the case that the major benefits of therapy can occur during the first three to eight sessions, but that such benefits may reduce rapidly thereafter (Westlake, 1987; Barkham, 1989).

With the exception of popular psychology texts of the 'understand your dreams' variety relatively little has been written by therapists about money, and yet much is said within sessions by clients on this subject. It is hardly surprising if the possession of money or the lack of it so often underpins discussion – it forms a staple of discussion among the general public.

Therapy has often laboured under the delusion that it operates in an economics free zone, finding its justification in a paradigm of help – deliverance through a personal relationship – which is impossible to quantify and evaluate. From this perspective it is understandable that therapists may be wary of an analysis of the validity of their work. Nevertheless, such an analysis is now inevitable and if they are to protect their clients from the worst ravages of the economists they had better begin to engage with the whole question of effectiveness from a philosophical perspective of their own devising – one which does justice to the richness and complexity of their work. The debate about effectiveness is not going to go away and if therapists are not to be radically deskilled over the next few years they had better make sure they have their say. Their unspoken role as conciliators between the economic system and their clients means that, although they observe the impact of economic disadvantage in their practice, they rarely make explicit the connections between this and psychological well-being. As Smail remarks:

> There is considerable irony in the fact that, at a time in our history when the successful pursuit of money has attained the status practically of a supreme moral injunction, we remain almost totally silent about what this means for our intra- and interpersonal conduct. (1993: 25)

Therapists are also surprisingly quiet about what it means for the very thing – effectiveness – about which there is now so much discussion. It seems as though they have sometimes been tempted to forget that the therapy session is a microcosm of the client's life and that the hopes and fears they express in the fifty minutes are real hopes and fears about how they can survive in the external world, and are not just symptoms of some underlying psychological trauma. Some of the assistance which clients seek in the therapeutic alliance may strike the more heady therapist as a tad too practical, but the way clients feel about themselves and about the world can be radically altered by practical change. The effectiveness of therapy can be undermined if we fail to take this into account:

> Whatever the temporary enthusiasm which may be fired in people through solidarity with a counsellor or therapist, the world will inexorably reassert its grip unless they can marshal against it powers and resources which are in themselves thoroughly mundane. Changing (or finding) jobs, moving house, forming new bonds or associations with others, acquiring knowledge or

abilities which can be put to use in changing one's circumstances: these are the kinds of events and activities which make a real difference to the way that people feel. (Smail, 1993: 188–9)

I became acutely aware of the truth of this observation during my time working in the outpatients of an inner city hospital. Very often the real changes came about as a result of the patient's taking up an evening class or finding their way from unemployment to part-time work. My task was to enable them to feel confident enough to be motivated to engage in the world but I often had to accept (and so did they) that the form this might take was greatly influenced by their poverty. A therapeutic approach which discounted the socio-economic position of the patient is likely to drive them deeper into a sense of failure and worthlessness.

Interestingly I found that these patients had a more positive prognosis than some more privileged private clients. Those who had private incomes and no immediate necessity to go out into the world to earn their living may lust for change as fervently as other clients but are less motivated because they do not need to change. In the final analysis one of the most dependable indications of successful therapy may, perhaps, be the extent to which individuals need directly to engage on a daily basis with the external world. Both extremes of poverty and of wealth may be injurious to psychological health, since both tend to limit or distort the interpersonal relationships on which it depends.

We are apt to think that clients can make changes in their lives only after they have addressed their psychological issues – indeed we can go back to Freud's injunction to those starting analysis that they should not begin any new venture or personal relationship for justification – but clients live in the real world where they need to deal with life events on a daily basis; life cannot be put on hold while they sort themselves out. This way of thinking about clients can go very deep: therapists often express surprise when they discover evidence that their clients have a life outside therapy. On a number of occasions I have had supervisees express shock (and sometimes delight) on running into clients in the street who are behaving differently or are dressed differently than the content of sessions led the therapist to expect, or who are clearly the centre of a group of friends of whose existence the therapist was ignorant.

Any emotional audit needs to take account not only of the economic realities of our clients, but also contribute to a shift in the way we view economics as a society.

The family

The work of psychotherapists and counsellors brings them on a daily basis into contact with evidence of the disparity between the reality of family life and the rhetoric about family values disseminated by politicians of every stripe. Therapists have for many years listened to stories about child abuse, violence, poverty and despair which are now supported by statistics and which are increasingly in the public domain. When we survey the therapy literature we could be forgiven for concluding that almost all of this work is concerned with repairing in adults the damage caused by unsatisfactory childhoods.

The insights on the reality of family life afforded by our clinical perspective place us in a unique position to critique the received wisdom about it under which individuals labour. Our psychological knowledge about the needs of human beings must urge us, however tentatively, to suggest new forms of family organization. For some practitioners this last may seem too radical and intrusive a role. Nevertheless we might suggest that there is an ethical problem if we observe certain things about the dysfunctioning of the family but do not use these observations for the general good. What if any other group of professionals should fail to contribute to the body of human knowledge in this way? If we are able to identify such a group we will probably question their right to be considered professionals.

The traditional model of the family – a married couple with two children who live together as an economic unit – exerts an enormous pressure of conformity on all those who live in different ways, a pressure so great that it frequently causes these people to consider themselves failures and often prevents unhappy couples from seeking other relationships. One of the most liberating things to happen in therapy is the realization by clients that they can make choices, that the way they are living need not be the way they continue into the future. Though counsellors and psychotherapists often shy away from saying that therapy can be educative since this smacks of an expert role, at its most useful it is often, as van Deurzen has claimed for existential therapy, a 'tutorial in the art of living'. Many people live in clumsy, restricted ways and damage themselves and others because they have not been vouchsafed a wide enough perspective on life. Institutions like the traditional family frequently function to limit, to provide a boundary on what is permissible and acceptable. The realization that this institution is a social construct, is in fact a fiction, can empower us to seek more adequate ways of living.

One of the primary functions of therapy is that of clarification, and perhaps the single most important question for us to raise concerns the status of this traditional family. Certainly there is little that is traditional about it. Politicians, particularly but not exclusively those on the right, promote Victorian values, but they, like us, lived in numerous different types of family structure and, arguably, enjoyed more flexible living arrangements than we do. The family did not become a shibboleth until late into the second half of the nineteenth century. When it did the middle and upper middle class who were promoted as role models tended to live in extended family structures within close geographical proximity, and not in the nuclear family which we consider the norm.

That the traditional family is not traditional might not matter so much if it clearly served its members, but our consulting rooms are packed with people who tell us otherwise. It can be argued that those who had happy childhoods and now have fulfilling families themselves are unlikely to begin therapy. In response to this we can observe that more and more people are now entering therapy. We also know from statistics on child abuse, youth suicide, divorce and what is euphemistically called 'domestic violence' that these people cannot be dismissed as in some ways the 'socially inadequate'; they are the vanguard of those who have suffered and wish to stop suffering. We cannot be impartial about this legacy of a normative model of a specific vision of traditional family and the problems which are endemic to it without denying the integrity of those who choose to live together in other, perhaps more innovative, ways.

Politicians of all parties are eager to champion family values at every opportunity but they rarely state what these are; it is assumed that we all know and agree about this subject. Is this, though, actually true? What values are there which are peculiar to families as against friends, colleagues, neighbours or any of the other relationships we have with others? Our popular image of the family is that it is a place of unconditional love of the sort mirrored by person-centred therapy in the concept of unconditional positive regard. The experiences which clients bring to us suggest that the values of the family and values which they had as children within the family structure were far from unconditional. Many of these clients found themselves enmeshed in a system which limited them and demanded dependency rather than nurturing their potential for growth and independence. Far from being respected as persons in their own right, clients found they were expected to meet their parents' unfulfilled desires or were expected to 'be a credit' to them.

Many people enter therapy because they are struggling with the role which their family of origin imposed on them. The psychologist Dorothy Rowe has remarked on the way in which value is accorded to children only to the extent that they unwaveringly fulfil their role – as the Stupid One or the Fat One – and allow other family members to feel secure:

> Perhaps worst of all is to be designated the Competent One. Many able children accept this role in the hope of gaining their family's love, but once you have accepted it you begin a life of servitude. You are expected to be always strong, helpful and available. Never disclose to your family that sometimes you feel weak, vulnerable and distressed, for if you do they will either ignore you or bully you until you shut up and go back to looking after them. (1997: 19)

Perhaps there is something even worse, and that is when parents shape their children to fit in with their own pathological needs. I recall a male client whose mother had a hatred of men and who repeatedly told him that he was the child of the devil and was cursed. This client was not able for many years to free himself of the conviction that he was evil and it was only as a result of intensive therapy that he was able to gain the courage to divest himself slowly of his family's values and to build his own life. In this case the damage was compounded by the fiction that the family was close and self-sufficient. This fiction had the practical result that the family was closed to external help; those who were not of it were against it. As Rowe has pointed out, while 'close knit' is bestowed by the media on families and communities as a term of approval it can make life outside this small group seem impossible: 'It is this family value, when "family" is extended to include those of the same religion or nationality, that makes war, conflict, terrorism, torture and persecution possible' (1997: 19).

It is not surprising that so much damage is done to children within the family. Our whole culture is split in its feelings about children, dividing them into good and bad, angels and demons. This unthinking dichotomization permits politicians to respond to bad behaviour with plans for curfews, smacking, boot camps and, finally, prison-building schemes. If we see children as inherently bad, rather than as reacting to their environment, then inevitably we will fear them and will seek to police them. As Orbach has stated:

> If we are to transform our culture's fear, and sometimes hatred, of children, we need to shift the conversation away from good parents and bad parents, good kids and bad kids, good teachers and bad teachers, and towards a consideration of what allows children to thrive, we need to undo the knots which tie those who parent or teach unhappy hurt children. (1997: 6)

Such direct input into public debate clearly signals a public appetite for guidance and an openness to more thoughtful ways of looking at the family than the knee-jerk reactions of politicians and certain elements in the media.

Discussion of the problems encountered in therapy in addressing the damage done to clients in childhood is commonplace. Counsellors and psychotherapists should also look to see what they can contribute from a therapeutic perspective in terms of preventative intervention to limit the harm which can be caused by inadequate parenting. The aim here is to support and empower parents. Therapists should not fall into the trap of prescribing a model of good parenting – to do so would be to emulate the arrogance often shown by politicians – but would support parents in providing their own 'good enough' parenting. Though even engagement in parenting education might be contentious and difficult to introduce, there are good grounds for giving it careful consideration. As Einzig points out:

> We know that abusive parenting produces abused children, many of whom in their turn will abuse themselves, their children, or those close to them. We

know now also that confident parenting can produce confident children and that 'good enough' parenting – that much over-used term – can be more than good enough. (1996: 220)

Politicians are, perhaps, more conservative and frightened of change than the general population. It was politicians who pilloried gays and lesbians at the end of the 1980s for living in 'pretend families', thus attempting to deny any legitimacy to this large group of their electorate who felt the need and had the courage to invent new support structures for themselves. Increasingly it is the model of the family championed by the politicians which is a pretence. To enter into the debate about what the family is as an ideology and what it can come to mean now and in the next century is not to devalue the 'traditional' family but to refuse to privilege it blindly and to work towards getting our real needs met as people for intimacy, support and growth.

Education

The accounts which clients give of their experiences of school are frequently accounts of active violence and brutalization or, and perhaps worse, a deadening of intellectual curiosity as the child was processed to value him or herself as just one more tiny cog in the machine. It may be this regimentation and discouragement of individuality which contributed most to distress, frustration, alienation and lessening of the human condition which children experience and attempt as adults to come to terms with. In the experience of large numbers of people, education was something which was done to them rather than a process they engaged in with teachers. If our education system is failing large numbers of children we will need to find new ways to promote what Fromm called our 'basic needs': for safety, belonging, love, self-esteem, knowledge and understanding. As therapists we know that when these basic needs go unmet the individual's internal world becomes distorted, and that this distortion is passed on to others and the wider environment. Good education strongly reinforces good mental health. Bad education can severely undermine the child, his or her family, and finally, all our collective social values. Educationalists have, over the last 30 to 40 years, recognized the crucial role of their profession in creating children's good-enough sense of themselves and their capabilities, and have looked to psychological theories to help them in this work. Tragically, the use of psychological knowledge is now under attack by politicians and the media who seem to attribute all sorts of social ills to it, including lack of discipline.

So important an activity as education should attract the attention of politicians and the media but this seems to take the form not of informed discussion but of a slanging match. At its most naive the debate can be reduced to one of apportioning blame for all the ills of society: from the decline in manners, litter in the streets and the demise of the orderly queue, through to long-term unemployment and violent crime. The jury seems to be constantly out on whether we should 'blame the parents' or 'blame the teachers'. Those who occupy both roles are, we might suppose, doubly guilty. The idea seems to be that teachers have in some way failed not children but Society, with a capital S; that we have poured money and resources into creating a responsible body (in Britain we would never aspire to an intellectual elite) for the trans-mission of moral values between generations only to discover, as if by sleight of hand, that the teachers are themselves feckless and, interested only in sociology and left-wing politics, at best simply incapable of setting the appropriate example to the nation's young.

Perhaps the most realistic way to make sense of this hostility is to see it not concerned so much with the process of education as with the maintenance of the 'system' itself. If politicians view the education system as responsible for socialization, social control and social engin-eering then it follows that they can lay almost any social problem at its door. This education system is not fundamentally concerned with safety, belonging, love or self-esteem. It is not even concerned with knowledge and understanding except where this is of the variety which will enable the young to enter the world of work with the skills an employer demands. British schools, with the notable exception of the elite public schools, have probably never been much concerned with culture or individuality but they are now blatantly intended to provide technical training rather than intellectual education. There may be too few books in the libraries but the main political parties are committed to ensuring that every teacher and every child can use a computer. There seems to be a measure of agreement among politicians, educationalists, employers and parents that young people must be adaptable if they are to meet the requirements of the rapidly changing workplace.

The needs of business are quite simply taken to be synonymous with those of the child. The child needs to have the skills and motivation to fit into the world of work with as little dissent or disruption to the machine as possible. To this end children now regularly have as many hours in education as the average working adult spends in their place of employment and politicians are talking about compulsory homework to be done at designated homework centres which will raise these hours even higher. As therapists we must be concerned about this encroach-ment on the child's time for being a child rather than a worker. As psychologists we may be able to show policy-makers that some of their plans are misguided. The current move, for example, to reject small group teaching in favour of traditional 'whole class' teaching, where the teacher stands at the front of the class and addresses all the pupils, may not, in fact, provide the best model for the innovative, team-based approach in most of modern industry and research.

Counsellors and psychotherapists need to find ways to become more fully engaged in discussion about curricula, classroom structures, classroom environment, and the quality of the teacher–pupil relationship to ensure that education promotes psychological well-being for all those involved in it. They need to promote an education system that serves the needs of young people in developing their emotional and social skills and does not simply standardize them in the service of industry.

Epilogue

In some respects the institutions of counselling and psychotherapy – now an increasingly vast edifice encompassing numerous distinct approaches to psychological distress – resemble nothing so much as the deregulated market economy the casualties of which form a large proportion of its clients. Few if any would wish to return to the situation where paternalistic psychiatry and classical analysis were almost the only treatments available, restricted to the inpatient and the wealthy, leaving the majority of the population in awe and fear of mental health practitioners and mental illness itself. It should not be forgotten that even fifty years ago mental distress was shrouded in shame and ignorance for the mass of the population. Yet the results of the deregulation of this market is a field so complex that the novice attempting to negotiate it, particularly in a state of anxiety or depression, is likely to become still more confused and distressed.

Part of the reason why therapy has thrived is the interest of the social system in promoting a view of psychological pain which conceives it as 'a problem caused and cured within the immediate ambit of people's personal lives' (Smail, 1993: 19). In fact there is little evidence for such a notion of individual psychopathology; rather 'psychology has consistently overlooked the more essential ingredient of distress: the ways in which power is exercised over people' (Smail, 1993: 23).

As van Deurzen has observed, 'the churches of psychotherapy have become oppressive forces that mould personalities and lives and that confuse pathology with the struggle to survive' (1997: 2). But psychotherapy need not side with all the other oppressive institutions of the late nineteenth century. Those approaches to therapy which have become ossified and dogmatic can no longer serve the goal of human life to be inquisitive, curious and reflective about its own nature. Those approaches are as suspect with regard to their ability to attend to us rather than to impose upon us as, at the other end of the scale, those approaches which pander to notions of self-actualization and the perfection of the individual. Both must be weighed and found wanting. Rather, therapy should contain within itself and hold dear the knowledge that we do not know very much about human nature. In this regard we might almost consider our endeavour to be one between researcher and co-researcher in collaboration, rather than between expert and patient or client. Therapy will refuse to split the troubled person off from everyday life and from the world of shared meanings in favour of a maze of theory replete with its own conventions and technical language and hidden understandings. To return to van Deurzen:

> We cannot dispense with theories and methods that seek to get a hold of the seemingly intangible thread of life. We should, however, have the courage to question any dogmas that monopolise claims to truth in this area. The domineering attitude of some psychoanalysts and other consecrated psychotherapists goes against common sense, which tells us that we are all in this business of living together and that there can be no authority higher than that of our own experience as it is understood in the light of reflection and in comparison with the experience of our fellow humans. (1997: 2)

The discontented function as the therapists of psychotherapy since those who critique the field prevent the rest of us from becoming complacent about either our profession or its relationship with wider society. Counsellors and psychotherapists will not be thanked for it very often and they should be wary of being paid for it. It might be objected that therapists identify social ills but shrink from offering solutions to them. Perhaps in the final analysis the most useful role for the therapist to take in any form of social therapy is, as is often the case in individual therapy, that of raising questions – daring to ask the most difficult questions, even those which make us unpopular – so that people begin to look more carefully at the way they live and begin to fashion their own answers.

As therapists we would do well to heed Edward S. Said's thoughts on the duties of the intellectual as he propounded them in his 1993 Reith lectures, 'Representations of the Intellectual':

> The intellectual today ought to be . . . someone who considers that to be a thinking and concerned member of society, one is entitled to raise moral issues at the heart of even the most technical and professionalized activity as it involves one's country, its power, its mode of interacting with its citizens, as well as with other societies. In addition, the intellectual's spirit as an amateur can enter and transform the merely professional routine most of us go through into something much more lively and radical; instead of doing what one is supposed to do, one can ask why one does it, who benefits from it, how it can reconnect with a personal project and original thoughts. (1994: 61–2)

If we only replace 'the intellectual' with the 'the therapist' we will arrive at the perfect description of the socially responsible psychotherapist or counsellor – a person in pursuit of integrity, living in a state of constant alertness to lies and half-truths, challenging rationalistic myths and phobias, eccentric in the etymological sense of being 'outside the centre', a marginal figure and questioner of the status quo, a hater of all systems, an undomesticated, anti-establishment figure who speaks the truth to power and lives in metaphorical exile. In so striving for authenticity we cannot but embody the questions which will clarify power relations and make those who exercise power more accountable and socially responsible.

References

Barkham, M. (1989) Towards designing a cost-effective counselling service: lessons from psychotherapy research and clinical psychology practice, *Counselling Section Review, The British Psychological Society*, 4 (2): 24–9.

Deurzen, E. van (1994) *Can Counselling Help?* Durham: University Press.

Deurzen, E. van (1997) *Everyday Mysteries, Existential Dimensions of Psychotherapy*. London: Routledge.

Einzig, H. (1996) Parenting education and support, in R. Bayne, I. Horton and J. Bimrose (eds), *New Directions in Counselling*. London: Routledge.

Freud, S. (1913) The claims of psycho-analysis to scientific interest, 13. *The Standard Edition of the Complete Psychological Works of Sigmund Freud*, translated and edited by James Strachey, London: Hogarth Press and The Institute of Psycho-Analysis, 1953–1974.

Horney, K. (1939) *New Ways in Psychoanalysis*. London: Routledge and Kegan Paul.

Nussbaum, M.C. (1994) *The Therapy of Desire: Theory and Practice in Hellenistic Ethics*. Princeton, NJ: Princeton University Press.

Orbach, S. (1997) A culture of child-hating, *The Weekend Guardian*, 4 January: 6.

Palmer, S., Dainow, S. and Milner, P. (eds) (1996) *Counselling: The BAC Counselling Reader*. London: Sage in association with the BAC.

Psychotherapists and Counsellors for Social Responsibility (1995) Founders Group statement, unpublished document.

Richards, B. (1986) Psychological practice and social democracy, *Free Associations*, 5: 105–36.

Rowe, D. (1997) Friends of the family, *The Guardian*, 4 January: 19.

Said, E.S. (1994) *Representations of the Intellectual*. London: Vintage.

Samuels, A. (1993) *The Political Psyche*. London: Routledge.

Smail, D. (1993) *The Origins of Unhappiness: A New Understanding of Personal Distress*. London: Harper Collins.

Usher, J.M. and Baker, C.D. (1993) *Psychological Perspectives on Sexual Problems*. London: Routledge.

Westlake, R. (1987) New futures: employee assistance programmes. Guidance and assessment review, *The British Psychological Society*, 3 (4): 2–3.

4

Self-development: Lifelong Learning?

Hazel Johns

To make a powerful case for the self-development of counsellors and psychotherapists is not difficult. Personal awareness and growth for all human beings have been advocated throughout the ages in arguments from philosophical, religious, sociological, literary and political thinking. From the 'examined life' of Socrates to the twentieth-century fascination with individual differences and 'self-fulfilment' through popular psychology, a consistent emphasis has evolved on the desirability of lifelong personal development, at least for those safe from poverty, danger and abuse. How much more crucial, then, is self-development likely to be for counsellors and therapists, who are using their personalities, communication skills and intimate understanding of human nature directly in the service of others?

Counselling and psychotherapy are relatively young 'professions', with divergent views on theory and practice generating sometimes more heat than light. Yet, in virtually all theoretical approaches, the actual relationship between the therapist and client is now accepted as central (McLeod, 1993). Whatever conceptual or philosophical differences in underpinning theory, the person, the self, of the worker must then be of primary significance in creating that relationship and maintaining its quality, appropriate to the needs of the client and the purposes of the therapeutic process. As Jersild (1955) emphasized, the questions 'Who and What and Why am I?' and 'Who am I and Who can I be for Others?' are key issues for any of us in 'helping relationships' of any kind. These questions are recognized as central in reputable training for counselling and psychotherapy, as evidenced by the course accreditation requirements of the BAC and UKCP: personal development is one of the core training elements. Selection, too, for such training normally includes an evaluation of personal qualities, emotional stability and flexibility of attitudes, as well as interpersonal skills, a degree of self-awareness and ability to reflect on experience.

This chapter is not primarily about training, since I shall take for granted in that context the high status and central contribution of personal development work. My focus here is rather on the need for self-development throughout the working life of a therapist, the range of motivation for such a focus and some of the methods by which it might be sustained. I have used throughout the chapter the terms psycho-therapist, counsellor and therapist, though I should record my own lack of differentiation between the roles of therapist and counsellor; my preferred use of the words 'counsellor' and 'counselling' to describe a range of therapeutic activities; and my irritation at the often hierarchical use of 'therapy' to suggest greater depth, seriousness or professionalism.

Paradoxes

Some of the assumptions which underpin this discussion give rise to a number of paradoxes. One such paradox is embedded in the focus of the chapter: a concentration on 'self', despite the consensus views of its centrality in the service of clients, has attendant dangers of selfishness and at worst narcissistic self-absorption. It must be understood here as 'self-in-relation'. 'Aloneness' (Gilmore, 1973) and its existential implications are at the heart of the self-development task, yet we must accept, especially in the context of counselling and therapy, that 'self-sufficiency is an illusion' (Hemming, 1977). Similarly, I would argue that working for knowledge and striving for some confidence in understanding of self and others are crucial for therapists and counsellors, yet it seems increasingly clear to me as I get older that maturity means being able to tolerate, on all sorts of planes, uncertainty and not knowing. Yet again, there may be paradoxical confusion in the very concept of 'self'. What understanding are we working on? What assumptions do I share with the reader? What theoretical models are influencing my thinking and yours? I find it helpful to think of 'the self' in a range of ways, influenced by different theoretical models: as a constantly changing and developing entity; as an existential being making and remaking itself by creating its own meaning; as an amalgam of conscious, subconscious and unconscious elements; as a collection of 'selves', social, sexual, philosophical, vocational and moral; or as a set of 'sub-personalities'.

The reader's own values and conceptual preferences will also influence which of these or other frameworks help make sense of the term. Other paradoxes include the need for confidence and self-belief in order to perform effectively in a therapeutic role, alongside the paramount demand that we retain sufficient humility and awareness of our own fallibility to avoid arrogance. Central to this chapter's exploration, too, is the core tension between accepting the need to work towards Egan's (1986) 'Ideal Helper', while acknowledging that to be human and stay sane, it is only reasonable to attempt to be 'good enough' (Connor, 1994).

Contexts

Within that framework of paradoxes, the contexts in which counselling, psychotherapy and self-development take place are also of considerable significance. In our culture at this moment, late in the 1990s, there are many pressures, stresses, confusions of values, current or imminent transitions, changes and uncertainties. We are approaching the end of a century and a millennium: one does not need to be a New Age fatalist to feel some sense of anticipation, excitement or tension surrounding the event. At the same time, early in 1997, after eighteen years of one-party dominated politics, we witnessed a general election which resulted in a change of government. However much some of us longed for that, there were others who felt a loss of security, even if of 'better the devil you know' variety. Employment patterns have changed dramatically; those who once could rely on settled jobs for life now face uncertainty at best and, at worst, unemployment and a non-work future. Tensions for both the 'work-rich' but 'time-poor' and the 'work-poor' but 'time-rich' (*Observer*, January 1997) are causing strains in individuals, relationships, homes and workplaces.

In addition, within families, work and social settings, some shifts in expectations and attitudes are occurring in gender relationships, both as a result of legislation and gradual social change, while similar, if slow, modifications are happening in ethnic, disability, sexual and age-related issues. Rampant consumerism, self-centred 'politics of greed and envy' and tabloid press influenced prurient gossip fight for supremacy of public concern with humanitarian tragedies around the world, ecological horror at the wilful damage inflicted on the earth and individual angst, as in Frankl's (1963) 'innate drive to search for meaning and purpose'.

How can counsellors and psychotherapists be unaffected by such potentially bewildering forces of change and uncertainty and by the struggle to manage the range of personal conflicts engendered by all the above? It is inevitable that such influences must exacerbate individual internal processes and intensify the core needs for self-awareness, self-knowledge and self-development. If, as Kierkegaard said, 'becoming human is a project', that project is faced no less by counsellors and psychotherapists, as human beings, than by their clients. At the heart of self-development, then, is 'the distinctively human characteristic' of the struggle for a sense of significance and purpose in life.

Defensive self-development

My starting point, then, is a non-apologetic reminder that counsellors/ therapists – as well as being professional or volunteer therapeutic helpers – are people who have particular needs to be self-aware and well grounded, yet open and sensitive to others. There is considerable consensus that the training of counsellors and therapists in all the 'talking therapies' and in all theoretical orientations should have self-development at its heart (Johns, 1996). After training, however, what particular needs – and demands – are there on skilled, qualified and experienced counsellors and therapists to continue their own professional and personal development?

There are two kinds of argument to reinforce these demands: the first set involves reactive responses to the range of critical attacks which bombard counselling and therapy, particularly in terms of accountability and ethical concerns. The other arguments, to be considered later in the chapter, are proactive and creative. The reactive reasons are defensive of the client, in the interests of protection of both client and counsellor and support the aim of strengthening the ethical frameworks within which counselling and psychotherapy operate. The knowledge, skills and awareness required to meet those demands are of course, as much responsibilities or obligations as needs. In the context of ethical propriety, responsibilities and needs must go in tandem and be seen as meeting the same or at least consistent ends. Nelson-Jones (1984), in emphasizing the capacity for 'choosing and making' one's life, and McLeod (1993), in stressing the need for 'personal soundness' to acquire sufficient 'sanity, knowledge and competence' to be a good-enough counsellor, both highlight this notion.

In order to protect clients, psychotherapists and counsellors must work consistently to develop their knowledge: of psychological theory, therapeutic models, human growth, development and change, social contexts, emotional health and illness, relationships, individual differences and philosophical, religious and existential frameworks for making sense of the world. They need to work, too, on their skills and competencies, so that they can operate with an appropriate range of approaches, techniques and modalities of relationship, relevant to individual clients at different points in the therapeutic process. If counsellors and therapists are to evaluate and apply all those elements effectively and sensitively, their greatest need in self-development is to struggle constantly for awareness, so that they can make accurate judgements about their clients, their contexts and – even more crucially – about themselves, their own motivations, responses and needs. Clients are likely to be most vulnerable to unaware practitioners who use inappropriately power, seduction, influence, pressure or emotion; who are unable to identify their own 'blind spots'; who are meeting their own unacknowledged needs; or who are unskilled or incompetent on any number of key dimensions.

As counselling and psychotherapy have become more accepted, understood and valued in some sections of society, so criticisms, attacks and challenges have multiplied. Some, such as mockery about clients' weakness or lack of moral fibre, are ill-informed, stem from traditional social attitudes and can be responded to by gradual attitude change and education over time. Others, which identify therapist manipulation, abuse or incompetence, must be incorporated into our collective and individual professional self-monitoring. There are, of course, unscrupulous practitioners who are perfectly aware of their malpractice: our shared aim must be to weed them out. Those of us (and that could be any of us) who might inadvertently abuse our clients in any way must accept the need for constant self-monitoring and striving for awareness. As the BAC Code of Ethics reminds us, 'Counsellors must not exploit their clients financially, sexually, emotionally or in any other way' (BAC, 1993). Bond (1996) has also written cogently of the urgent need to take into account differences in cross-cultural and gender experiences, which should alert us to further ethical questioning of our practice, attitudes and assumptions.

In parallel with this process, we have to recognize that clients may, deliberately or unconsciously, seek to manipulate, abuse or deceive their therapists. For therapist self-protection, there is a key need for self- and other-awareness of feelings, thoughts, intra and interpersonal process, the ability to notice in the counsellor herself early signals of discomfort, unease or legitimate doubt, clearly differentiated from a lack of empathy or non-acceptance of the client. The skills of appropriate challenge, of self-disclosure and immediacy, are crucial in this context, as is the ability to self-challenge. Counsellors and therapists may also be skilled at deceiving themselves: it is no accident that exhaustion, stress and what has popularly become known as burn-out are familiar experiences for many in the helping professions. Any of us may fall into the trap of ignoring our limits – whether of energy and health; of competence, in terms of kinds of clients, depth of therapeutic work, or areas of human concern and struggle; of will, motivation and commitment. Those all too human fallibilities may also be affected by the inevitable developmental, age-and-stage pressures of living, ageing and changing, or by the crisis events, large and small catastrophes, which all of us will suffer.

There may also be issues about performance over time and experience: there are obvious dangers of inexperienced workers missing key cues or making errors of judgement; if experienced workers take their own judgement for granted and begin to operate on a kind of 'automatic pilot', their work might be just as inefficient, incompetent, arrogant or unethical. The Sufi path to personal development involves a series of travels: for counsellors and psychotherapists, one of the essential internal journeys is the constant quest for focus, purpose and motivation, in order to combat weariness, staleness, cynicism or despair at the pain or frustration of aspects of human existence to which they may be exposed. There is, at times, a slender tightrope to tread between the need to stay fully open to others' often harrowing experiences and the need to defend ourselves against anguish. If, as practitioners, we mismanage this balancing act, we may betray our clients and ourselves. However, to sustain the sensitivity, empathy and congruence to manage that huge task, we must constantly strive for our own self-awareness and self-development – or we and our clients are at risk.

Bond (1993) has explored the ethical demands facing both individual counsellors and the emerging profession of counselling. Organizations such as the British Association for Counselling (BAC), the British

Psychological Society (BPS) and the United Kingdom Council for Psychotherapy (UKCP) have all worked hard to draw up codes of ethics and practice, to provide at least broad guidelines within which practitioners might operate safely and appropriately. There might at times be conflict between the organizational needs of the 'profession' of counselling and therapy and matters of individual conscience or belief, for example, in relation to friendships, social or sexual relationships after counselling or therapy has ceased. Since so much of our work is rooted in values and beliefs, we all still have a duty (responsibilities and needs, again) to monitor our work conscientiously against both those agreed codes and our personal creed or code of practice. Supervision facilitates the evaluation of the broad questions of ethics and practice, particularly in relation to the safety of the client. Only personal work on the unique pattern of moral, emotional, sexual, social and intellectual concerns will enable any individual counsellor or therapist to identify her own strengths, limitations and oddities – a 'spiral curriculum' to which she will need to return throughout professional life. Instead of the 'Persecutor', 'Rescuer' and 'Victim' of the 'drama triangle', therapists need constantly to revisit their Pressures, Resources and Vision – and the moral sense at the heart of their theory and practice. Accountability, competence and conscience are tough but necessary companions on a counsellor's or psychotherapist's journey of self-development.

Proactive and creative self-development

'The greater our awareness, the greater our possibility for freedom.' Corey's (1994) assertion reminds us that there is more to human and professional self-development than the defensive, reactive drivers outlined above, however important those are. It should be axiomatic that an emphasis on creative renewal and growth should operate throughout professional life, yet my knowledge of counsellors and therapists with a wide spectrum of years of experience does not bear that out. There are, of course, individuals who plan and control their lives to allow for new learning, adequate rest, sufficient new stimuli and restorative experiences, but many others seem to allow themselves to be steadily drained and exhausted by the demands of their work and their lives until they feel ill, defeated or diminished in a range of ways. (Glasshouses and stones come to mind here.) Some key values in counselling and therapy cluster around the search for wholeness and balance; for integration of head and heart; for increasing awareness, understanding and growth; for the possibility of working towards a reliable belief system; for ways in which to identify, accept and meet enough of our own needs for life to be purposeful and rewarding; and for the learning that enjoying dependence, independence and interdependence is a lifelong task. These values lie at the heart of much therapeutic work for clients and should have an equal importance for therapists. If lifelong learning is increasingly accepted as a central intellectual task in the field of continuing education, then we might fruitfully acknowledge and live out more consistently the need for lifelong emotional and social learning. If that is so for any adequately functioning adult, how much more necessary for counsellors and psychotherapists, for whom feelings and relationships are the central currency of their life and work?

There are many arguments to reinforce this view, not least that if the abilities to communicate well, respond to and process human interaction are central to therapy, then therapists might be expected to model such features in their 'ordinary' lives. Reality, of course, provides us with sufficient evidence that paragons are hard to find, since some counsellors' relationships fail, organizational conflicts occur and therapists have unhappy, confused times in their lives. There should, however, be great potential in counsellors and psychotherapists who continue to work to develop the core qualities of empathy, acceptance and, above all, genuineness. They are perhaps more likely to sustain high quality relationships, be of positive significance in others' lives and manage their own journey through the vicissitudes of life with some sense of purpose and relative equanimity – or even hope.

Some readers might consider such a view unrealistically optimistic: if you believe, as I mostly do, that hope is better than despair and that human beings are capable of improving the quality of their immediate worlds by small and imperceptible changes, then those values will continue to feed the concept of therapeutic workers as possible role models for effective living. A key aim might be to reduce the likelihood of practitioners being seen as, or indeed, living as 'morally ambiguous' people, a contentious concept much in focus in current social and political contexts. Before words such as pious, arrogant, foolish or silly are flung my way, I should record my own awareness of the philosophical, spiritual and pragmatic complexities of that concept, which other chapters in this book and many other tomes might elucidate. Struggling to move beyond such ambiguity does not imply an easy attainment of perfection, but, as the poet Robert Browning expressed it: 'Man's reach must exceed his grasp, Or what's a heaven for?' Similarly and convincingly, May (1969) argued: 'We must have the courage of imperfection . . . to triumph over the burden of unnecessary fears.'

Another encouragement for continual self-development comes from the psychological interpretation of modern quantum physics, which posits the interconnectedness of all things and prompts a consequent reviewing of our relationships with each other and the universe. Again, the acceptance of such a view is bound to be linked to values and beliefs, but even a grudging willingness to consider the possibilities allows for potential reward in both general and therapeutic terms. The 'quantum world view' offers an emphasis on creative dialogue between body and mind, individual and context, human culture and the world of nature. It suggests a picture of the human self which is 'free and responsible, responsive to others and its environment, essentially related and naturally committed, and at every moment creative' (Zohar, 1991). How could that not be relevant to and beneficial for counsellors and psychotherapists? Given that we are 'never exempt from the human condition', and 'never perfectly equipped to help others' (van Deurzen-Smith, 1992), there would yet be huge potential in continuing to work on ourselves which, in turn, might have reverberations for good in the emotional, social and environmental climate around us. Any of us in the therapeutic world ignore at our peril the complex relationships between individuals and the other people intimately or distantly involved in their lives; the interactions between any of us and the social systems and networks in which we live; and the invisible or all too evident wider connections between those systems and the physical or metaphysical world in which we exist. The human ecology, the symbiotic network of relationships underpinning human existence, has to be continuously nourished and replenished or it will wither, diminishing the quality of life for all.

In this context, it is perhaps crucial (especially for counsellors and therapists) to differentiate between the need for self-development in order to survive professionally and the need in order to flourish as human beings, who then bring more than the minimum to their therapeutic work. As Ignatieff (1984) points out, in writing about 'the needs of strangers', it is 'notorious how self-deceiving we are about our needs' and yet we are 'the only species with the capacity to create and transform our needs'. He argues powerfully that, both for ourselves and others, we can and should work towards realizing the full extent of our potential in human and community terms – with no more specific and therefore constraining an aim, but no less ambitious. Self-development, then, is not only a professional expectation but a human obligation, to explore, like King Lear, our blindness to our own needs. Key in that exploration is the ability to distinguish between needs we have a right to have met by others and those we do not: a central theme in any therapeutic relationship.

There are three other interrelated aspects which underpin the above and reinforce the drive for creative self-development. One is the concept of 'emotional intelligence'; the second is the contribution of culture, in the sense of literature, art, music, dance, theatre, film and so on; and the third is the necessary – for me at least – notion of individuals in context, socially, politically and spiritually. Those form an image of concentric circles of development, the ripples of each spreading irresistably through the others. The wellspring for development – and I would argue, particularly for counsellors and therapists – is the challenge of harnessing our emotions in order to optimize our thinking, acting, choosing, changing, leaving, loving and surviving – or flourishing.

The case for 'bringing intelligence to our emotions' is cogently argued by Goleman (1996), who outlines emotional intelligence as including self-awareness, impulse control, persistence, zeal and motivation, empathy and social deftness. It is – or could be – central in altering the qualitative experience of people in aspects of life as diverse as medicine and health, management, the family and relationships, and, above all, in and through education. It is indeed hard to differ from his view that 'emotional illiteracy' is at the core of many of the painful issues of modern life and certainly those brought to counselling and therapy. I would argue further that a constant striving for 'emotional intelligence' and 'emotional literacy' should form the heart not only of counselling training (as I have written elsewhere, Johns, 1996), but of a lifelong curriculum for self-development for all counsellors and psycho-therapists. This is especially relevant in any (that is, most) models of counselling and therapy which assume a capacity in the therapist for reflection and self-monitoring as a central element of the counselling process, so that feelings and responses are a purposeful part of the therapeutic relationship.

If the centrality of emotional education is accepted, then the links become self-evident with cultural stimuli and all the art forms mentioned earlier (and returned to later in this chapter). The possibilities are endless for meeting, exploring, absorbing or debating all human emotions through the diversity of art forms now available to us, at least if we have sufficient resources, freedom or energy to access them. I recognize that not all therapists have the desire or means to do so and may, indeed, not share my values about their worth. I suppose a challenge of white/ Western/ middle-class elitism could be levelled at the expectation that all practitioners should attempt to extend their emotional range by experiencing 'culture' in this way. I can only respond that such an attack would be ironic, since my own route to both culture and counselling came through such exposure in my Welsh working-class origins.

There may, however, be other relevance in those origins for my equally firm conviction that counsellor/therapist self-development should also encompass awareness of and exposure to wider contexts, social, political, philosophical or spiritual, than their immediate personal world. Kearney (1996) argues, as suggested by her book's subtitle 'Undeclared Influences in Therapy', that many practitioners are unaware of the implicit political attitudes or values which govern their view of the world, rarely challenge them or even evaluate their influence on their perspectives on clients, theories or psychotherapeutic issues. Training should have provided the impetus for such an evaluation; further questioning of and exposure to different world views and experiences should form a central and continuing part of counsellor/ therapist self-development, if 'tunnel vision' is not to result. Any training of quality should, of course, have stimulated exploration of that kind and should equally have inculcated the concept of lifelong self-challenge, since many values and beliefs change over time, are rarely immutable but may be influencing responses to clients in unexpected ways. Counsellors and psychotherapists may also be located in organizations or working with clients who are; they need a clear understanding of organizational issues and processes. In addition to these arguments for a broader political, social or philosophical world view, I also have a belief that having some passion, some strength of feeling attached to more than the immediately personal, helps to maintain a practitioner's energy and lifeforce, so sustaining his or her sense of purpose. This also offers some protection against the pain and hopelessness which may dominate the work, at least in some circumstances.

Finally, and perhaps most convincingly, the therapist's need to keep on growing and developing, as Mearns and Thorne (1988) suggest, is 'a glorious invitation to live life to the full!'.

Self-development: how to meet the need?

The case, then, is strong for continued self-development for both defensive and creative reasons. How might counsellors and psychotherapists, at all stages of their working lives, manage this complex task? There are many ways in which personal development can be pursued: including further training; opportunities to be involved in groups; recreational, cultural and learning activities or challenges; a commitment to reflection and self-review; working for a solidly centred and satisfying life of personal relationships; and, existentially, and perhaps especially as mid-life transitions come and pass, seeking actively to identify and explore key questions concerning the meaning of life, art and work. One of the most obvious methods, given the field we are considering, is personal therapy for the therapist.

Personal counselling and therapy

There are many views, depending particularly on theoretical allegiance, on the place of personal therapy/counselling before and during training. Despite the lack of consistent research evidence (Aveline, 1990; Norcross and Goldfried, 1992) to demonstrate the greater effectiveness of therapists who have undertaken it, there is a general anecdotal view (often expressed with great conviction) that the opportunity to explore personal issues in a safe therapeutic relationship is desirable and probably essential for counsellors and therapists. There is, of course, strong evidence that the 'therapeutic alliance' is significant in terms of outcomes for the client (Orlinsky et al., 1994); the person of the counsellor and his 'soundness' (McLeod, 1993) are clearly central in that. Certainly all the principal professional bodies, BAC, BPS and UKCP, reinforce that view in the expectations expressed in their Codes of Practice, accreditation procedures or chartered status process. Most (though not all) psychotherapists and counsellors in training who commit themselves to therapy acknowledge gains in insight, awareness or emotional resolution.

Many commentators would argue that personal counselling/therapy is equally necessary as a protection throughout the rigours of professional counselling life – at least, at recurring times of stress, if personal life becomes difficult, in life crises or in relation to responses to particular clients. If, as practitioners, we believe in counselling/therapy as a creative contribution to development for clients, we might also value its developmental potential for ourselves. My own view is that the emphasis on personal therapy as obligatory for practitioners entirely misses the point: its optimal value is likely to emerge at a time of readiness, through reflective self-awareness which identifies a need, triggered by discomfort, uncertainty, the presence or absence of expected or unexpected feelings, unresolved personal issues, challenge to accepted beliefs or crisis or developmental transitions in both professional and personal maturity. As such, there may be recurring moments of choice throughout professional life when a period of personal counselling will be valuable, most productively, perhaps, with a range of practitioner approaches.

A central but important irony is that counsellors, like any human beings, have to have sufficient resilience and strength in order to risk feeling and being vulnerable. That experience, which parallels the client's, may be at the heart of the processes and blocks of the therapeutic relationship. In addition, such a valuable learning opportunity, which reinforces empathy and offers insight into client perspectives on therapy, provides a healthy reminder that not all issues, conflicts or confusions are susceptible to solutions or neat outcomes. Indeed, the recognition that both therapists and clients are freed from the obligation of being perfect may be a gift to both, and contribute to genuine other- and self-acceptance. Further consideration might be given to the differing focus of therapy for workers belonging to different theoretical schools, to practitioners' needs for personal work to vary over time and, of course, to the inevitable overlap and fusion of concerns between therapy and supervision (Wilkins, 1997).

Other approaches

It would be naive and protectionist to assume that personal therapy is the only means to meeting the need for self-development. I have written at length about the range of activities possible in counsellor training (Johns, 1996). All of those are equally relevant for experienced practitioners, though given the range of settings and geographical areas in which counsellors and therapists work, it will not always be possible for practitioners to have easy access to, for example, participation in groups, sophisticated further training, or structured activities with peers. It is, of course, important that counsellors and psychotherapists see continuing personal and professional development as a responsibility, as well as a need. They have to identify gaps in training to date or monitor new demands as they arise through changes in client group, modifications in depth of work or shifts in theoretical approach or perceived needs in competencies.

There is perhaps no substitute for interpersonal interaction with peers in groups, in order to sharpen perceptions, make oneself available for feedback or engage in deeper exploration or debate; practitioners have some responsibility to continue to seek such experiences as part of their personal development. Groups have, however, become something of a 'sacred cow' in training circles, and I now have a pragmatic recognition that there are other equally valuable, if different, ways of increasing self-monitoring and self-awareness. The techniques of IPR (*Interpersonal Process Recall*, Kagan, 1967) can be adapted and other sources of feedback sought from clients or colleagues, all in the service of extending the capacities of our 'internal supervisor' (Casement, 1985). Supervision itself must be a key support in and stimulus for that self-monitoring, but at the heart of self-development there needs to be a commitment to and skill in being a reflective practitioner, using all means at our disposal.

Writing journals, poetry or creative recording of any kind, seeking and responding to the magical spectrum of literature which can offer so many modes of cognitive and affective learning, using physical activities and the natural world as therapeutic 'play space', and reaching out into art forms of all kinds to deepen insight, understanding and emotional range are all ways of intensifying awareness and furthering personal development. Knights (1995) explores vividly the potential in literature for counsellors, while many writers have examined the creative potential of journal writing (Progoff, 1975; Rainer, 1980). Any process which stimulates the right brain as well as the left, therapist hearts and spirits as well as heads, will contribute to client well-being and practitioner self-development. This allows full use to be made of life experience and maturity, founded on and integrated with training and professional practice. I referred earlier to the potentially damaging influences of moral ambiguity; in contrast, I am arguing here that counsellors and psychotherapists should strive to be as open as they dare to all the moral complexity, emotional, social and intellectual nuances that life, art and literature offer.

Individual differences; common needs

There are individual ways of perceiving and responding to the world; preferred modes of learning which affect interpersonal interaction and receptiveness in groups (Honey and Mumford, 1986; Irving and Williams, 1995); and a range of personality types (Bayne, 1995). In addition to the variety of emphases stemming from theoretical orientation, all these are factors in the differing commitment to self-development (Bergin and Garfield, 1994) which therapists and counsellors display. It seems unarguable (at least to me) that, whatever those variables, personal development, before, during and after training, is a core need of counsellors and psychotherapists, in the interests of the community, their clients and themselves. As Gilmore (1984) advocated, counsellors have a responsibility to undertake continuously a 'systematic audit' of their strengths, limits and capacity for change, under, she suggests, the key headings of Skills, Style, Stamina, Situation, Spirit. Such an audit should increase the likelihood of therapists managing more effectively, ethically and openly the central and often distorting issues of power, oppression and empowering, belonging and not belonging, shame and blame, other- and, perhaps most importantly, self-acceptance.

Self-development is a crucial need. In order that both individuals and society should benefit, Holmes and Lindley (1991) argue for the centrality of moral development, including ethical sensitivity and a sense of our own fallibility, in our struggles toward maturity and autonomy or 'self-government'. Adding emotional intelligence, creativity – and even the capacity for fun – might enable counsellors and psychotherapists to grow within a flexible yet robust framework which offers both challenge and support. When I can acknowledge who and what frightens me, as well as what, for me as a counsellor and even more for me as a human being, I truly care about and value, then I feel at my most grounded; without aiming for unrealistic or sanctimonious perfection, I can truly attempt to live in the moment and work for the future. In a BBC Radio 4 programme (January, 1997), the politician Tony Benn movingly described the 'flame of anger' and the 'flame of hope': I am able to glimpse the possibility of keeping both alive – each, I believe, a powerful motivator and essential companion for counsellors and psychotherapists.

References

Aveline, M.O. (1990) The training and supervision of individual therapists, in W. Dryden (ed.), *Individual Therapy: A Handbook*. Buckingham: Open University Press.

BAC (1993) *Code of Ethics and Practice for Counsellors*. Rugby: British Association for Counselling.

BAC (1996) *The Recognition of Counsellor Training Courses*. Rugby: British Association for Counselling.

BPS (1993) *Code of Conduct, Ethical Principles and Guidelines*. Leicester: British Psychological Society.

Bayne, R. (1995) *The Myers-Briggs Type Indicator: A Critical Review and Practical Guide*. London: Chapman and Hall.

Bergin, A.E. and Garfield, S.L. (1994) *Handbook of Psychotherapy and Behavior Change*. New York: Wiley.

Bond, T. (1993) *Standards and Ethics for Counsellors in Action*. London: Sage.
Bond, T. (1996) *Future Developments for Ethical Standards in Counselling*, in R. Bayne, I. Horton and J. Bimrose (eds), *New Directions in Counselling*. London: Routledge.
Casement, P. (1985) *On Learning from the Patient*. London: Tavistock.
Connor, M. (1994) *Training the Counsellor*. London: Routledge.
Corey, G. (1994) *Group Counselling*, 4th edn. Pacific Grove, CA: Brooks/Cole.
Deurzen-Smith, E. van (1988) *Existential Counselling in Practice*. London: Sage.
Deurzen-Smith, E. van (1992) in W. Dryden (ed.), *Hard-Earned Lessons from Counselling in Action*. London: Sage. pp. 26–45.
Egan, G. (1986) *The Skilled Helper*, 3rd edn. Monterey: Brooks/Cole.
Frankl, V.E. (1963) *Man's Search for Meaning*. New York: Washington Square.
Gilmore, S.K. (1973) *The Counselor-in-Training*. Englewood Cliffs, NJ: Prentice-Hall.
Gilmore, S.K. (1984) Unpublished lecture. London.
Goleman, D. (1996) *Emotional Intelligence*. London: Bloomsbury.
Hemming, J. (1977) Personal development through education, in J.B. Annand (ed.), *Education for Self-Discovery*. London: Hodder and Stoughton.
Holmes, J. and Lindley, R. (1991) *The Values of Psychotherapy*. Oxford: Oxford University Press.
Honey, P. and Mumford, A. (1986) *The Manual of Learning Styles*. Maidenhead: Honey and Mumford.
Ignatieff, M. (1984) *The Needs of Strangers*. London: Hogarth Press.
Irving, J.A. and Williams, D.I. (1995) Experience of group work in counsellor training and preferred learning styles, *Counselling Quarterly*, 8 (2): 139–44.
Jersild, A.T. (1955) *When Teachers Face Themselves*. New York: Teachers College Press.
Johns, H. (1996) *Personal Development in Counselling Training*. London: Cassell.
Kagan, N. (1967) *Studies in Human Interaction: Interpersonal Process Recall Stimulated by Videotape*. Michigan: Education Publications.
Kearney, A. (1996) *Counselling, Class and Politics*. Manchester: PCCS Books.
Knights, B. (1995) *The Listening Reader*. London: Jessica Kingsley.
May, R. (1969) *Love and Will*. New York: W.W. Norton.
McLeod, J. (1993) *An Introduction to Counselling*. Buckingham: Open University Press.
Mearns, D. and Thorne, B. (1988) *Person-Centred Counselling in Action*. London: Sage.
Nelson-Jones, R. (1984) *Personal Responsibility Counselling and Therapy*. London: Harper and Row.
Norcross, J.C. and Goldfried, M.R. (1992) *Handbook of Psychotherapy Integration*. New York: Basic Books.
Orlinsky, D.E., Grawe, K. and Parks, B.K. (1994) Process and outcome in psychotherapy – noch einmal, in A.E. Bergin and S.L. Garfield (eds), *Handbook of Psychotherapy and Behaviour Change*. New York: John Wiley.
Progoff, I. (1975) *At a Journal Workshop*. New York: Dialogue House Library.
Rainer, T. (1980) *The New Diary*. London: Angus and Robertson.
UKCP (1997) *Ethical Guidelines. In National Register of Psychotherapists*. London: Routledge.
Wilkins, P. (1997) *Personal and Professional Development for Counsellors*. London: Sage.
Zohar, D. (1991) *The Quantum Self*. London: Flamingo.

5

Cultural Differences in the Therapeutic Process

Zack Eleftheriadou

Western counselling and psychotherapy training has arisen from a pre-dominantly ethnocentric philosophy. Most of the tutors, clinicians and supervisors are white middle-class Anglo-Saxons, which inevitably places a particular ideology on training and practice. Demographical shifts have meant that, as therapists, increasingly we have to work with people who originate from different parts of the world. Although the cross-cultural field is still relatively new, innovative methods of multi-disciplinary theoretical and clinical work have been formulated in the areas individual therapy, family therapy and medical consultations (see Pedersen, 1987; D'Ardenne and Mahtani, 1990; Kareem and Littlewood, 1992; Eleftheriadou, 1994, 1996a; Holland, 1995). As Pedersen predicted:

> Multiculturalism has become a powerful fourth force (complementing the psychodynamic, behavioural and humanistic perspectives) not just for understanding foreign based nationality groups or ethnic minorities but for constructing accurate and intentional relationships generally. (1996: 20)

The purpose of this chapter is to transcend the different theoretical frameworks (as much as one is able to) and to highlight some of the essential areas for exploration. The aim is to explore the effect of cultural differences on the therapeutic relationship and process. It describes cross-cultural therapeutic skills which are necessary if we are to serve the mental health needs of the ethnic minority population. The under-lying philosophy is that there are effective ways in which a counsellor can incorporate cultural issues in clinical work. However, cross-cultural therapy does not mean that there are distinct ways of working with particular cultural groups, such as West Indians or Italians. Cross-cultural practice is an attempt to encourage cross-cultural communica-tion, rather than ostracize or highlight ethnic minority clients as being 'different'. Cross-cultural work also aims to support people who wish to understand or regain respect for their roots and cultural heritage.

Wherever appropriate, case material is used to highlight clinical practice. The reader is urged to consider the material, but not to perceive the case vignettes as representing the cultural group as a whole.

Throughout the text the words therapy, counselling and psychotherapy, and similarly counsellor and therapist, are used interchangeably.

The nature of prejudice and racism

Many people in Britain today are living away from their country of origin and struggling to find their sense of identity in a multicultural world. Living in a different culture from one's country of origin, or growing up in a family that has its cultural roots elsewhere, introduces its own themes and concerns. Those who have connections with cultures other than the dominant one experience culture shock (including confusion, anger and loss of their culture), as well as discrimination and prejudice because of their cultural or racial differences. Inevitably, the daily social experience of being perceived as different and thought of purely as part of a group rather than as an individual filters into the psychological level. For some people this can create a sense of inadequacy and can aggravate other psycho-social issues. It is common that if a person is going through social or emotional difficulties then racism and cultural alienation can intensify feelings such as despair and helplessness.

The relationship of culture to identity development

> Culture is a vast system of meanings, behaviours and rituals. Culture is a way of creating shared ways of functioning, in order to communicate effectively . . . we create shared events, practices, roles, values, myths, rules, beliefs, habits, symbols, illusions and realities. . . . Cultural information is like a flexible dictionary which is handed down [through intergenerational transmission] and gives the appropriate cultural definition of every single event, object or concept. (Eleftheriadou, 1994: 1–2)

Lago and Thomson (1996) discuss culture using the image of an iceberg. This is a useful metaphor because it reminds us of the numerous observable, visible cultural characteristics, such as customs, language and literature, but equally the plethora of invisible ones, such as motivational styles and ways of carrying out tasks. Confusion and misunderstandings in cross-cultural communication are most likely to occur in the area below the tip of the iceberg which is often made less explicit. Often the 'passport' (which comes from the French word meaning 'to pass through doors or barriers') to these signals is membership of the cultural group or close affiliation to it.

All psychological approaches, albeit in their own disparate ways, discuss the notion of self, using words such as ego or personality. This is not a universal concept that we can apply to all cultures. A person's sense of self will depend on the psychological make-up of the parents, their own familial experiences and the wider socio-cultural milieu. Clients may have a more individualistic or more extended notion of self.

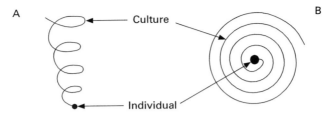

Figure 5.1   *The relationship of individual and culture*

Harwood et al. (1995), in their innovative book *Culture and Attachment*, challenge the commonly discussed notion of the micro-system of caregiver and child in the formation of intimate relationships. They demonstrate that from the period of infancy personality formation and generally the most intimate relationships will be largely shaped by cultural socialization. Culture and the self are linked almost as a spiral. If we extend this notion, some people have moved away from their culture and therefore the spiral has stretched (see Figure 5.1, state A) and for others, who are still extremely involved with their culture (Figure 5.1, state B) the spiral is closer together.

     This does not mean that either of the states is following a so-called 'normal progression', but it indicates the type of relationship between the person and the culture at a particular point in time. There is often the pressure that people need to become 'integrated' or 'acculturated' into the culture in which they reside. Becoming integrated can take place at different levels and in different areas, depending on the person's motivation and the environment. For example, some people may learn the language in order to find work or study, while others may engage more fully by taking on values and practices. Acculturation may be desirable to the new society for many reasons, including the wish to view everyone as the same. However, it is a well-known fact, demonstrated repeatedly by extensive research (Pedersen, 1995), that people who change environments do not necessarily change or move away from their cultural roots. On the contrary, some people adhere even more closely to what was practised in their home country. Furthermore, people can shift from states A to B (Figure 5.1) and vice versa depending on their psycho-social state. It is often the case that when people experience stressful life events, such as a relationship break-up or a bereavement, they seek a closer connection to their culture or spirituality. This process is represented by a move towards state A. Clients can also change during the course of therapy. An illustration of this is a client who not only changed allegiance back to her country of origin but also began to wear the traditional cultural dress which she had battled against for years, prior to the therapy.

     The counsellor's sensitivity to the different patterns of relating can help the client to relate in ways which are comfortable and congruent with their upbringing. Nevertheless, this is not an easy task as many of these patterns are unknown to the therapist because they are subtle; hence they need careful consideration. For example, among many other subtle non-verbal and social communication signals, which of the following client qualities does the therapist validate or encourage – co-operation, politeness, addressing the therapist indirectly, wish to protect family reputation, level of eye contact/gazing which is acceptable, tone of voice, facial expressions, emotional expression, physical distance? Similarly, is a counsellor encouraging behaviours which involve seeking help, sharing of concerns with family or friends, competition and separation from the familial or cultural group? Unless there is awareness and rigorous cross-cultural therapy supervision these elements, determined by what is acceptable in different cultures, can often be ignored.

Matching or a cross-cultural relationship?

Many clients who seek help find themselves working with someone from a different culture. This may be out of lack of choice or wishing to work with someone from another background. This section will address ways of establishing, from the beginning of the therapy, how the client feels about being in a cross-cultural relationship. Cross-cultural counselling implies two people working together who come from different cultures. The most common case is that the therapist comes from the dominant culture and the communication with the client takes place in the dominant culture's language. A second scenario is that they are both from a different culture and use the dominant culture's language. The third may be that the therapist comes from the minority culture and uses the client's language to communicate. These combinations will all create their own unique dynamics which have to be addressed from the beginning. The different relationships require not only that the counsellor moves out of his/her prospective theoretical and cultural framework, but also the client, although to a considerably lesser degree.

During the assessment stage or initial sessions, information is gathered which may indicate the potential course of the cross-cultural therapeutic relationship and outcome. As stated earlier, one of the first indicators is whether the client had a choice about the cultural background of the therapist. Grieger and Ponterotto outline six components which need consideration during the assessment stage. These include:

the client's level of psychological mindedness (defined as familiarity with the western middle-class conception of the term), the family's level of psychological mindedness, the client's/family's attitude toward counseling, the client's level of acculturation, the family's level of acculturation, and the family's attitude toward acculturation. (1995: 360)

These components are extremely useful, but perhaps it is more relevant to think about the 'type of individual and family psychological minded-ness' rather than the 'level of psychological mindedness'. The reason for this is that clients from different cultures have a different way of con-ceptualizing emotions and interactions rather than possessing a higher or lower level of psychological mindedness. This has often been used as a case against the provision of cross-cultural therapy services.

The first assessment factor, the individual's type of psychological mindedness, includes all the ways in which individuals conceptualize or make a 'diagnosis' about their emotional state. This would indicate whether they had a choice or understood the referral, whether they attribute the distress to biological or psychological factors, whether they manifest bodily or verbally, and generally how these fit within the client's socio-cultural construct. This point also raises the question of how much do therapists need to inform their client about psychological constructs. At times clients may find it useful to have names for their distress and ways that it can be worked with.

Second, the type of familial psychological mindedness requires investi-gation. When clients and their families have different notions of distress it is likely to increase conflict. Third, the attitude of the the client/family towards counselling will have an impact on the therapeutic outcome. Grieger and Ponterotto provide the example of Irish-American families:

> There is a cultural value on stoicism, on keeping a stiff upper lip, and on not 'feeling sorry' for oneself. In a family of this background, an individual who is depressed and trying to express that as a psychological or emotional phenomenon may receive little support. . . . For a client from a background in which the family does not believe in emotional disturbance or psychological explanations for unhappiness, entering the therapeutic process may be conflictual. (1995: 363)

It is also more common that clients from cultural backgrounds where there is more emphasis on the extended family, often from Asian and Southern Mediterranean populations, to be accompanied by family members.

The fourth point on acculturation refers to how much the client has incorporated the dominant culture: for example, whether their choice of partner, social groups or support systems include people of the same culture or of different cultures, how would the community judge them as successful or unsuccessful, among other information. The relationship to one's culture (Figure 5.1) can be used as an indication of how much the client accepts or rejects culture and therefore how much they will engage in the therapeutic process with a therapist of another culture. If there is too much distance the therapeutic relationship may not work successfully. According to Grieger and Ponterotto (1995: 359) the research results 'indicate that levels of acculturation and ethnic identity development are related to client's attitudes toward Western-type mental health services and to levels of mental health functioning'.

There are times when it is sufficient for clients to know that the therapist is also a member of the same or another culture to that of the majority culture, because they feel it gives them a closer connection and a better understanding of their experience. Some clients may be threatened by contact with someone from an obviously different background. An example may be a Muslim woman working with a male counsellor or a Muslim man being alone with a female counsellor. These are obvious mismatches that create conflict from the beginning. Of course, the opposite can also take place where it may be safer to confide to someone of another culture because the fears of someone being connected to their family or community are relatively limited. This may mean that extra assurance regarding confidentiality will be required. When working with Muslim girls, for example, any potential leakage of material means not only community gossip but possible ostracization or punishment from their family or cultural group.

The fifth factor, family level of acculturation, may provide indicators for the individual's relationships. For example, what language was or is spoken at home, whether cross-cultural friendships or partnerships are encouraged or discouraged. Last, the family's attitude towards acculturation can have an impact on the client's cultural identity. If the individual and familial ideas on acculturation are dissimilar, which include the type of engagement a client makes to the therapy, it can often be extremely stressful and become the focus of the therapy. This is common in people who have been brought up in the dominant culture. They may have learnt to speak the language and behave in ways which fit into what are considered 'appropriate behaviours' of that culture, but they still hold another cultural pattern which warrants exploration in the therapy.

Case vignette

Andrea, a Greek-Cypriot client in her mid-fifties, was referred for counselling after repeated visits to her new Greek doctor. Her doctor was British-educated and believed that the client was suffering from depression which could be helped by a therapist. The client agreed and made an appointment to attend counselling shortly after. She explained that she has been suffering for years, but she could not confide in anyone who was 'foreign'. The reason for this is that her spoken English was poor and she would rarely mix with anyone non-Greek. She was able to speak to the Greek doctor because a male doctor in her culture holds high status.

Andrea responded readily to my enquiry about her thoughts regarding the counselling; it was her first experience so she did not know what it entailed. She had strong doubts as to whether talking would alleviate her problems, but she agreed to co-operate to please her doctor and her family, who made her promise that she would attend at least the first few sessions. She believed that there had already been a 'cathartic' effect by breaking her silence and so we met regularly for a brief period of time. Counselling was experienced as companionship which took place once a week. She wanted to return the 'favour' of my attentiveness and listening and invited me to her home to offer me 'a coffee and a sweet', which is a common gesture of hospitality in a Greek-Cypriot household. Although I declined, this is a regular event with Greek-Cypriot clients, especially first generation immigrants, that I have to address in the course of the therapy.

How much do we need to know about the client's culture?

As therapists, we may not need to know all the details about a person's culture, but there are some significant factors which have to be taken into account. Some behaviours are culturally specific and if they are removed from their context they become meaningless. There are also behaviours and emotions which may be understood even when they are taken out of their context. These commonalities, which transcend cultural barriers, can be used as the main building blocks in cross-cultural therapy work.

We can prepare ourselves for cross-cultural work by undertaking a certain amount of cross-cultural training and by learning about other cultural systems, but the rest will also depend on factors such as the counsellor and client relationship, length of therapeutic contact and the level of trust which has developed. Usually clients will outline the significant elements of their culture during the process of the therapy. For example, if they feel their culture is validated they will talk about religious holidays in depth. Where clients feel mistrustful of the therapist they will not share any meaningful cultural elements. Instead, they may talk about cultural information in detail, leaving out the affect. This creates a distancing effect with the counsellor and conveys such messages as 'you do not understand my culture' and 'you are not one of us' or 'you do not know the culture and therefore it will be kept a secret', among many others. The therapist has to be able to address these messages without feeling threatened or the alienated outsider. After all, this experience of being an outsider is what the client may want to convey to the therapist in the most emotive way. If clients feel comfortable enough with the therapist then they will be able to step back from their culture far enough to be able to make a critique, be it positive or negative. The therapist's role is to remain open during such delicate exploration.

The therapeutic process is an open one which can not be predicted. The task of the therapist is to listen and observe with an open mind. This state is not a blank one. The cultural background, experiences, values and attitudes influence the psychological processes for both the client and the therapist. The therapist cannot claim that he or she is culturally neutral. Instead it is vital that therapists have awareness of their own culture and its impact on their development before working with someone of a different culture or race. As Thomas states:

> Claiming neutrality on the therapist's part puts the client in a difficult position because the therapist has thereby divested herself/himself of those things that might connect with the client's culture and background, be this positively or otherwise. A therapist who claims cultural neutrality also robs the client of the opportunity to speculate or to make observations about the therapist's background, particularly if this has an effect on the therapy in terms of connection or fit. (1995: 172)

When is the presenting issue about culture?

Clients seek therapy when they feel they have reached a point where they can no longer cope alone with their emotions and need another person to support and listen to them. One of the counsellor's functions is to mirror back to clients their feelings, especially if they feel they do not know what image/person they are projecting in their relationships. The counsellor can only empathize in relation to her or his own experience which may have different socio-cultural referents.

It does not necessarily mean though that all clients from different backgrounds will present cross-cultural issues as problematic. Culture is part of their context and should be addressed as such. When the distress is about cross-cultural issues the client may indicate this. Often the more conflict there is about cross-cultural issues the more likely it is that the issues will be presented in a rather 'disguised' form. By disguised I mean the material is presented in a hidden manner, either because it is out of the client's awareness or because the client is really unsure of how the therapist will react. This perhaps communicates the level of the emotional intensity attached to the material. Being from a minority background, the client may not have had the opportunity to discuss her or his experiences of moving from one culture to another or of racism or prejudice. Nevertheless, at the Inter-cultural Therapy Centre, Nafsiyat (London) race and cultural issues seem to arise from the first therapy session. Clients appear to have the 'freedom' to talk about cultural issues or racism because they are aware of what the Centre stands for and that the staff originate from all over the world. This inevitably brings myriad other assumptions and it is therefore just as important to avoid collusion or over-identification with the client.

How cultural background, experiences, values, attitudes influence the psychological process: integrating the inner and outer world

It is useful to begin the clinical work with the clients' assumptions of what the therapeutic process entails. If clients are not familiar with the counselling process it may be necessary to establish their notion of care and support. 'Caring' for clients may incorporate their cultural notion of what is appropriate support/care/counselling, who the appropriate 'healer' might be, what type of process and length of the support is required. It is always vital to find out where clients stand in relation to their culture and how much they wish to move out of their cultural framework. This implies the motivation to learn/understand other cultural ways of viewing the world.

In order to understand the role of culture in the client's life we can begin by obtaining a psycho-social biography, which incorporates both psycho-racial and psycho-cultural material. As Kareem and Littlewood (1992: 14) state, cross-cultural therapy 'takes into account the whole being of the patient – not only the individual concepts and constructs as presented to the therapist, but also the patient's communal life experience – both past and present'. In other words the client's 'worldview' (Deurzen-Smith, 1988) is explored. This consists of the different elements of our experiences. First, clients are encouraged to explore their relationship to their culture or social group – an exploration of the shared characteristics which the person has with their social group and the practices they reject, where they belong in terms of their race and what impact societal views have had on the formulation of this image.

Second, the experience of being in different physical and architectural landscapes and climatic conditions may also be discussed. Third, the spiritual element of a client's culture can provide the therapist with invaluable information. This is the case even when clients claim that they are 'not religious'. In this context spiritual is a broad construct, whether it is a more traditional or a combination of different philosophies. Through exploration of ideas and values taken from religious upbringing, powerful cultural visual images, icons and symbols can be uncovered.

Adequate time and thought needs to be given to the client's material before distinguishing when it is their own perception or that of other people. However, clients may also have internalized societal views, for example, their cultural group is portrayed in the media and hence it has become embedded in their psyche as their own self-perception.

In the therapy the concept of 'pre-transference' or 'societal transference' (Curry, 1964) incorporates all that clients may transfer from their societal experiences to the therapeutic relationship, for example, how clients perceive their status within the majority culture. This notion refers to all the feelings that clients experience even before they have met the therapist. In the same way the therapist will have views on what the client will be like. As the encounter progresses, the therapist takes into account the dynamics of transference and countertransference. Transference and countertransference are psychoanalytic concepts which are used to describe the feelings evoked between the client and the therapist. Transference includes the feelings a client holds for those who are most intimate to them (usually stemming from childhood relationships with their primary caregivers) and how they were treated by them. These are projected (or placed onto) the therapist. Similarly, countertransference refers to the way in which therapists may also project their own feelings onto clients or their own feelings can be triggered by a similar emotional experience with their client. These feelings can often be intensified when the therapist belongs to the same culture as the person or their caregivers.

A mixed race client who had a Greek-Cypriot mother and an African father talked to me about how she knew immediately that I was Greek and often thought I looked at her in the same way as her mother. For this client the mere fact I was of the same cultural background as her mother evoked material that had not been touched before. She never felt accepted by her mother or her (mother's) cultural group and yet she found herself in a therapeutic relationship with someone who was accepting, despite the cultural differences. She often enquired about my cross-cultural involvements, but I would usually refrain from responding. On two occasions when she enquired directly about my ethnic origins, I did respond as I felt it would be helpful to the therapeutic relationship, although I avoided elaborate answers. It is important to allow room for the client's imagination to flourish rather than feel obliged to respond to cultural questions because, as this example illustrates, transference and countertransference feelings are complicated by issues of culture. The therapist needs to be able to judge whether an answer about her country of origin will help the client examine further material or whether it will interfere with the relationship at that particular moment. Therapists disclosure should aim to help bridge the client's internal and external reality, but not to highlight the therapist's own relationship between higher psychological state and socio-cultural position.

There is a strong tradition in psychoanalysis and psychoanalytic psychotherapy and indeed other forms of counselling and psychotherapy to be suspicious and view the client's material as being about something else, something which has been significantly altered and deeply hidden. The client's material can fall under one of the following three categories: there may be material which stands for something else and is yet out of the client's awareness; the material may be events which have taken place (for example, the client's experiences of prejudice due to their accent, appearance or name); or a combination of both. This is illustrated in the case vignette of Angela below. Caution is necessary before giving feedback to the client's racial and cultural material. For example, an adolescent who had just started therapy asked me whether my colleagues were also friends of mine. Since my colleagues are from different cultures I asked her whether she was wondering how I relate to people of different cultures, but of course how she and I would relate since we were from different backgrounds.

This opened up issues of having to negotiate a therapeutic relationship with someone who has probably had rather different socio-cultural experiences. She needed to know about how much exposure I had had to different cultural viewpoints and whether I would allow room for the differences between us.

Some clients come to therapy with the wish to explore their cultural milieu and the process may entail some accepting, reviewing and leaving behind other cultural patterns. Other clients will want to work specifically within their cultural setting. Each person will make it clear what is negotiable during the process of therapy. It is a complicated process to establish how much of a client's distress is linked to cultural issues and how much is linked to more personal issues (which are still embedded in a cultural milieu, but culture is not the main focus). At any rate, clients seem to work best with someone who can take into account their cultural milieu and recognizes racism so that they do not feel it is a personal problem. Numerous research projects in the early 1990s conclude that cultural responsiveness 'counselors should be aware of, show recognition of, demonstrate knowledge of, and express interest in the client's ethnic identification and cultural background and how both may or may not relate to the client's problem' (Atkinson and Lowe, 1995: 408).

Cultural responsiveness seems to supersede any preference for a particular therapeutic approach (whether directive or non-directive, depending on what is congruent with the client's cultural healing patterns) and matching counsellor and client according to culture or race (Atkinson and Lowe, 1995).

The following vignette illustrates the complex link between the clients experience of racism, and how it becomes linked to her personal issues as well as how it filters into the therapeutic relationship.

Case vignette

Angela, a West Indian client in her late thirties, came to therapy to discuss her anxiety. It had become generalized into different areas of her life and one of her main concerns was that it was preventing her from going out of the house and interacting with other people. Early on in the therapy she revealed that she had been sexually abused by a member of her own culture. She often reported dreams with intruders, but she had not made the emotional connection to the earlier events in her life. One of these dreams was about a white man who came into her house and attempted to enter her bedroom. She tried to stop him and after a difficult struggle he quickly entered her room and stole her bedcover, records and other personal belongings. She remembered him as having a 'distinctly English appearance'. When she reported the dream she was confused because the man was of another race. We slowly explored what it meant and we were able to unravel how she linked the childhood abuse with her experience of racism during the same week. This enabled us to explore what it meant to be in a cross-cultural counselling relationship.

Initially she had told me that she did not mind what type of therapist she consulted and 'whether they were black or white'. However, at this stage it was clear that I was seen as white. When I addressed this in the therapy she felt embarrassed and wondered what I would think of her. She felt she was being ungrateful for the help she was receiving. I told her I thought it would actually be important for our work together to think about what it meant to be working with someone she did not perceive as 'black'. It was a step closer to exploring our relationship and her own ambivalence about needing support, but being frightened whether I would understand her experiences since I belonged to another race and culture. She had West Indian roots, but was born and brought up in Britain while I was brought up in three different countries. The client also needs to know that their own culture will not be criticized as a result of their own critique and disappointment with the behaviour of another member of their culture, as in this client's case.

Angela had experienced racism, but the sexual abuse was actually perpetrated by a man from her own culture. However, in the dream 'reality' becomes an amalgamation of events. Moreover, this reflects the complexity of the transference when cultural factors come into play. The therapist may not only be seen as a parental figure, but also as a representative of a cultural group, either the client's or as part of another culture. In Angela's case, for a brief period I became part of the dominant culture. All of these components have to be unravelled slowly in the process of the therapy.

Objectives and competencies of culturally skilled counsellors and psychotherapists

In this section I will identify the most important themes which should be considered by counsellors and psychotherapists. These have to be considered prior to embarking in cross-cultural clinical work and they are equally essential for ongoing work.

1 To undergo experiential training in order to understand one's worldview, including a sense of racial and cultural identity development. Furthermore awareness of how this correlates with the client's notions of normality and abnormality and the implications for the psychological process (Sue et al., 1995).
2 To undergo personal development or experiential training with people from other cultures can be a way of understanding one's conscious and unconscious reactions to people of other cultures, including negative emotional reactions such as prejudices, stereo-

types and racism. The aim of this process is not to observe others as objects or as 'exotic', but as human beings who are embedded in different socio-cultural systems.

3   To understand social factors such as culture, gender, sexual orientation and class, as well as their interactive effect on the client's psycho-social thinking and behaviour.

4   To be informed about oppression, colonialism and its impact on group and individual identity development, as well as the result of this experience on the psychotherapeutic process.

5   To be informed about other cultural practices and ideas in order to understand cultural informants. This information can be kept in mind by the therapist, not as rigid knowledge but almost as a 'mental checklist'. Knowing about the cultural backgrounds of our clients is useful as a way of understanding a completely different system of practices, beliefs and family systems. Therapists have to learn how and when to use cultural knowledge to prevent the introduction and reinforcement of stereotypes in the therapeutic relationship.

6   To know the shared experiences due to a particular cultural membership. For example, what it might feel like to be a first or second generation immigrant, reasons for the move and whether it was voluntary or involuntary due to political circumstances. The change of socio-political environment of ethnic minorities often leads to a change of status and common problems of poverty, scapegoating and racism may be experienced.

7   To value biculturalism or bilingualism.

8   To be familiar with cross-cultural literature and research.

9   To pursue enhancement of theoretical and clinical skills as ongoing professional development (Sue and Sue, 1990).

Guidelines for cross-cultural counselling

In this section I will explore further poignant cross-cultural issues of the initial encounter, process and ongoing relationship between the counsellor or psychotherapist and client.

1   To engage in clinical work with clients from different cultures and facilitate the counselling process, taking into account their cultural milieu. Involvement in cross-cultural work has to be emotional, behavioural and intellectual.

2   To be able to understand and work with the dynamic interaction between individuals and their culture. A skilled therapist will aim to achieve a delicate balance; to include the cultural background of the client, but not to make it the prime issue unless the client has already indicated that it is an area of importance in the therapy.

3   Awareness of appropriateness of certain greetings, gestures, facial expressions and behaviours; to be able to generate these and receive them.
4   To be aware of and able to tolerate the differences between the client and themselves, to explore the client's (ethnic) choice of therapist, respect and work with cultural diversity.
5   Not to rely solely on personal factual knowledge about a client's culture, but to obtain information directly from the client.
6   To feel comfortable enough to introduce or challenge the client on cultural issues and their meanings for the client. The therapist should feel at ease to do this from the beginning of the therapy if necessary (Ridley, 1995).
7   To avoid deliberate racial or cultural matching unless it has been requested by the client.
8   To be aware of professional boundaries and skill and acknowledge one's own limitations.
9   To facilitate referrals to other sources when the therapist clearly does not understand the cultural background. Referral to a therapist of the same race, culture and/or language should be discussed openly with the client. This will prevent the notion that the majority culture is rejecting them.
10 To undergo supervision with racially/culturally different therapists can be important in unravelling one's impact on the client, particularly to do with issues of inferiority and/or superiority and race and cultural expectations of emotion, behaviour and therapeutic outcome. The supervisor will also help the counsellor or psychotherapist to determine what behaviours and values are culturally embedded.
11 To have information on resources for interpreters if necessary.
12 To feel comfortable seeking advice, if necessary, from advocate workers who share the client's background or to work with interpreters, work/liaise with relatives of the client and appropriate religious and spiritual leaders.

The process of carrying out successful cross-cultural counselling and psychotherapy requires the counsellor or psychotherapist to engage with the dynamic relationship between the client's culture(s) and the self, the client's interaction with the therapist and (the therapist's) worldview and to take into account the socio-cultural context of the therapy.

Conclusion

This chapter provides an outline of some of the key issues in cross-cultural clinical work. Issues have been raised on the nature of the relationship between culture and the self and how this has an impact on the psychological process. The relationship between the client and the counsellor or psychotherapist will parallel what the person has learnt about relationships from their familial as well as cultural upbringing. This will include all forms of verbal and non-verbal communication. In cross-cultural counselling and psychotherapy the context of the person has to be understood and the nature of their relationship with that context. Through becoming aware and sensitive to the client's cultural context it enables clients to examine their whole experience in a context that is safe and meaningful to them. Addressing cross-cultural issues is a way of raising them into awareness rather than minimizing them or making them vanish.

What I have tried to do in this chapter is demonstrate that cross-cultural therapy is a highly complex process. Counsellors and psycho-therapists need to develop new creative ways of thinking to complement their existing psychological theory, clinical practice and training.

References

Adams, M.V. (1996) *The Multicultural Imagination*. London: Routledge.

d'Ardenne, P. and Mahtani, A. (1990) *Transcultural Counselling in Action*. London: Sage.

American Psychological Association (1995) Guidelines for providers of psychological services to ethnic, linguistic, and culturally diverse populations, in Ponterotto et al. (eds), *Handbook of Multicultural Counseling*. London: Sage. pp. 609–14.

Atkinson, D.R. and Lowe, S.M. (1995) The role of ethnicity, cultural knowledge, and conventional techniques in counseling and psychotherapy, in Ponterotto et al. (eds), *Handbook of Multicultural Counseling*. London: Sage. pp. 387–414.

Curry, A. (1964) Myth, transference and the black psychotherapist, *International Review of Psychoanalysis*, 45.

Deurzen-Smith, E. van (1988) *Existential Counselling in Practice*. London: Sage.

Eleftheriadou, Z. (1992) Multi-cultural counselling and psychotherapy: a philosophical framework, *Psychologos: International Review of Psychology*, 3: 21–9.

Eleftheriadou, Z. (1993) Application of a philosophical framework to transcultural counselling, *Journal of the Society for Existential Analysis*, 4: 116–23.

Eleftheriadou, Z. (1994) *Transcultural Counselling*. London: Central Publishing House.

Eleftheriadou, Z. (1995) Psycho-social aspects of Thalassaemia: a psychodynamic understanding, *Psychodynamic Counselling*, 2.

Eleftheriadou, Z. (1996a) Communicating with patients from different cultural backgrounds, in R. Bor and M. Lloyd (eds), *Communication Skills for Medicine*. Edinburgh: Churchill Livingstone.

Eleftheriadou, Z. (1996b) Notions of culture: the impact of culture on international students, in S. Sharples (ed.), *Changing Cultures: Developments in Cross-Cultural Theory and Practice*. London: UKCOSA.

Eleftheriadou, Z. (in progress) Assessing the counselling needs of ethnic minorities in Britain, in P. Laungani and S. Palmer (eds), *Counselling Across Cultures*. London: Sage.

Fernando, S. (1991) *Mental Health, Race and Culture*. London: Macmillan.

Furnham, A. and Bochner, S. (1986) *Culture Shock: Psychological Reactions to Unfamiliar Environments*. London: Methuen.

Grieger, I. and Ponterotto, J.G. (1995) A framework for assessment in multicultural counselling, in Ponterotto et al. (eds), *Handbook of Multicultural Counseling*. London: Sage. pp. 357–74.

Grinberg, L. and Grinberg, R. (1989) *Psychoanalytic Perspectives on Migration and Exile*. London: Yale.

Harwood, R.L. et al. (1995) *Culture and Attachment*. London: Guilford.

Holland, S. (1995) Interaction in women's mental health and neighbourhood development, in S. Fernando (ed.), *Mental Health in a Multi-Ethnic Society*. London: Routledge.

Ibrahim, F.A. (1985) Effective cross-cultural counselling and psychotherapy: a framework, *The Counselling Psychologist*, 13: 625–38.

Kareem, J. and Littlewood, R. (1992) *Intercultural Therapy: Themes, Interpretations and Practice*. Oxford: Blackwell Scientific Publications.

Krause, I.B. and Miller, A. (1995) Culture and family therapy, in S. Fernando (ed.), *Mental Health in a Multi-Ethnic Society*. London: Routledge.

Lago, C. and Thomson, J. (1996) *Race, Culture and Counselling*. Buckingham: Open University Press.

Littlewood, R. and Lipsedge, M. (1989) *Aliens and Alienists: Ethnic Minorities and Psychiatry*, 2nd edn. London: Unwin Hyman.

Pedersen, P. (ed.) (1987) *Handbook of Cross-Cultural Counselling and Therapy*. London: Praeger.

Pedersen, P. (1995) *Five Stages of Culture Shock: Critical Incidents Around the World*. Westport, CT: Greenwood Press.

Pedersen, P. (1996) Recent trends and developments in cross-cultural theories, in *Changing Cultures: Developments in Cross-Cultural Theory and Practice*. London: UKCOSA Seminar Report.

Pedersen, P.B., Draguns, J.G., Lonner, W.J. and Trimble, J.E. (eds) (1989) *Counselling Across Cultures*, 3rd edn. Honolulu: University of Hawaii Press.

Ponterotto, J.G. et al. (1995) *Handbook of Multicultural Counseling*. London: Sage.

Ridley, C.R. (1995) *Overcoming Unintentional Racism in Counseling and Therapy*. London: Sage.

Shweder, R.A. (1991) *Thinking Through Cultures: Expeditions in Cultural Psychology*. London: Harvard.

Sue, W.S. and Sue, D. (1990) *Counselling the Culturally Different: Theory and Practice*. New York: John Wiley.

Sue, W.S. et al. (1995) Multicultural counseling competencies and standards, in Ponterotto et al. (eds), *Handbook of Multicultural Counseling*. London: Sage. pp. 624–44.

Thomas, L. (1995) Psychotherapy in the context of race and culture: an inter-cultural therapeutic approach, in S. Fernando (ed.), *Mental Health in a Multi-Ethnic Society*. London: Routledge.

6

The Nature and Role of Theory

Joyce Cramond

All approaches to counselling and psychotherapy are based implicitly or explicitly on a theoretical framework. The professional bodies responsible for the training and registration of counsellors and psychotherapists make clear reference to the importance of theory. Although particular theories are generally not specified, different views are expressed regarding whether it is advisable for the counsellor or therapist to adhere to a single theory or to explore a range of theories. The British Association for Counselling (BAC) emphasizes that counsellors should be trained in a core theoretical model (BAC, 1996). Counsellors are encouraged to explore other approaches in order that comparisons may be made with the core theoretical model. BAC points out that the core theoretical model may be eclectic or integrative. The British Psychological Society (BPS), on the other hand, advocates that the counsellor in training should explore a 'broad overview of the main schools of counselling and counselling psychology in terms of their assumptions, methods and aims. This should include dynamic, cognitive-behavioural, humanistic, existential and integrative schools' (BPS, 1993: 5). Additionally, it indicates that at a later stage 'detailed knowledge of at least two distinct theoretical approaches' is required. The UK Council for Psychotherapy (UKCP) also emphasizes that the psychotherapist should explore a range of psychotherapies and counselling perspectives at an introductory level, to develop a knowledge of the approaches available (UKCP, 1993). In practice, however, registration with UKCP is through a section which is represented on the Council and identified by one of the broad theoretical schools.

The literature on theoretical models in counselling and psychotherapy is vast. The beginning counsellor or psychotherapist may be overwhelmed by the range of theoretical perspectives available and faced by a number of questions. Why is theory needed? Which theory is most useful? Can all theories be used? This chapter considers the significance of theory to the work of counsellors and psychotherapists. It examines the nature of theory in relation to counselling and psychotherapy and then presents an overview of the major theoretical perspectives. The relationship between theory and outcome is considered, identifying the role of common factors in effective therapy. With increasing recognition of the role of common factors in counselling and psychotherapy, the advantage of adherence to single theories is questioned. The limitations of single theories have led to the development of the integration movement. The possibilities of integration are thus explored in some depth and some of the obstacles to this development are considered.

Why have a theory?

There appears, therefore, to be a consensus on the need for theory, but different views regarding allegiance to one particular theory. Why is the need for a theory given such emphasis? A theory is an attempt to organize and integrate knowledge and to answer the question 'why'. Faced with a person experiencing psychological difficulties, therapists need to be able to make sense of them before they can begin to help the person. Before they act they need to have a plan of what to do. Patterson (1980) has suggested that operating on the basis of a theory is the difference between being a technician and a professional. A theory enables professional practitioners to organize their thinking and helps them to move beyond the use of techniques on a trial-and-error basis. A theory allows therapists to adopt a more systematic and logical approach in their work. A formal theory has certain characteristics (Patterson, 1980: 4):

1   Assumptions: these are the premises, the taken-for-granted elements which do not require proof.
2   Definitions: of the terms or concepts in the theory.
3   Hypotheses: from the assumptions and definitions, hypotheses are constructed. These are the predictions about what would be true if the theory is valid.

Various criteria have been identified to assess the validity or usefulness of theories (Patterson, 1980; Cramer, 1992). They include:

1   Testability: theories which can be tested are more valuable than those that cannot be tested. If theories cannot be tested it is not possible to prove whether they are true or false. In order to test a theory, assumptions and propositions need to be expressed in a way that can be measured. This is often difficult in practice.
2   Empirical support: a theory is more useful if it is supported by experience or experiments.
3   Clarity and logical consistency: theories which are understandable and free from contradiction are more useful.
4   Simplicity: a theory is easier to use if it is uncomplicated and straightforward.
5   Comprehensiveness: the more the theory attempts to explain, the more useful it is.

6   Fruitfulness: a theory which leads to further predictions is more likely to lead to the development of new knowledge.
7   Practicality: a good theory (in counselling and psychotherapy) is one that practitioners find useful as a basis for practice.

If we looked for a theory of counselling or psychotherapy that met all those criteria, we would probably not find one. This may be one of the reasons why the terms model, perspective, school or approach are often used instead of 'theory'. These terms are viewed as less rigorous, yet still emphasize the need to organize information in some coherent form.

Most approaches to counselling and psychotherapy embody a theory of personality which to some extent informs the practice of therapy. There is often an assumption that an aetiological theory automatically implies a therapy; that knowing what is wrong leads quite naturally to a method of therapy. Smail (1987) challenges this assumption on the basis that there is no reason to suppose that knowledge of cause leads automatically to prescription of cure. He cites the example of psychodynamic therapy which emphasizes the importance of understanding symptoms of distress in terms of the client's personal history. He acknowledges that this makes sense but argues that there is no reason to believe that laying bare the history of this experience will make any difference at all to the experience of psychological pain it has engendered.

Mahrer (1989) argues that a theory of psychotherapy is not the same as a theory of personality. The components of a theory of psychotherapy are different and so too are the issues and questions it addresses. A theory of personality may imply a theory of therapy and most theories of counselling and psychotherapy are based on a theory of personality but the latter is not the same as the former. Mahrer suggests that theories of personality consider a vast range of issues including those relating to human development and behaviour, the nature of feelings and relationships and the nature of social influences. A theory of counselling and psychotherapy, however, involves issues relating to the therapeutic contract, therapeutic interventions and the relationship between client and therapist.

Why so many theories?

There has been a proliferation of schools of counselling and psychotherapy over the last thirty years. Karusu (1986) suggests there are currently over 400 schools of counselling and psychotherapy. Few approaches (if any) reach the optimum criteria for a good theory and many cannot really claim to call themselves theories. Theories, as indicated earlier, are based on certain assumptions. It is not surprising, therefore, that there is a range of theoretical perspectives in counselling and psychotherapy, reflecting the diversity of assumptions about human

Table 6.1   *Assumptions of major theories of counselling and psychotherapy*

	Psychoanalytic/ psychodynamic	Cognitive/ behavioural	Humanistic/ existential
Human nature	Determined by psychic energy and early experience	Determined by learning experiences	Natural tendency towards self-actualization
Concept of psychological disturbance	Intrapsychic conflict	Learned maladaptive behaviour and thoughts	Potential blocked by circumstances and/or other people
Goals of therapy	Develop insights into unconscious processes	Modify behaviour and thoughts	Help clients become more fully themselves
Therapist attitude	Neutral. Interprets transference, defences and unconscious processes	Educative and directive	Non-directive, warm, empathic, genuine
Role of client	Free associates. Develops understanding	Active. Experiments with new behaviour and thoughts	Client takes responsibility for direction of therapy. Self-exploration

nature, the concept of psychological disturbance, the role of social factors, and the nature of change and how it can be achieved. The majority of theories can be categorized within three main strands:

1   Psychoanalytic/psychodynamic.
2   Cognitive/behavioural.
3   Humanistic/existential.

Table 6.1 illustrates the assumptions of the three main schools. This table excludes a number of significant approaches which have been less influential in mainstream statutory provision, for example, gestalt, trans-actional analysis, existential-phenomenological. While these assumptions are sometimes viewed as contradictory or competing, in that they reflect different basic philosophies and views of human nature, Corey (1995) argues that adopting one perspective need not necessarily lead to discarding models which appear to conflict. He points out that each theory contributes to our understanding of human behaviour and our therapeutic endeavours. Each theory may be viewed as considering different aspects of the person. Goldfried et al. (1992) point out that the theoretical premises of the major schools emphasize different components of psychological functioning, namely thoughts, behaviour and affect.

Which theory to choose?

Faced with the range of approaches in counselling and psychotherapy, how does the beginning therapist proceed? One strategy might be to select the most effective therapy. Interestingly, although this may appear as a valid basis for choice, it is not the most popular. The question of how therapists select their theoretical orientation has been explored by Norcross and Prochaska (1983: 201). They report that the major influences on selection of theoretical orientation in a sample of clinical psychologists were 'clinical experience' and 'values and personal philosophy'. Outcome research was listed as relatively uninfluential, appearing as the tenth influence on choice of orientation. Vasco and Dryden (1994) support the influence of personal values and philosophy in choice of orientation. They further indicate that therapists from different orientations cite different variables as influential in their choice.

Although Norcross and Prochaska (1983) reported outcome research to be rated as rather insignificant as a basis for choice, extensive research has been conducted into the effectiveness of therapy. Lambert and Bergin report in their comprehensive review that 'a broad range of therapies, when offered by skilful, wise and stable therapists is likely to result in appreciable gains for the client' (1994: 180); and further 'that differences in outcomes between various forms of therapy are not as pronounced as might have been expected' (1994: 181).

There seems to be general support for the view that psychological therapy can be a valuable means of helping people. However, there is little evidence to suggest that theoretical orientation makes much difference to the outcome of counselling and psychotherapy. Most reviews of outcome studies report what is widely referred to as the Dodo bird effect. In *Alice's Adventures in Wonderland* (Carroll, 1962), when the Dodo was asked who had won the Caucus race, he replied 'Everybody has won and all must have prizes.'

Lambert and Bergin (1994) suggest a range of explanations for the general finding that differences in outcome appear to be unrelated to particular theoretical perspectives.

1   The success of different therapies results from different processes.
2   Different outcomes occur but are not identified in the research.
3   Different therapies share common factors which determine outcome.

They point out that all these explanations may be valid as there is not enough evidence to exclude any of them.

Common factors

The possibility that different therapies share common factors has been explored extensively. Lambert and Bergin (1994) suggest these common

factors may account for most of the success of counselling and psychotherapy. As early as 1974, Frank identified four shared features of
successful therapies:

1 The particular type of relationship between clients and therapists in
   which the clients have confidence in their therapists' competence
   and desire to be of help.
2 The setting for therapy is defined as a place of healing and thereby
   arouses the client's expectation of help. The setting is also characterized by clear boundaries related to time and place. The setting
   offers clients a safe place in which to concentrate on therapeutic
   activities.
3 The therapy is 'based on a rationale or myth which includes an
   explanation of illness and health, deviancy, and normality'. For
   therapy to be successful, Frank (1974: 327) argued that the therapeutic myth must be compatible with the worldview shared by the
   client and the therapist. He points out that therapies based on the
   view, characteristic of almost all Western therapies, that psychological distress results from damaging early life experiences, would be
   ineffective for clients who, for example, attribute psychological
   distress to spirit possession.
4 The therapy provides a task or procedure, which usually requires
   some effort on the part of the client.

Frank reported that these four components contributed to the success of
therapy for the following reasons:

1 They provide the client with new opportunities for learning at both
   a cognitive and experiential level.
2 They improve the client's hope of change.
3 They contribute to the client's experience of enhanced self-efficacy.
4 They help the client to overcome his or her sense of alienation in
   that the client discovers that other people do understand and care.
5 The client, in the process of therapy, experiences emotional arousal.
   Frank reports this to be important in facilitating therapeutic change.

Over the last twenty years there has been increasing research into
non-specific or common factors. The terms common factors and non-
specific factors are often used interchangeably. Castonguay (1993) advocates discarding the term non-specific variables and retaining the term
common factors. He points out that non-specific factors continue to be
viewed as vague aspects of the therapeutic process which are not easily
defined. On the other hand common factors refer to aspects of the
therapeutic process that are present in a range of approaches. Some of
these factors, he argues, are well defined and researched, whereas others
need further attention. Castonguay argues that, for example, operant

conditioning has been well defined and research has shown it to be a commonality in humanistic, psychodynamic and behavioural therapies. Additionally he points out that the importance of the therapist qualities of empathy, congruence and unconditional positive regard is recognized by a range of therapeutic perspectives. He considers factors which require further research include the cognitive, emotional and behavioural aspects of a client's experience of therapy.

Common factors have been represented in different ways. Grencavage and Norcross (1990) reviewed fifty publications to identify common factors across therapies. They reported all the factors referred to by at least 10 per cent of the authors. They categorized the factors into five groups:

1   Client characteristics (positive expectations, distressed client).
2   Therapist qualities (warmth, empathy, acceptance).
3   Change processes (opportunity for catharsis, practice of new behaviours, foster awareness).
4   Treatment structures (use of techniques, a healing setting, adherence to theory).
5   Relationship elements (alliance, transference).

The common factors most often referred to were the development of a therapeutic alliance, the opportunity for catharsis, the acquisition and practice of new behaviours, the client's positive expectations, beneficial therapist qualities and the provision of a rationale for change.

Lambert and Bergin (1994) grouped common factors associated with positive outcomes into support, learning and action factors based on a sequence which they consider operates in therapy. They suggest that the supportive factors operate initially, followed by changes in beliefs and attitudes after which the therapist encourages the client to act.

Orlinsky et al. (1994) outline a generic model of psychotherapy which emphasizes commonalities across psychotherapies. They identify six aspects of process that, they argue, may be found in all forms of therapy:

1   The therapeutic contract. This specifies the aim and limits of therapy, and where and when it takes place.
2   Therapeutic operations. These are the techniques, interventions, methods used to accomplish therapeutic change.
3   Therapeutic bond. This refers to the relationship between the therapist and the client including the therapeutic alliance and the care and concern that develops in the relationship.
4   Self-relatedness. This is the way in which both the client and therapist experience and deal with their thoughts and feelings in the therapy. For example, self-relatedness may be characterized by openness on the one hand and defensiveness on the other.

5   In-session impacts or therapeutic realizations. These are experiences occurring during therapy which effect change. Examples include insight, reduction of anxiety, changing irrational thoughts, enhancement of self-efficacy.

6   Sequential flow. This refers to the role of time and relates to the development of changes within and across therapy sessions.

There is then, substantial recognition of the place of common factors in different therapies. If therapeutic success is associated with common factors rather than theoretical orientation, what then is the role of theory? The previously stated argument for theory would still stand. A theory enables counsellors and therapists to make sense of the complexities presented by an individual and in the words of Mahrer (1989: 50) 'to know what to do, when to do what, or what to try and do it for'.

Eclecticism and integration

The evidence for common factors has contributed to a move towards eclecticism and integration in counselling and psychotherapy. Many other factors have supported this development. Norcross and Grencavage (1990: 4) identify four additional factors.

1   Proliferation of therapies. The considerable number of therapies available has led to the concern that 'psychotherapy is in a state of theoretical clutter and disorder' (Hanna, 1994: 124).

2   Inadequacy of single theories. There is increasing agreement that no single approach can adequately benefit all clients and their complex difficulties. While failures in therapy may be due to a number of factors, Davison (1995: 111) argues that, at times, they may be due to the inadequacy of the theoretical approach. He reports the case of a man whom he treated with behaviour therapy. The client terminated therapy before the therapist considered it appropriate. Davison surmises that this was due to behavioural interventions which in retrospect he now considers to have been unsuitable. He suggests that, in this particular case, it may have been useful to have considered underlying causes that the client may have been unaware of or may have been reluctant to explore with the therapist. Davison gives an account of how these considerations led him to take a more integrative approach in his work.

Recognition of the limitations of single theories has also been reported by therapists who find themselves practising in ways which do not adhere to their espoused theoretical approach. Field (1990) gives an account of his concern when he found himself deviating from analytic principles relating to 'benevolent neutrality'. He reports being more challenging with some clients, more empathic with others. Although both approaches seemed to deviate from the required neutrality of his model, he considered them to result in useful therapeutic gain. He concludes: 'I began to reconsider whether what I had feared were serious lapses from good practice might, in fact, be time honoured therapeutic responses appropriate to the patient at the time' (Field, 1990: 275).

An additional concern is noted by Beutler et al. (1994) who observed that therapists whose theoretical commitments are similar frequently use very different interventions. While some psychodynamic therapists may adhere strictly to consistent use of transference and neutrality, others may be more fluid. These deviations may be regarded as errors but they are not uncommon. Many of the 'theoretical tenets' of particular theoretical schools are debated within them as practitioners strive to work in more effective ways with their clients.

3   Equality of outcomes. Research has shown little evidence for differences in outcome for different therapies. Lambert and Bergin (1994) report that in some studies on specific disorders, behaviour therapy, cognitive therapy and behavioural-cognitive approaches have appeared to be more effective than traditional verbal therapies, but that this is by no means always the case.

4   Socio-economic contingencies. As counselling and therapy services continue to grow and providers of services are under increasing pressure to be accountable, there may be a need to present a unified coherent view of practice. There is increasing emphasis on audit and fundholders are questioning the effectiveness of the range of counselling and therapy approaches. Without some change, Norcross and Grencavage (1990) argue, psychotherapists may lose status and money. They consider that as demands escalate, therapeutic integration will develop.

Increasingly counsellors and psychotherapists are describing themselves as 'eclectic' or 'integrationist' in approach. Although integration and eclecticism in counselling and psychotherapy are generally regarded as a recent development, a study carried out by Kelly (1961) reported the popularity of eclecticism. He explored the theoretical preferences of the members of the Division of Clinical Psychology of the American Psychological Association. Of the 1,024 clinical psychologists studied, 40 per cent declared themselves to be eclectic, as opposed to 41 per cent who described themselves as subscribing to psychoanalytic and related psychodynamic orientations. Garfield (1994) reports the results of a number of other studies carried out in the USA showing continued interest in eclecticism.

Fewer studies of theoretical orientation have been conducted in the UK, although there is evidence of a similar trend. O'Sullivan and Dryden (1990) reported that 32 per cent of a group of clinical psychologists in one area of the UK described themselves as eclectic.

Approaches to integration

Norcross and Newman (1992: 10) identify three major approaches to integration: technical eclectism, theoretical integration and common factor integration.

Technical eclecticism

McLeod (1993: 99) defines the eclectic approach as 'one in which the counsellor chooses the best or most appropriate ideas and techniques from a range of theories or models, in order to meet the needs of the client'. Lazarus (1990: 35) appears to be the most vociferous exponent of eclecticism. He points out that eclecticism is not a single entity and makes a distinction between 'idiosyncratic or unsystematic eclecticism' and 'systematic eclecticism'. Lazarus describes the former as an approach which selects methods on the basis of subject appeal, and, he argues, offers no coherent rationale or empirical validation. This approach should not be confused with the 'systematic eclecticism' which, he emphasizes, is based on 'years of painstaking research and clinical work'. He refutes Eysenck's (1986: 378) statement that 'an eclectic point of view by definition means an anti-scientific point of view: eclecticism has always been the enemy of scientific understanding'. Lazarus defines his approach as technical eclecticism, which draws on social and cognitive learning theory, arguing that this provides a framework grounded in research. He explains that by operating from a consistent, testable theoretical base and then drawing on useful techniques from any discipline without necessarily subscribing to the theoretical underpinnings that gave rise to the techniques in question, one avoids the jumble, the melange, and the subjective bias of theoretical eclecticism or integrationism (Lazarus, 1990: 37).

Although Lazarus acknowledges that psychotherapy is in need of unification and would benefit from eventual integration to reconcile theoretical differences and provide a coherent framework, he considers that this is far from possible at present. He argues that attempts to integrate theories are doomed because of their irreconcilable differences.

The fact that therapists identify themselves as eclectic does not indicate the nature of what occurs in therapy. All that we know is that the counsellor or therapist is not following one theoretical orientation, but is incorporating techniques from other approaches. A consideration in eclecticism is not only whether the therapy works but whether it works best for a particular client (Norcross and Grencavage, 1990).

Theoretical integration

Integration refers to the attempt to combine different theories or elements of theories to create a new theory. Integration goes beyond the combination of different methods or techniques characteristic of technical eclecticism. Norcross and Grencavage (1990) outline the differences between eclecticism and integration. Eclecticism is defined as technical, atheoretical but empirical. Additionally, it involves the selection of strategies from a range of alternatives. Integration, on the other hand, is viewed as theoretical, involving the identification of commonalities and the synthesis of elements to create something new. Although eclecticism was initially more popular, counsellors and therapists who do not adhere to a single theory increasingly identify themselves as integrationist.

In the study carried out by Norcross and Prochaska (1988), respondents were asked to identify the type of eclecticism which best represented their practice. The largest group (62 per cent) selected 'synthetic eclecticism', which was defined as the integration of multiple theories. Another group (27 per cent) selected 'technical eclecticism', described as integrating a variety of techniques within a particular theory. The remainder (11 per cent) selected 'atheoretical eclecticism'. The respondents were also asked whether they preferred the term 'eclectic' or 'integrative'. The latter term was most popular with 40 per cent of the group preferring to define themselves as integrative, 25 per cent preferring eclectic and the remainder (35 per cent) indicating no preference. These figures give us an indication of the extent to which counsellors and therapists describe themselves as integrative but do not inform us about the nature of the integration. The most frequent combinations identified by Norcross and Prochaska (1988) were cognitive and behavioural (12 per cent), humanistic and cognitive (11 per cent) and psychoanalytic and cognitive (10 per cent). It may be that this is not representative of the current situation in the UK but the information offers a view of the range of integrative possibilities. How successful these integrative enterprises have been is an interesting question which requires further research.

Common factor integration

Beitman (1990: 51) makes a distinction between common factor integration and theoretical integration and claims that his own predisposition is towards the former. He is interested in identifying common factors in a variety of approaches which then forms the basis of an integrated therapeutic approach. He presents a detailed matrix outlining the stages of therapy and the elements which are involved at all stages. The stages he identifies are engagement (attempts to work together), pattern search (efforts to define maladaptive behaviours), change (attempts to initiate and maintain change) and termination. He acknowledges that these steps are characteristic of a range of approaches adopted to work with people to solve problems. The elements he suggests addressing at each stage are goals, techniques, content, resistance, transference and countertransference. Although he distinguishes his approach from theoretical integration, Beitman does not expand on how it would differ. In examining his model there is clear reference to different theoretical approaches including psychodynamic, cognitive, person-centred and behavioural. His framework includes a comprehensive account of psychotherapy. Beitman points out that he does not view eclecticism and integration as being in opposition and considers the technical eclecticism of Lazarus as being part of the integration movement. Beitman does, however, suggest

Table 6.2 *Components of a theoretical model of counselling*

Process structures and themes	Structures:	Stages
		Contracting
	Themes:	Therapeutic operations and strategies
		Relationship/therapeutic alliance
		Reflection on clinical problems/counsellor's feelings
Principles of change	Focus for change	
	Assume client responsible for change	
	Use client resources	
	Confront resistance to change	
	Recognize systemic influences (gender, race, family)	
	Facilitate learning and new perspectives	
	Encourage application of learning	
Process of change	Assimilation of problematic experiences	
Mechanisms of change	Common therapeutic factors – relationship between counsellor and client:	
	• emotional release	
	• provision of rationale	
	• reinforcement of client resources	
	• exposure	
	• information or skills training	

Source: Adapted from Horton, 1996

that Lazarus ignores some crucial issues. These include aspects of the therapeutic relationship including the therapeutic alliance, the personality of the therapist and the transference relationship.

Butler and Strupp (1986: 30) also point to the interpersonal context of counselling and psychotherapy, emphasizing the need to 'understand how therapist qualities interact with patient characteristics to produce or fail to produce, the interpersonal conditions necessary for therapeutic change'. The question is no longer 'Does it work best for this client?' but 'Does it work best for this client with this therapist?'

Horton (1996) presents another model based on common factors, incorporating and expanding Beitman's framework. He identifies four components which reflect 'the active ingredients of all or most approaches to counselling or psychotherapy'. These are represented in Table 6.2. This is a clear summary of the range of issues that needs to be considered by any comprehensive model of counselling or psychotherapy.

Obstacles to integration

The above discussion underlines the significant move towards an integrative approach in counselling and psychotherapy. The rivalry between different theoretical perspectives has become more muted, and to some extent has been replaced by debates about the nature of integration. Alongside this, however, various concerns are expressed about the future development of integration. In order to highlight these concerns, Norcross and Thomas (1988: 78) explored the views of a number of integrative practitioners. They were asked to rate the severity of a number of potential obstacles. The obstacles rated as most powerful include investment in single theories; divergent assumptions; inadequate research base; absence of a common language.

Investment in single theories

Although studies reported above indicate that an increasing number of counsellors and psychotherapists identify themselves as eclectic or inte-grationist, there are still large numbers who describe their orientation in terms of single theories. The number of integrationists may be an underestimate as therapists who identify themselves in terms of a particular model do, in fact, diverge from their model. The adherence to single theories is strongly encouraged by professional bodies, particu-larly BAC and UKCP. Although the rationale for this is based on the clear need for counsellors in training to have 'a secure frame of reference in which to conceptualise their clients' concerns' (Wheeler, 1993: 87), this position has implications for the development of integrative approaches.

Divergent assumptions

One of the main questions acknowledged by Norcross and Thomas (1988) is whether it is possible to integrate theories which are based on fundamentally different assumptions about human nature and the pro-cess of therapy. It is argued that the basic philosophies of the different approaches to counselling and psychotherapy do not lend themselves to unification (Corey, 1995).

   Messer (1990) presents a detailed analysis of some of the obstacles facing integration. He illustrates the problems relating to clinical issues by addressing the nature of the relationship between therapist and client. He asks: 'Can one be integrative or eclectic in the kind of relationship that one establishes in counselling or psychotherapy without undermining the very premises of the theory of therapy upon which one draws?' (Messer, 1990: 72). Table 6.1 outlined the nature of the therapeutic rela-tionship characteristic of the psychoanalytic, cognitive-behavioural and humanistic/existential approaches. The pychoanalytic therapist, in prin-ciple, adopts a neutral attitude; the cognitive-behaviourist assumes a directive educational approach and the humanistic therapist offers warmth, empathy and genuineness. Messer enquires: 'How can one be, simultaneously, neutral in the service of transference, real and genuine in the service of authenticity, and didactic in the service of guiding the client, when each role interferes to some extent with the other?' (Messer, 1990: 76). The answer is complex. It is possible to explore strategies for change within the context of a warm empathic relationship (Linehan, 1988) and address transference issues relating to the situation in terms of the feelings and attitudes which are aroused.

An additional issue identified by Messer as problematic for integration in terms of divergent assumptions is the method used by counsellors and psychotherapists to understand clients and their problems. He describes a dichotomy between a scientific versus humanistic approach to understanding. The former he characterizes by observation and objectivity; the latter by case study and subjectivity. While behavioural and cognitive schools epitomize the scientific approach, Messer considers the humanistic approach to typify both psychoanalytic and humanistic perspectives. He now asks whether it is possible to accept both the empiricist and the interpretive perspective. Both approaches may be considered useful, offering different and complementary avenues for understanding.

Inadequate research base

An additional obstacle identified by Norcross and Thomas is the lack of research on the effectiveness of integrative approaches. While this neglect is being addressed (Norcross and Goldfried, 1992), the research on common factors in counselling and therapy (Lambert and Bergin, 1994) suggests that approaches incorporating these factors would likely prove to be effective.

Absence of a common language

The absence of a common language is listed as yet another obstacle to integration. Each theoretical approach uses a particular terminology which often leads to difficulties in communication between adherents of different theoretical schools. However, the behaviourist's mind need not wander when discussions turn to 'transference issues' (Norcross and Newman, 1992). With a commitment to exploring and understanding different theoretical terminology, a position where discussion can take place may be achieved. It may then be possible to answer the question of whether punitive super-ego, negative self-statements and poor self-image are similar or not. This task is already underway. Beitman (1990), in his discussion of common factors, points out ways in which commonalities may be obscured by different terms. Self-observation is referred to in various ways, including 'self-monitoring' and 'self-reflection'. 'Resistance' may be called 'non-compliance' or 'blocks', depending on the theoretical perspective.

Social context

There is increasing recognition of the neglect of social factors in theories of counselling and psychotherapy. The contribution of, for example,

gender, ethnic minority and social class to the development of psychological difficulties is not addressed. This has led to attempts to integrate
a consideration of such factors into therapeutic work. For example,
cross-cultural counselling emphasizes the need for counsellors and
therapists to develop an approach which reflects the cultural needs of
their clients (d'Ardenne and Mahtani, 1990). In relation to gender,
Eichenbaum and Orbach (1985) integrate psychodynamic and feminist
perspectives in their understanding of emotional difficulties. They argue
that people internalize the assumptions, expectations and attitudes of
society relating to gender roles which in turn influences psychological
development.

A personal integrative perspective

Several writers emphasize the development of a personal integrative
perspective. McLeod (1993: 105) suggests that 'a more fertile approach to
understanding integrationism may be to view it as a personal process
undertaken by individual counsellors and therapists'. He cites the work
of Smail (1978) who stresses the need for any counsellor to develop his
or her own personal approach. Corey (1995) advises counsellors and
therapists to explore the range of theoretical perspectives available, to
resist commitment to a single theory and to consider what each theory
has to offer in developing an integrative basis for practice. He does not
advocate an undisciplined eclectic approach and warns against mixing
theories with incompatible assumptions. He also emphasizes that an
integrative perspective necessarily involves 'a great deal of study,
clinical practice, research and theorising' (Corey, 1995: 454).

References

d'Ardenne, P. and Mahtani, A. (1990) *Transcultural Counselling in Action*. London: Sage.
BAC (1996) *The Recognition of Counsellor Training Courses*, 3rd edn. Rugby: British
    Association for Counselling.
Beitman, B.D. (1990) Why I am an integrationist (not an eclectic), in W. Dryden and J.C.
    Norcross (eds), *Eclecticism and Integration in Counselling and Psychotherapy*. Exeter: Gale
    Centre.
Beutler, L.E., Machado, P.P.P. and Neufeldt, S.A. (1994) Therapist variables, in A.E. Bergin
    and S.L. Garfield (eds), *Handbook of Psychotherapy and Behaviour Change*, 4th edn. New
    York: John Wiley.
BPS (1993) *Membership and Qualifications Board Training Committee in Counselling Psychology.
    Guidelines for the Assessment of Postgraduate Training Courses in Counselling Psychology*.
    Leicester: British Psychological Society.
Butler, S.F. and Strupp, H.H. (1986) Specific and non-specific factors in psychotherapy: a
    problematic paradigm for psychotherapy research, *Psychotherapy*, 23 (1): 30–40.
Carroll, L. (1962) *Alice's Adventures in Wonderland*. Harmondsworth: Penguin.
Castonguay, L.G. (1993) 'Common factors' and 'nonspecific variables': clarification of the
    two concepts and recommendations for research, *Journal of Psychotherapy Integration*,
    3 (3): 267–86.

Corey, G. (1995) *Theory and Practice of Counselling and Psychotherapy*, 5th edn. Pacific Grove, CA: Brooks/Cole.

Cramer, D. (1992) *Personality and Psychotherapy*. Milton Keynes: Open University.

Davison, G.C. (1995) A failure of early behaviour therapy (circa 1966), or, why I learned to stop worrying and to embrace psychotherapy integration, *Journal of Psychotherapy Integration*, 5 (2): 107–12.

Eichenbaum, L. and Orbach, S. (1985) *Understanding Women*. Harmondsworth: Penguin.

Eysenck, H.J. (1986) Consensus and controversy: two types of science, in S. Modgil and C. Modgil (eds), *Hans Eysenck: Consensus and Controversy*. London: Falmer.

Field, N. (1990) Healing, exorcism and object relations theory, *British Journal of Psychotherapy*, 6 (3): 274–84.

Frank, J.D. (1974) *Persuasion and Healing*. New York: Schocken Books.

Garfield, S.L. (1994) Eclecticism and integration in psychotherapy: developments and issues, *Clinical Psychology: Science and Practice*, 1 (2): 123–37.

Goldfried, M.R., Castonguay, L.G. and Safran, J.D. (1992) Core issues and future directions in psychotherapy integration, in J.C. Norcross and M.R. Goldfried (eds), *Handbook of Psychotherapy Integration*. New York: Basic Books.

Grencavage, L.M. and Norcross, J.C. (1990) Where are the commonalities among the therapeutic common factors?, *Professional Psychology: Research and Practice*, 21 (5): 372–8.

Hanna, F.J. (1994) A dialectic of experience: a radical empiricist approach to conflicting theories in psychotherapy, *Psychotherapy*, 31 (1): 124–36.

Horton, I. (1996) Towards the construction of a model of counselling: some issues, in R. Bayne, I. Horton and J. Bimrose (eds), *New Directions in Counselling*. London: Routledge.

Karusu, T.B. (1986) The specificity versus nonspecificity dilemma: toward identifying therapeutic change agents, *American Journal of Psychiatry*, 143 (6): 687–95.

Kelly, E.L. (1961) Clinical psychology–1960: report of survey findings, *American Psychological Association, Division of Clinical Psychology Newsletter*, 14 (1): 1–11.

Kelly, E.L., Goldberg, L.R., Fiske, D.W. and Kilkowski, J.M. (1978) Twenty-five years later, *American Psychologist*, 33: 746–55.

Lambert, M.J. and Bergin, A.E. (1994) The effectiveness of psychotherapy, in A.E. Bergin and S.L. Garfield (eds), *Handbook of Psychotherapy and Behaviour Change*, 4th edn. New York: John Wiley.

Lazarus, A.A. (1990) Why I am an eclectic (not an integrationist), in W. Dryden and J.C. Norcross (eds), *Eclecticism and Integration in Counselling and Psychotherapy*. Exeter: Gale Centre.

Linehan, M. (1988) Perspectives on the interpersonal relationship in behaviour therapy, *Journal of Integrative and Eclectic Psychotherapy*, 7 (3): 278–90.

McLeod, J. (1993) *An Introduction to Counselling*. Buckingham: Open University Press.

Mahrer, A.H. (1989) *The Integration of the Psychotherapies*. New York: Human Sciences Press.

Messer, S.B. (1990) Integration and eclecticism in counselling and psychotherapy: some cautionary notes, in W. Dryden and J.C. Norcross (eds), *Eclecticism and Integration in Counselling and Psychotherapy*. Exeter: Gale Centre.

Messer, S.B. and Winokur, M. (1981) Therapeutic change principles: are commonalities more apparent than real?, *American Psychologist*, 36: 1547–8.

Norcross, J.C. and Goldfried, M.R. (eds) (1992) *Handbook of Psychotherapy Integration*. New York: Basic Books.

Norcross, J.C. and Grencavage, L.M. (1990) Eclecticism and integration in counselling and psychotherapy: major themes and obstacles, in W. Dryden and J.C. Norcross (eds), *Eclecticism and Integration in Counselling and Psychotherapy*. Exeter: Gale Centre.

Norcross, J.C. and Newman, C.F. (1992) Psychotherapy integration: setting the context, in J.C. Norcross and M.R. Goldfried (eds), *Handbook of Psychotherapy Integration*. New York: Basic Books.

Norcross, J.C. and Prochaska, J.O. (1983) Clinicians' theoretical orientations: selection, utilization, and efficacy, *Professional Psychology: Research and Practice*, 14 (2): 197–208.

Norcross, J.C. and Prochaska, J.O. (1988) A study of eclectic (and integrative) views revisited, *Professional Psychology: Research and Practice*, 19 (2): 170–4.

Norcross, J.C. and Thomas, B.L. (1988) What's stopping us now? Obstacles to psychotherapy integration, *Journal of Integrative and Eclectic Psychotherapy*, 7 (1): 74–80.

Orlinsky, D.E., Grawe, K. and Parks, B.K. (1994) Process and outcome in psychotherapy – noch einmal, in A.E. Bergin and S.L. Garfield (eds), *Handbook of Psychotherapy and Behaviour Change*, 4th edn. New York: John Wiley.

O'Sullivan, K.R. and Dryden, W. (1990) A survey of clinical psychologists in the South East Thames Region: activities, role and theoretical orientation, *Clinical Psychology Forum*, 29: 21–6.

Patterson, C. (1980) *Theories of Counselling and Psychotherapy*, 3rd edn. New York: Harper & Row.

Smail, D. (1978) *Psychotherapy: A Personal Approach*. London: Dent.

Smail, D. (1987) Psychotherapy and 'change': some ethical considerations, in S. Fairbairn and G. Fairbairn (eds), *Psychology, Ethics and Change*. London: Routledge and Kegan Paul.

UKCP (1993) *Training Requirements Information Sheet*. London: Regent's College.

Vasco, A.B. and Dryden, W. (1994) The development of psychotherapists' theoretical orientation and clinical practice, *British Journal of Guidance and Counselling*, 22 (3): 327–41.

Wheeler, S. (1993) Reservations about eclectic and integrative approaches to counselling, in W. Dryden (ed.), *Questions and Answers on Counselling in Action*. London: Sage.

7

Professional Training: Politics and Needs

Alan Lidmila

The established, if unproven, assumption is that in order to practise a trade a practitioner needs training. Historically, training has taken place before, during or even after an increasing immersion in the craft in question. The purpose of this chapter is to outline some of the major aspects of this assumption in relation to counselling and psychotherapy through a consideration of the needs and provision of professional training. The chapter falls into two main headings concerned with the needs of counsellors and psychotherapists and the training imperatives or the form training takes as an institutionalization and definition of need. The relation of need to training is critically reviewed through an aerial mapping of current training provision and the rationales that inform and drive such structures.

Why training: who needs what?

In simple form my concern is with who needs what, and who decides – or to paraphrase the bards: 'Do you get what you need, and do you need what you get?' (Jagger and Richards, 1970). This raises a number of interesting questions as to when does training start. Can you practise something before you are trained, is training a licensing procedure prior to practice, or does training necessarily include hands-on experience as in most apprenticeship systems? In terms of professional development, is training for the novice or for the profession? Is there any room for idiosyncrasy or differential training needs? Individuals may need to acquire or improve something in order to practise better but they may not need a training. Needs may be defined at the level of those in the process of becoming counsellors and psychotherapists and are also defined by training or accrediting bodies, that is, the institutional structure and ideology of the profession. This distinction inclines us to ask a third, and far from idle question. Are these needs the same or, alternatively, is professional training the expression of the training needs of counsellors and psychotherapists?

What is professional training?

Professional training does not exist in an evolutionary vacuum but typically arises under given circumstances and at particular times. Historically it has been the case in many trades that practice took place prior to, as well as alongside, subsequently professionalized work. This was the case with medicine, social work and currently with counselling and psychotherapy. It is possible to be both an accredited and ordinary member of the British Association for Counselling (BAC) and it is possible to advertise services as a 'psychotherapist' without membership of a professional body. Psychotherapy provides a recent example of this with the development of the Rugby Conference, later the UKCP, following the publication of the Sieghart Report (1978) which itself arose following public concern over the claims of the Scientology movement (Dyne, 1985; Hinshelwood, 1985; Pokorny, 1995).

The development of a profession quite quickly involves the recognition of a need for training structures which also facilitate the acquisition of professional status and public recognition. People who have been involved often for many years in an increasingly professionalized activity may or may not recognize the need to be trained, although the carrot of professional status usually provides an ultimate inducement to train in something they 'do already'. There is often debate in the early stages of professionalization as to whether or not experienced practitioners can be trained to do something better. This controversy can be expressed in terms of costs and resentments as to the sacrifices or even offences to self-esteem that further training will involve. 'Grandparenting', or the automatic registration of experienced first-generation practitioners, as in the recent case of the UKCP, can of course reduce unease by providing a structure for transitional anomalies of experience, training and status. A level playing field has to be created at some point, even if the competitors may seem at first glance to be a trifle ill-assorted.

Professional training may therefore be regarded as enshrining two sets of needs, intrinsic and extrinsic. The former is concerned with personal development, with a subjectivist investment in skills and identification with a practice. The extrinsic component of training complements the former need as it is concerned with the ways and means of formal, or public, recognition. Unfortunately it is insufficient to be good at something unless someone else concurs in a voice vested with some sort of authority (whether this is grudgingly or freely accorded). Practitioners therefore need professional training, whether they perceive an intrinsic need or not. Even if they feel they can train themselves, be self-taught, they cannot accredit themselves in a way that is consensually validated. In this sense a licence to practise does not necessarily have anything whatsoever to do with the skill level of the practitioner so licensed; it is still possible to be in the anomalous position of being extremely skilled at a craft but for one reason or another falling outside of a licensing net.

Even in the future, when licensing will become more formally tied to competence, it does not follow that training guarantees good practice. Interestingly, this dual understanding of the motivation and function of training often forms some part of the selection process for training programmes. An orientation to training that is merely instrumental, bordering on the grandiose and cynical, would be as worrying as its mirror image, whereby institutions become increasingly concerned to keep up numbers and to standardize production at the expense of idiosyncratic trainee needs. This would not be a wholly authentic investment in professional training by educational or training institutes, although it would be based on sound principles of commercial self-interest.

The tension between intrinsic and extrinsic needs which ramifies at institutional and subjective levels can lead to peculiar, yet not uncommon, experiences to do with real as opposed to symbolic meaning. An example of this is the circumstance where a practitioner is recognized as having been trained (or even 'properly trained') but does not feel trained, thereby remaining dependent on and idealizing the training parent body. It is however appreciated, at least by some trainers, that there is such a thing as consolidation and integration of training, so that people may come to feel trained and their external recognition becomes internally recognized some years following formal training. This discussion therefore raises the question: what is realistic to expect from training in relation to the needs of the neophyte, as well as the untrained but experienced practitioner? It may be that professional training provides at best a limited, if crucial, preliminary function rather along the lines of ambulation as a necessary precursor to athleticism. This involves among other things evaluative accrediting functions which are concerned with containment: a psychological holding of the practitioner's anxieties as to what the parent body cannot provide and what the newly trained will have to provide for themselves in the way of clinical 'life experience'. During this painful developmental period to mature adulthood, the knowledge of having been accredited or 'approved of' is vital as a transitional signifier.

The needs of practitioners

The definition of training needs is typically specified by those who have already trained or have been around a long time before formal training was established. What a trainee 'needs' from training is therefore determined not by the consumer but by the supplier and, moreover, gate-keeper. (This determination is exacerbated by the restrictiveness of opportunities or routes to training.) This sounds like the logic of monopoly capital that lurks within free market competition and indeed it is – the advertiser and supplier express what the consumer needs (holidays in the sun) and then supply them, possibly as exclusive or scarce commodities. The recent evolution of training in psychotherapy and counselling has given rise to much wry and at times resentful discussion peppered with phrases such as: 'the goalposts are moving', 'pulling the ladder up after they've climbed it', and 'the jumps get higher each time'. It is not that this process is cynical but that it underscores the tension between what the practitioner needs and what professional bodies and others that provide the training think the practitioner needs. At its most extreme, training is either a necessary evil or a perennial tension between the idealized and the disappointed, but it is better to speak more realistically about the ordinary needs that training may be able to meet in a good enough way.

Therefore it is a myth to argue that training arises exclusively as a benign intervention in response to people's need to be trained. People are always trying to sell other people something they had not realized they needed. This salutary reminder does not at the same time deny the benefits that can accrue from being shown how to do something better – which is what training should be. It is this latter consideration to which our attention now appropriately turns.

The intrinsic needs of practitioners

First, for children to develop and separate they have to internalize and come to terms with their parents, good, bad and indifferent, warts and all, with some gratitude and inevitable disappointment. It is difficult for this identificatory process to occur meaningfully if training bears little resemblance to practice in the realities of life in that particular professional world. A trainee therefore needs a training to be consonant with expectations and with a job they are trained to do and not presented with theorizations that are hopelessly idealized. As my friendly local mechanic chides me, when I want to talk about 'why' things happen in the car (the phenomenology of the machine) he tells me I need to know what to do in or to the engine and that I am 'all talk'. He has a point. The practitioner needs to identify with principles and practices that may be usefully and realistically applied.

Second, a practitioner needs help in integrating realistic principles and practices. A supervisor or teacher should, therefore, like the parent, model and articulate this need as part of the solution – 'you do your best, we can't cure everyone, perhaps you could think a little bit more about this', etc.

Third, this is why practitioners need – and I speak as a practitioner here, not as a trainer – post-professional training, even if that takes the form mainly of clinical consultation or supervision. Post-professional training in this sense involves the 'how's it going then?' supportive function that facilitates gradual separation and autonomy along with the encouragement of self-monitoring following training – 'I can see now I need to know more about 'x' or 'y' so I will attend 'b' course or read 'c' paper.' This mature need may have existed already, or been developed over training, and is a marker of independent practice. The individual is not doing post-professional training because they 'have to' but because they want to – their own development must represent their own desire.

The fourth item is the pivotal need for confidence and security as interrelated emotional states of mind. Training cannot provide such dynamic qualities (by providing a module of six seminars) but the overall experience can facilitate the capacity for growth and consolidation of these requisites through the provision of resources and setting, that is, feeding and caretaking. Practitioners need this because training, quite severely in the case of analytic psychotherapy, always deskills and deprives comfort by heightening anxiety. It is training in the management of uncertainty and it does not provide certainty through the naming of parts (Reed, 1965).

Fifth, exposure to living with uncertainty or anxiety is not persecutory, but neither does a trainee need to complete a training in an anxious or disturbed state. On the contrary, an understanding and tolerance of uncertainty should be in place or at least seen as a possibility in time. Qualification is the concrete means of assisting this developmental point. It is a transitional phenomena, a status role that is an enveloping blanket, a second skin very necessary to keep out the cold air of real practice. It has the same function as the medical coat or the doorman's uniform – we could not do the job without the props and gongs that are talismanic to touch and help us strike a public stance in front of a private doubt. The exhibitionist and obsessional attachments to newly won insignia seem fairly universal examples of this phenomena; the warrior may not feel brave or have accomplished very much but certainly looks the part. Showing off, as well as the sometimes quite hostile wish to prevent others from obtaining the same head-dress/qualification are defences against anxiety associated with an insecurity of status. This is more likely to occur with greater intensity among those young adults of the species or in this context the newly trained counsellor or psychotherapist. To be qualified is therefore a fifth need.

Sixth, as in the Arthurian and Greek romances, qualifications, certificates and fur stoles, like magic shields or sacred benedictions, assist practitioners in their perilous and often uncertain journeys, as does a sense of purpose. By sense of purpose I am thinking of the practitioner having and being helped to have a sense of self-justification. At its most mundane this simply means a faith that talking and listening are helpful. This sense that one's actions are justified is essential to a sense of self-esteem, confidence and purpose and implies the management of uncertainty because it is a faith, not a belief (Halmos, 1975). Counsellors and psychotherapists therefore need to feel justified in what they have been trained to do, even if the scope of their project is limited or the proof of their endeavours evades positivist reason. This is a sixth need.

Seventh, practitioners need to 'belong' to something larger with protective umbrella features and this helps fulfil a need to consolidate identifications. I think that training and professional membership can provide for this primitive albeit transitional need, which is stronger in the novice than the more phlegmatic or experienced practitioner. Belonging can take forms that are offensive to adult sensibilities ('you can be in my gang, my gang') which in turn reduces the potency of belonging in the same way that children can become disillusioned by the squabbles and rigidity of the parents. We all feel saddened by the parental arguments, pomposity or discovery that they do not really know and we all struggle to try and forgive this in them, and in ourselves. I think training needs to assist the development of a mind that can contain ambivalence about its own professional identifications and the identifications of others without resorting to adhesive attachment or paranoia, without being blind to limitations or overvaluing one's own specialness. This seventh need is the most difficult need to fulfil, as it has been to describe: the need to belong and to possess a professional identity, without sectarianism or the unassailable refuge of correctness.

Eighth, a further need, easier to describe, is the enduring need for meaningful rites of passage, for ceremonies, initiations and graduations that signify entry and place. Personal therapy, especially towards the analytic end of therapeutic practice, is regarded by some, in and out of the profession, as the sine qua non of professional and personal development and certainly has ritualistic features, describable as purification involving psychic revelation (Cremerius, 1990; Bierenbroodspot, 1991; Rycroft, 1995; Kendall and Crossley, 1996). Points of accreditation and transition need to be ritualized, otherwise although the act may be completed it is instrumental and bureaucratic, that is, less meaningful. In an age when tradition and ritual have been in decline there might be a need to reinvest in that which is in danger of being eroded.

Finally, counselling and psychotherapy have, of course, produced a literature and a highly literate constituency. Yet in some ways, not unconnected to the apparently ineffable and highly personal nature of the work, there is an anti-intellectual tendency or at least anti-theoretical strain evident in the profession and so I would argue also for a need for theory. There is a debate that runs along the art versus science axis as to whether or not the language we employ to describe things in the therapy world is doomed to one of three outcomes, none of which is ultimately helpful:

1   to diminish or reduce meaning;
2   to obfuscate or complicate meaning and purpose;
3   to fail to capture or describe meaning and purpose.

This debate manifests itself quite seriously at times and so, for example, there are those concerned that clinical wisdom suffers through too much exposure to academic discourse, either because the critique implied, the intellectual scepticism, erodes (it is unattached chatter) or it does not have the grounded ballast of a hands-on clinical practice. In the psychotherapy world this view has surfaced in relation to the expansion of training in universities and higher education colleges where, of course, the reverse prejudice is sometimes celebrated. In caricatured form this goes along the lines that clinicians have their well-meaning heads in the sand, they have not been trained to question and think objectively, and they eulogize inter-subjectivity at the expense of critical rigour and research-based knowledge. I find both of these perspectives embarrassing to write down, but even in exaggerated form there is no invention. Not only have I heard these conversations, because I occupy both settings, but I find that I share elements of the split. But it is a split I think we can and do try to integrate as trainers in the interests of our own trainees. Clear thinking about one's practice, the integration of clinical and intellectual knowledge in a critical yet also receptive way, is a vital accompaniment to independent practice.

To assume that the need for theory is obvious is a dangerous assumption and so the importance of a theoretical language as a ninth practitioner need is worth outlining.

Without theory we are reduced to aimlessly kicking around in the dust. Theory, the word, is a language of containment that makes possible the project of dealing with experience (Bion, 1967). The authority of language and thought functions as a necessary defence against what is unintelligible and permits some distance from enmeshment with the client. The practitioner needs to assimilate or digest theory in order to internalize this means of understanding their own intention and actions. Training is incomplete if the trainee is not provided with theory, including that which not only purports to explain but also challenges our actions: if there is nothing to cut teeth on the diet is reassuring pap. The need to be immersed in the interpersonal and highly subjective emotional world to an equivalent depth is not questioned here, but what is asserted is the importance of theory as a counterbalancing need (Craib, 1987). Without theory we are reduced to seeking a solution like that of Humpty Dumpty: 'When I use a word . . . it means just what I choose it to mean' (Carroll, 1972: 209).

Training standards and professionalization: the evolution of political identities

As fairly robust organisms grown in diverse conditions over varying lengths of time, counselling and psychotherapy have flourished in an ad hoc manner, only recently susceptible to a more centralizing horticultural control. Training takes place in private institutes, public health associated institutions and in the decreasingly subsidized state education sector. This pattern is likely to continue but with increased tendencies to harmonize and supervise the content of training provided. It is also likely that under conditions of change there will be a tension between the untested but orthodox and the heterodox and innovative that up-end training assumptions. This could be an exciting fillip or highly destabilizing and accounts for divisions apparent in the field, the most notable example being the development of the British Confederation of Psychotherapists (BCP) as an offshoot from the UKCP. This split is a good example of developmental tension and, as in most family disputes, matters of opinion become embalmed as cause célèbres. Another example would be the UKCP and BAC debate over personal therapy as a concurrent training requirement which expresses itself at its most radical and ridiculous by those who say: 'Why personal psychotherapy when there is no proven correlation with therapists' effectiveness?' Conversely there are those who consider themselves as the Only True Representatives Of The Proper Way Who Do Not Deviate From Prescriptive Paths Of Mathematically Stated Integrity (for example, anything less than three times weekly with one of the bloodline is inadequate). To those more psychodynamically inclined the importance of personal therapy may seem incontestable, yet for some it is at best optional and for others even questionable; evidential claims are lost within sacraments and dogma.[1]

The BAC watches the squabble with interest, as do many within other non-analytic sections of the UKCP, conscious also that what happens in Rome today happens in Rimini tomorrow (unless, of course, a different route is followed by claiming that what counsellors do is different). But to choose the route of difference compromises another view which may gain increasing credence and this is the path of harmonization of all counselling/psychotherapy activity as, for example, expressed in the idea of the Lead Body and NVQs.

A new profession seeks to reassure itself and others that it is purposeful and respectable. It seeks to protect those who belong and the public that consumes its services. Insofar as it makes claims about its practice it provides a basis for the advance of its knowledge base. It also attempts a commonality of purpose that affirms, partly by enclosing and demarcating identity. Psychotherapy as a body of diverse but related practices has been seeking to establish structures that address such needs over the last decade and since inauguration of the UKCP in 1989 the profession has sought to frame its practice in capital letters. This is not an automatically smooth transition in terms of superior rights to practice based on either modality or training because differences are expressed between various approaches. For example, there is no consensus as to the practice and training for psychoanalytic psychotherapy so there exists a separate body for those analytic practitioners who for a variety of reasons wish to retain a separate identity – the BCP (Richards,

1993). The ins and outs, the gossip and invective of the latter debate would require separate discussions, as would a serious consideration of the issues (Lidmila, 1996; Young, 1997). Suffice to say that the argument hinges on whether an analytic psychotherapist may be trained and practices in diverse contexts, under a professional organization that is inclusive and, as with the UKCP's federalist structure, ecumenical and tolerant. Or, whether practitioners at the analytic end of the spectrum (which for some is privately viewed as the only valid form of psychotherapy anyway) need to belong to an exclusive model of training and practice, which is then claimed to determine the exact nature of analytic psychotherapy (there is only one way to make an omelette).

Similarly there have been various working parties within the UKCP and BAC that have attempted and, some would say by definition, failed adequately to define the differences between counselling and psychotherapy. It is possible to find adherence to the view, especially in the psychoanalytic tradition, that counselling is concerned with conscious problems, whereas psychotherapy is concerned with the unconscious psyche, one with coping and problem-solving, the other with illness and long-term treatment (for change). It is equally possible to be persuaded that 'the view that counselling and psychotherapy are the same activity will eventually become paradigmatic' (Ellingham, 1995: 289; see also Lefebure, 1991; Thorne, 1992; Jacobs, 1994). As often the debate is interesting but frustratingly inconclusive (Hawkins, 1990; McLeod and Wheeler, 1995).

In discussions of training standards across the sections of the UKCP it has already become apparent that different therapeutic modalities have different requirements concerning not only personal therapy but also the duration of both training and treatment. To a degree that amazes the outsider, demarcation disputes rage within modalities as much as between them. These disagreements (or splits) within organizations are not only of a technical/theoretical nature but concern questions of status and professional identity. As a trainee asked recently, having completed a psychodynamic counselling training that was difficult to distinguish from psychotherapy training, 'Can I call myself a psychotherapist?' Of course, one way to respond to the question is to ask, 'Why do you want to?' The reader might answer, rightly, that one important reason is to do with the politics of professionalism, which *name* would we prefer.

Professional training: the public expression of practitioner needs?

What is the relationship of professional training to the needs of the practitioner? Simply, that training imperatives claim to be an institutionalization of needs which simultaneously concern both the public and the trainee and therefore represent definitions of need. Typically these are referred to as training standards and refer to the acquisition of skills and adherence to ethical guidelines for practice. It is fortunate that in many ways the core features of professional training actually reflect the needs of the practitioner. Claims and reputations will always be made as to which particular training context, or even course, achieves a better product outcome. Nonetheless the work of scrutinizing trainings in the UKCP Analytic Section and the early stages of a parallel procedure in the Universities Psychotherapy Association (UPA) to accredit university trainings has convinced me of a high degree of compatibility and over-lap in the broad field of counselling and psychotherapy trainings. (It is with training standards across different modalities that the broad church bodies like the UPA, UKCP and BAC face difficulties.)

Core components

Trainings are almost without exception organized around the following core elements and take place within identifiable structures that include staffing and resourcing. If one is involved in deciding whether a training 'fits the bill', the following checklist applies:

1   Are there selection procedures?
2   Is there a core organizational infrastructure?
3   Does the training run a minimal length of time?
4   Are there clear evaluation and assessment procedures?
5   Are there standards measurable at a comparative level, and con-sistent with related professional trainings?

There are many other questions which are concerned with detail but in my experience some sort of variation on these core questions sets the tone for the exercise and sets the agenda for accreditation visits. For comparison, the BAC Scheme for the Accreditation of Counsellor Train-ing Courses established in 1989 requires nine elements that begin the course recognition procedure: Admission, Self-Development (personal counselling), Client Work, Supervision, Skills Training, Theory, Profes-sional Development, Assessment and Evaluation.

Similarly the UKCP accreditation visitation procedure within sections has been based on 'Training Requirements' formalized in 1993 which enumerate a large number of criteria for deciding whether a body can claim to be providing a bona fide training. These criteria include super-vision, academic content, trainee consultation, clinical contact, means of assessment, registration procedures; with more specific guidelines according to theoretical orientations and UKCP section membership.

Furthermore a parent body like the BAC or UKCP will also have to develop a base line understanding of high and low common denomi-nators with respect to quality control. To pursue an earlier analogy, all cars have wheels but some provide better equipment and a more durable driving experience. (Full details of training requirements are obtainable from BAC and UKCP.)

It is relatively easy beyond this point to assess whether professional trainings fulfil the needs of practitioners-to-be because the scrutineer, representing the profession, and peers can get on with a more manageable focus job of evaluating procedures, content and quality control – is there enough of 'x', should they not have read 'y'? A visiting panel can have a mind as to whether a training has or is likely to meet the sort of practitioner needs outlined earlier or whether the training is somewhat designer led and following fashion (or is even outmoded). Meeting external validation criteria is a realistic aim for a training but on its own would not make the training, and therefore the criteria, true reflectors of practitioner need.

Language in a changing world

Children are often begotten under conditions of love or passion (or darkness). The decisions may be ill-considered, accidental or hopelessly romantic and the relationship may change. A sociology of the helping professions would show that counselling and psychotherapy grew as a post-war phenomena and boomed in the post-1960s because the ideas and practices were reflections of a contemporary zeitgeist (Rogers, 1961; Southgate and Randall, 1976; Rosen, 1978; Rossman, 1979; Miller and Rose, 1988). Many aspects of such beliefs, of course, continue to inform practice belief and would include respect for persons, the healing power of love, the importance of quality of life rather than wealth-orientated productivity, the significance of emotional life and the expressive value of getting the 'inside out', and so on. It would not be difficult to show the continuance of these early parental values, a first generation language in the practices and writings of practitioners today, but an ice age has followed a summer of love and the socio-cultural climate in the mid-1990s is very different. The radical or idealist adolescent of counselling and psychotherapy is growing into an adult with somewhat different priorities. (For similar discussions see, for example, Frosh, 1986; Hinshelwood and Rowan, 1988; Smail, 1987; Rowan, 1992; BAC, 1990).

Under present conditions amateurism has clearly given way to professionalism: the days of the 'barefoot psychoanalyst' seem to be numbered. The competing demands for professional recognition have been following certain predictable pathways and these include the following features:

- the tendency to centralize organizational and professional control of training;
- the increase in tension between diversity, and harmonization of training practices;

- the development of uniform or standard procedures and criteria to facilitate the inevitability of the above (the bureaucratic solution of categories and serial numbers);
- the development of therapeutic interventions as packagable commodities, marketed by human relations technicians, fluent in a second language that is technical, yet, in the terms of the dominant contemporary media, 'user-friendly'.

The shift in language in the counselling and psychotherapy worlds should not be underemphasized as a cursory flip through the advertising sections of professional publications will reveal. The second business-professional language that has developed tends to be employed increasingly in the public domain and at the (reified) institutional level to define practice. It coincides to varying degrees with the first-generation language that may still enshrine the core beliefs but practitioners may well be developing a bilingual facility in using the first language while increasingly speaking the second. This is a tension, and may be resolvable by the reassertion of primary linguistic identities. Alternatively, the dissonance may be resolved by the gradual decline in old usage and the increasing adoption of a second language of meaning more compatible with the location of human relations practices in changed milieu.

This change in language reflects a societal shift to a concern with cost effectiveness, saleability, quality control, product effectiveness and the development of procedures to control monopoly and competition. It does not sound much like a description of what you do in your consulting room does it? The language, however, is increasingly claiming descriptive power as any NHS trust or university department will testify. Far from being immune, private practitioners have also developed quite an interest in, for example, employee assistance programmes which have blossomed in the last decade. Counsellor/therapists as private individuals have become more comfortable at defining themselves within the cash nexus rather than, as in earlier incarnations, to the left of and outside of mammon. Training is increasingly reflecting a tension between the instrumental creation of human relations technicians intent upon acquiring skills helpful in the relief of disorders like occupational stress and the aftermath of bank robberies while taking place within a first language tradition that maintains a socially critical perspective which in some ways celebrates values counter to the prevailing winds.

A further example of such tendencies would be the fairly recent development of the 'mission statement', adopted by many counselling organizations and HE institutions and increasingly de rigeur at the beginning or end of any advertising publicity. The mission statement is itself part of a wider cultural process, in which political correctness, the sound-bite and 'enterprise culture' come most quickly to mind, and it is a phenomenon worthy of special study. However, for the purposes of

The Counselling and Psychotherapy World

COUNSELLING   **PSYCHOTHERAPY**

[Institute of Psychoanalysis]

BAC   ⟵ [LEAD BODY:] ⟶   UKCP ⟵ – – – ⟶ [BCP]
              Advice, Guidance,
              Counselling &
              Psychotherapy

Counsellor	Counsellor	The Psychotherapies	Institutional
Accreditation	Training Accreditation	(Sections)	Members [UPA]
(Individual)	(Institutional)		
		Psychotherapy	Psychotherapy
		Training	Training
		Accreditation	Accreditation
		(Institutional)	(Courses)
	(EEC: now EU	[EAP]	
	Sectoral		
	Directives for		
	professions)		

Note:

BAC: Credit accumulation model and recognized training; the individual route to accreditation: UK Register of Counsellors

UKCP: Recognized training and the institutional route to accredition: UKCP Register of Psychotherapists

Figure 7.1   *Towards the millennium – an incomplete mappa mundi*

this argument it will suffice to note that form determines content, with the ensuing prose aiming for a tone that is a strange brew of the robust, breezy and, most particularly, reassuring. It is not so much a question of accuracy or otherwise of the claims but more that the mission statement is fundamentally rhetoric and probably a good example of post-modernism in that the head is detached from the body, the signifier floats and in one's worst nightmare may not even require a body. In examples of such statements there is little substantive content. There is, however, in the deployment of language, an emphasis on scale (high, all), the reassuring yet bold (tradition, frontiers) and the ever-popular clarion that banishes all uncertainty (commitment); a retrospective reinvention of the Protestant ethic?

Like all maps Figure 7.1 presents us with a pleasing simplicity that provides a soothingly omnipotent illusion of order. But, rather like ancient cartographical principles that designated essentially unknown, let alone unexplored, territory as 'there be dragons', or 'heaven', knowledge of the real world is constantly under revision.

The visual scheme does help by illustrating the potential for complexity and confused professional identities that persist in these novice professions. A practitioner may be a clinical psychologist who by virtue of training will have a de facto right to practise psychotherapy and counselling, although not necessarily trained as a psychotherapist or counsellor. The practitioner may then also take a specialist training in, say, psychotherapy, but in one modality, for example, person-centred therapy. Nonetheless, the practitioner may continue to practise cognitive-behavioural techniques as part of her employment contract. They may receive supervision in different modalities, in both public and private settings and subscribe to, or be governed by three different ethical codes. I become confused as I write this and wonder how it reads. Are they psychologists/counsellors, a person-centred psychotherapist, a specialist or generalist, on 'level 2 or 3'? (Dyne and Figlio, 1989; Pedder, 1989).

The bureaucratic solution, or different bedrooms, larger beds?

There is a number of complex relationships that exists between and within bodies that claim parentage of professional training practice. The formation of these relationships has not been without conflict, acri-monious and even destructive at times, and in some cases separation and divorce represents the compromise to perceived incompatibilities. In the part of the world where dwell the analytic psychotherapies and forms of psychoanalysis, squabbles over inheritance and lineage, even divinity, have resulted in paths of separate development and cordial but uneasy political truths. Much of this of course, is unwritten, or unexpressed; we are left with some fairly formal documents to chart history (Figlio et al., 1993; Deurzen-Smith, 1993, 1995; Oakley, 1994; Balfour and Richards, 1995; Tantam and Zeal, 1996).

In a way that exacerbates but may paradoxically solve many of the internecine rivalries and prejudices within the profession, the meteoric ascendancy of the Lead Body could prove decisive. This rise is viewed as regrettable or exciting depending on the practitioner's position on the vertical and horizontal axis of professional development; whether standing to gain or lose in terms of esteem and safety. The Lead Body solution is a levelling and standardizing procedure and as such offers much to those seeking this kind of remedy. Although the psychotherapy world seems more cautious than that of the BAC, the argument that unit cost packaging is persuasive to fundholders has some mileage. The claim that long-term psychotherapy is not researchable, is concerned with the essentially uncertain and ineffable (and is costly) may be true but remains a handicap in the politico-economic world. We are as ever concerned with hidden agendas and the advent of the mapping process initiated by the Lead Body has had an exhilarating effect in tandem with other trends on the task of refining professional training needs.

The drive to define, to map, sets of competencies and standards is moving into a second phase that opens the way forward for a revision of the world map of psychotherapy and counselling in that NVQs may be developed in psychotherapy and counselling and with different types of practice modality. At its inception the UKCP was cooler than BAC towards the Lead Body, concerned as to the point of the exercise and the style of defining complex work. Temporarily, due to the concern that whatever would prove to be distinct between counselling and psychotherapy would be lost, the UKCP suspended its involvement in the consultative workshops, later rejoining. The point had been made, without making it precisely: 'the boundary between counselling and psychotherapy has become increasingly muddled' (Lepper, 1995). The project gathered together practitioners across modalities who had training experience with the following outcomes in mind:

> An initial mapping of psychotherapeutic competencies taking a broad definition of the latter term to include performance and capability.
> This involved a comparison of such competencies together with the draft therapeutic counselling units, produced as a set of draft competencies of psychotherapy which capture aspects of capability and performance within the technical parameters of the standards programme definition of competence.
> The differences and commonalities between the distinct but overlapping worlds of therapeutic counselling, psychotherapy and couples counselling were then delineated as far as possible. (Inniss and Bell, 1996: 2)

Rather in the way that research forces one to define one's terms a little better, the problem of defining competencies has not been uninteresting or invalid. The question of whether this categorizing methodology should become the marker for professional competence and can hope to express meaning remains in the profession of psychotherapy: the instrumental advantages are more clearly perceivable (Whyte, 1994; Morgan-Jones, 1995).

The Lead Body is but one of a group of factors that may exercise a determining influence on what we understand by professional training. With the development of Credit Accumulation Transfer Systems (CATS) and Accreditation of Prior Experiential Learning (APEL), together with access and introductory training modules, increasing discussion of post-professional training requirements, the modularization of clinical and non-clinical educational components within and between institutions, the established routes to learning a craft through apprenticeship and tutelage are under question. The development of the Universities Psychotherapy Association (UPA) as a relative latecomer to the training scene is part of this shake-up which, while raising anxieties in the independent sector, is also stimulating some rapprochement between the independent and university sectors.

The independent sector is increasingly aware of the potential influence of the European Community directives and training scene whereby virtually all training in psychotherapy takes place in the universities. Furthermore there is not a clear institutional definition of counselling in the European training scene. Together with the anomaly of counselling and psychotherapy training traditionally taking place in the private sector in the UK, this combines to suggest an interesting future for the development of psychotherapy and counselling professions. A recent UPA initiative, the development of a Network in Psychotherapy and Counselling designed to map the points of contact in counselling and psychotherapy training courses, may prove to be illuminating in this respect. In a world where it is possible to advance a model of clinical training through distance learning via the Internet, it is all the more important that conventional pedagogic and clinical structures stake a claim, however absurd but commercially attractive some innovations may appear.

Conclusion

It is an inevitable, if disappointing, fact that professionalization and training are not immune from the most primitive drives, anxieties and defences. Another way of expressing this is to address the point at an institutional level and to remind ourselves that the world is political, not least where power, prestige and money are concerned. Any under-standing of the development of training in relation to psychotherapy and counselling, and in turn in relation to psychiatry or clinical psy-chology, has to embrace the political dimension that is present, if at times concealed behind the earnest rhetoric of appeals to training standards and professional respectability. The confluence of the psychic and the political has become part of contemporary critical discourse and has been explored elsewhere, as have the observable psychodynamics present in live groupings of practitioners meeting in ritual contexts (Bosanquet, 1988; Black, 1990; Holmes, 1993; Young, 1997).

The training needs of counsellors and psychotherapists are therefore inextricably part of this wider discussion. I have noted the importance of history in reminding us that the culture of counselling and psycho-therapy in many ways developed as an alternative to the commodifica-tion of everyday life, to advertising and the attendant features of industrial capitalist social organization. This seems to have changed through an increasing professionalization of the field which in turn has affected, perhaps shaped, the parameters of practice and professional identity. Counselling and psychotherapy are now service products to be consumed, and training is therefore quite consistently concerned with the creation of technicians, proficient in a practice. The training needs of counsellors and psychotherapists will increasingly match these impera-tives while possibly continuing to entertain the ideological need to view self and practice as in some way 'alternative', and therefore helpful, to the dominant culture. Perhaps we should be reminded that one of the founding fathers of this movement, Sigmund Freud, also attempted to address these needs and potential dilemmas when he spoke of a 'salvation army' which had a mission that was in some way an alternative to the discontents of civilization (Freud, 1970).

It may be that languages can be integrated, generations of meaning can co-exist and that the professional needs of practitioners will be reflected in professional training. It is to be hoped that the statutory regulation of practice will legitimize, rationalize, make as effective and safe as possible, what was once alternative and without status in the dominant culture. Therefore it is desirable that the needs of psycho-therapists and counsellors will be reflected in the institutional provision of training as part of the dialectic of wider societal change.

Note

1   In book three of Swift's satire *Gulliver's Travels*, our hero travels to Laputa, a place where there are many examples of the trivial extremes to which otherwise quite learned people can go to prove their way is the only way. 'Debates,' in the UKCP's formative years, degenerated into a 'big-enders, little-enders' fall-out along similar lines as to which is the correct end of the egg to open, an argument that provokes periodic and violent confrontations between two factions, rather like there being only one way to train.

References

BAC (1990) *Towards a Sane Society: 14th Annual Training Conference.* Rugby: British Association for Counselling.

BAC (1996) *Scheme for the Recognition of Counsellor Training Courses.* Rugby: British Association for Counselling.

Balfour, F. and Richards, J. (1995) History of the British Confederation of Psychotherapists, *British Journal of Psychotherapy*, 11 (3): 422–6.

Bierenbroodspot, P. (1991) Shame, guilt and penance in the psychoanalyst: the therapist super-ego in psychoanalysis, *British Journal of Psychotherapy*, 8 (1): 71–81.

Bion, W. (1967) *A Theory of Thinking in Second Thoughts.* London: Heinemann.

Black, D. (1990) A note on 'core professions', *British Journal of Psychotherapy*, 6 (4): 458–9.

Bosanquet, C. (1988) The confusion of tongues and the Rugby conference, *British Journal of Psychotherapy*, 5 (2): 228–40.

Carroll, L. (1972) *Alice Through the Looking Glass.* London: Collins. pp. 209–10.

Craib, I. (1987) The psychodynamics of theory, *Free Associations*, 10: 32–56.

Cremerius, J. (1990) Training analysis and power, *Free Associations*, 20: 114–38.

Deurzen-Smith, E. van (1993) UKCP and the National Register for Psychotherapy, *British Journal of Psychotherapy*, 9 (4): 513–17.

Deurzen-Smith, E. van (1995) Psychotherapy: a profession for troubled times, *British Journal of Psychotherapy*, 11 (3): 458–66.

Dyne, D. (1985) Questions of 'training?', *Free Associations*, 3: 92–147.

Dyne, D. and Figlio, K. (1989) A comment on Jonathon Pedder's 'courses in psychotherapy', *British Journal of Psychotherapy*, 6 (2): 222–6.

Ellingham, I. (1995) Quest for a paradigm: person centred counselling/psychotherapy versus psychodynamic counselling and psychotherapy, *Counselling*, November.

Figlio, K., Martindale, B., Oakley, H., Richards, J., Sandler, A.M. and Young, R. (1993) The psychotherapy profession, *Free Associations*, 29: 79–116.

Freud, S. (1970) The question of lay analysis, in S. Freud, *Two Short Accounts of Psychoanalysis*. London: Penguin. p. 170.

Frosh, S. (1986) Beyond the analytic attitude: radical aims and psychoanalytic psychotherapy, *Free Associations*, 7: 38–58.

Halmos, P. (1975) *The Faith of the Counsellors*. London: Constable.

Hawkins, P. (1990) Chairman, Joint Working Party, BAC/UKCP, psychotherapy and counselling: an exploration of differences. Unpublished.

Hinshelwood, R. (1985) Questions of training, *Free Associations*, 2: 7–18.

Hinshelwood, R. and Rowan, J. (1988) Is psychoanalysis humanistic? A correspondence, *British Journal of Psychotherapy*, 4 (2): 142–7.

Holmes, J. (1993) Who owns psychoanalysis?, *British Journal of Psychotherapy*, 10 (2): 249–52.

Inniss, S. and Bell, D. (1996) Final Project Report for Therapeutic Counselling, Couple Counselling and Competencies (Report 39, May), Welwyn: The Advice, Guidance, Counselling and Psychotherapy Lead Body.

Jacobs, M. (1994) Psychodynamic counselling: an identity achieved, *Psychodynamic Counselling*, 1 (1): 79–92.

Jagger, M. and Richards, K. (1970) You can't always get what you want, in *Let it Bleed*. London: Decca Records, Abkco Music Inc. (BMI).

Kendall, T. and Crossley, N. (1996) Governing love: on the tactical control of the countertransference in the psychoanalytic community, *Economy and Society*, 25 (2).

Lefebure, M. (1991) The relationship between counselling and psychotherapy: on learning from casement, *Counselling*, February.

Lepper, G. (1995) Memo re: Lead Body/UKCP, *UKCP*, 7 November.

Lidmila, A. (1996) What do we mean by 'psychodynamic'? A contribution to the development of a model, *British Journal of Psychotherapy*, 12 (4): 435–46.

McLeod, J. and Wheeler, S. (1995) Person centred and psychodynamic counselling: a dialogue, *Counselling*, November.

Miller, P. and Rose, N. (1988) The Tavistock programme: the government of subjectivity and social life, *Sociology*, 22 (2): 171–92.

Morgan-Jones, R. (1995) Competencies: reservations, risks and developments – a response to Chris Whyte, *British Journal of Psychotherapy*, 11 (3): 436–47.

North, M. (1972) *The Secular Priests*. London: Allen & Unwin.

Oakley, H. (1994) Correspondence, *British Journal of Psychotherapy*, 10 (3): 464.

Pedder, J. (1989) Courses in psychotherapy: evolution and current trends, *British Journal of Psychotherapy*, 6 (2): 203–21.

Pokorny, M. (1995) History of the United Kingdom Council for Psychotherapy, *British Journal of Psychotherapy*, 11 (3): 415–21.

Reed, H. (1965) Naming of parts and judging distances, the lessons of war, *The Penguin Book of Contemporary Verse*. London: Penguin Books.

Richards, J. (1993) The BCP up-date, *British Journal of Psychotherapy*, 10 (2): 298–9.

Rogers, C. (1961) *Becoming a Person*. London: Constable.

Rosen, R. (1978) *Psychobabble: Fast Talk and Quick Cure in the Era of Feeling*. New York: Wildwood.

Rossman, M. (1979) *New Age Blues: On the Politics of Consciousness*. New York: Dutton.

Rowan, J. (1992) What is humanistic psychotherapy?, *British Journal of Psychotherapy*, 9 (1): 74–83.

Rycroft, C. (1995) On beginning treatment, *British Journal of Psychotherapy*, 11 (4): 514–21.

Sieghart, P. (1978) *Report of a Profession's Joint Working Party on Statutory Registration of Psychotherapists*. London.

Smail, D. (1987) Psychotherapy as subversion in a make-believe world, *Changes*, 5 (4): 398–402.

Southgate, J. and Randall, R. (1976) *The Barefoot Psychoanalyst*. London: Barefoot Books.

Swift, J. (1963) *Gulliver's Travels (Book 3)*. London: Longman.

Tantam, D. and Zeal, P. (1996) Letter, *UKCP*, 7 August.

Thorne, B. (1992) Psychotherapy and counselling: the quest for differences, *Counselling, BAC Journal*, 2 (4): 244–8.

Whyte, C. (1994) Competencies, *British Journal of Psychotherapy*, 10 (4): 568–9.

Young, R. (1997) The psychodynamics of psychoanalytic organisations, in *The Culture of British Psychoanalysis and Related Essays*. London: Process Press.

8

Achieving and Maintaining Competence

Sue Wheeler

Counselling and psychotherapy are activities practised by many in all walks of life. The offer of time and space, close attention to personal disclosure, support, encouragement and understanding are the essence of interpersonal relationships. It is probably true that the more adept people are at exercising these interpersonal skills, the more likely they are to forge deep and satisfying relationships with others. However the focus of this chapter is the overall competence of counsellors and psychotherapists who choose to work professionally with a wide range of clients from diverse cultural backgrounds, providing a service for which they would usually expect to be paid. Such professionals must have confidence in their own ability to practise competently and be able to inspire confidence in others, both at an individual level and in the community in which they are located. The incompetence or mistakes of individual therapists, when publicized, undermine the confidence of the public and may deter some from seeking vital help. This chapter will address what makes a good counsellor or psychotherapist and a competent practitioner.

What do we mean by competence?

The Oxford Dictionary defines competence as 'properly qualified', while the Collins Thesaurus (1991: 75) offers the following synonyms: able, adapted, appropriate, clever, equal, fit, proficient, sufficient and suitable. Schon (1987) sees competence as an outcome of being a reflective practitioner that leads to enlightened action, involving a complex mix of skill and judgement in which critical capacities are all important. He describes professional practice as reflection in action and knowledge in use (Barnett, 1994: 76). Barnett has analysed the notion of competence in depth and argues that knowledge and skill are essential components that cannot be separated. He describes the application of skills involving:

1 A situation of some complexity.
2 A performance that addresses the situation, is deliberate and is not just a matter of chance.

3   An assessment that the performance has met the demands of the situation.
4   A sense that the performance was commendable. (Barnett, 1994: 56)

He distinguishes between skills that require a high level of cognitive insight, such as those performed by a surgeon or airline pilot (or a therapist it might be argued) and those required to perform tasks that have a less sophisticated knowledge base such as driving a car or operating a machine. McLeod (1992: 360) refers to 'competence' as 'any qualities or abilities of the person which contribute to effective per- formance of a role or task', a broader description that takes account of the qualities of a relationship that are so essential to counselling and psychotherapy.

Competence as a professional practitioner encompasses a complex mix of theoretical knowledge, advanced skills, practical experience, con- fidence in performance, ability to manage unpredictable, unexpected and hitherto unencountered events using problem-solving experience, all of which lead to an acceptable or positive outcome for those using the service provided. Competencies, as currently described in the National Vocational Qualification (NVQ) scheme, describe the micro application of skills to complex activities and may be a useful measure of aspects of professional competence, but competence is more than a sum of the parts.

Competence

Counsellor or psychotherapist competence is multifaceted. There are many models of counselling and psychotherapy and hence competence is required in the specific model to which a practitioner aspires. To discuss the complexities of even the most popular paradigms would be beyond the scope of this chapter. Nonetheless, Figure 8.1 provides a framework for thinking about the generic components of practitioner competence developed by the author (Wheeler, 1996). The five com- ponents of the frame are described as follows:

1   Self-presentation, preservation and professionalism.
2   Other-centredness.
3   The relationship.
4   The therapeutic frame.
5   Environment.

Self

For therapists to feel able to practise competently, they must have a secure sense of their own identity and be emotionally stable. Therapists, like everyone else, will experience life problems and difficulties, will have

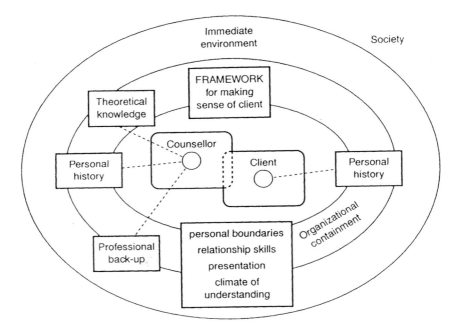

Figure 8.1 *The components of counsellor competence*

good and bad times and will sometimes feel vulnerable or pressured, but they must have sufficient insight into their own personal history and relationship style to be able to manage their own conflicts sufficiently. Alternatively they must have enough self-awareness to recognize their own distress if it becomes incapacitating, when, for the benefit of their clients, they need to withdraw from work until they can function more effectively. Johns (1996) has written at length about the need for personal development in counsellor training and gives her own view of aspects of personal work that must be a focus, including:

- identifying and exploring the uniqueness and patterning of our values, attitudes and constructs;
- the elements in our personal family, relationship and educational history which facilitate or hinder our ability to feel, perceive, relate or protect/ assert ourselves;
- the balance of our personal and interpersonal strengths and limitations;
- a sense of our emotional world, our capacity for intimacy with others and ability to stay separate and appropriately distanced from them;
- a knowledge of our needs, our fears, our intolerances;
- and perhaps most significant, our passions and powers, our tendencies, inappropriately, to invade or deprive others. (Johns, 1996: 9)

Clients also need to perceive their therapists as being confident in their potential to be helpful. Confidence will be inspired through the way in which therapists present themselves physically, their dress and grooming, their way of expressing themselves and ability to make a relationship. Some research studies have shown that clients are influenced by the therapist's personal presentation which has an effect on the therapeutic alliance and subsequently on the outcome of the work. Strong (1968) deduced that clients had more faith in the therapist's ability to facilitate change if they were perceived as attractive, trustworthy and expert. LaCrosse (1980) and Grimes and Murdock (1989) confirmed this with their work on initial interviews and subsequent attendance rates.

Self-preservation is also crucial for a therapist's continued competence. Listening to clients' concerns, bearing their distress, managing boundaries and intense thinking about the world of another, sometimes in an environment that adds pressures or with a caseload that pushes the limits of tolerance, make for a stressful occupation. Therapists need to be able to leave work behind at the end of a day and to find ways of relaxing and offloading some of their own distress. Cushway writes about stress in mental health professionals and reminds us that 'counsellors are human too'. She refers to work on 'wounded healers' and notes that 'the consensus of the literature is that an important determinant for becoming a therapist may be a conscious or unconscious wish to make good the unresolved difficulties of early childhood' (1996: 177). Clearly such motivation would be explored through personal development processes such as personal therapy, and in the opinion of Guy (1987), if properly managed through training and supervision, may enhance effectiveness of the therapist. Cushway (1996) advocates four coping strategies that should be built into the practice of all counsellors and therapists. These are: experience, training, supervision, and personal therapy.

What Cushway describes as coping strategies would also be the key elements of maintaining professionalism. Competent practitioners need to be able to communicate with other mental health professionals, keep accurate records and accounts, adhere to codes of ethics and monitor and evaluate their own work. They need to be able to recognize the limits of their competence and to make referrals when appropriate. This leads back to the discussion of self-awareness. Counsellors and psychotherapists must be secure enough in themselves to be able to tolerate their lack of perfection and the gaps in their knowledge and experience that mean that they cannot help everyone. In other words they must have given up their sense of omnipotence.

Other-centredness

Counsellors and psychotherapists must be self-aware, able to recognize their own thoughts and feelings and to manage their own distress, but they must also be able to suspend their own thoughts and fantasies, in order to give their full attention to the client. They need a natural curiosity and concern for others that can be channelled into attentive listening and focusing on the words, behaviour and other communication from the client. Rogers (1951) emphasizes the need to be nonjudgemental and to show the client positive regard. On some occasions this can be more easily said than done. For example, when working with a known sex offender who has committed crimes against women and children, positive regard may not be automatic. The task is to suspend judgement and work with the person and the inner world that is presented in the session, rather than dwelling on the behaviour that has been so unacceptable. Therapists must be able to set aside their own history, value system, beliefs and ideas about punishment or solution in order to begin to hear, understand and make sense of the world of the client, which requires considerable skill. Johns writes about the counsellor's need to work towards:

- identifying her own needs, fears and blocks to self-acceptance and self-love – and therefore her acceptance of others;
- uncovering and challenging her own implicit personal theories about human growth and development, so that theories and beliefs can be used helpfully, not as predictions for individuals to fit into;
- being centred, stability, congruence in the counsellor of all aspects of her own experience;
- to use opportunities to release sensitivity so that empathic responsiveness to others is increased. (Johns, 1996: 34)

What Johns is emphasizing is that the agenda for counselling belongs to the client, which can be a major source of frustration for the therapist, particularly when issues of paramount importance (to the therapist) seem to be avoided. The therapist must tolerate decisions that the client makes, without overt interference, even if they are anxious about the outcome. That is not to say that some of that anxiety cannot be shared, but ultimately clients are responsible for themselves and have the same potential as children to learn from their mistakes.

Being 'other' focused could be the core of a definition of psychological therapy. A competent practitioner must be able to face whatever the client brings to the therapeutic encounter, including strong feelings of rage, despair, depression and eroticism. They must be prepared to face a wide range of presenting problems including abuse, illness, disability, loneliness, depression, eating disorders, addictions, self-harm, bereavement, trauma through loss or displacement, to name but a few. That is not to say that the counsellor or psychotherapist must choose to work with everyone who comes. On the contrary, the ability to make an assessment of the difficulties presented and a decision about suitability for counselling or psychotherapy or referral to another agency is crucial.

Relationship

There is little dissent amongst the various schools of thought about psychological therapy that the relationship between practitioner and client is an essential aspect of the therapeutic work. Positive outcome in counselling and psychotherapy has been consistently predicted by the therapeutic alliance (Luborsky, 1976). This encompasses trust, respect, understanding, empathy and co-operation in the therapeutic relationship and is a description of the real relationship between the two or more people in the room, as opposed to a representation of past relationships (transference) that may also be present. Our understanding of the therapeutic alliance has evolved from the work of Rogers (1957) on the core conditions that should be present in a therapeutic relationship for change to take place. The core conditions are summarized here:

1   The therapist should be genuine in relation to the client, being aware of his/her own feelings and not hiding them from the client.
2   The therapist should regard the client positively, as someone of unconditional self-worth, of value regardless of his or her behaviour or feelings.
3   The therapist responds to the client with empathy, attempting to understand his or her communication by adopting the client's internal frame of reference.

Rogers described the core conditions as necessary and sufficient for exploration and personal change to take place. Other therapy theoreticians would disagree, particularly about the word 'sufficient'. Various models of counselling have developed their own range of skills and techniques that contribute to therapeutic outcome. Clarkson writes that 'the therapeutic relationship is one of the most, if not the most important factor in successful psychotherapy' (1994: 31). She describes the therapeutic relationship as having five components: the working alliance, transferential–countertransferential, reparative or developmentally needed, I–you, and the transpersonal.

The working alliance or therapeutic alliance has already been described here. The transference relationship refers to an aspect of the relationship that relates to significant figures in the client's past life; the client relates to the counsellor at times as if they were that significant other. The countertransferential relationship is in part the reverse of this and describes the way in which the psychotherapist responds to the client as if he or she were a significant person from their personal life. It also describes the therapist's instinctual response to the material that clients present or their way of being. The reparative or developmentally needed relationship describes the corrective emotional experience that the therapist may from time to time offer clients, for example, by being consistent and therefore helping them to develop confidence, which their upbringing has failed to do. The I–thou or I–you relationship is the real relationship between the two human beings engaged in the therapy. Finally the transpersonal relationship refers to the spiritual dimension of the therapeutic relationship, qualities that transcend the limits of our understanding and are beyond words or description. It might be described as a communication between the unconscious of the therapist and that of the client.

The therapeutic frame

The therapeutic frame includes the agency within which the counselling or psychotherapy is offered, the code of ethics to which the practitioner adheres, the core theoretical model used in practice and skills and interventions used to promote change. A competent therapist will have organized the best possible environment to see clients, having taken care of the details such as an accessible soundproof room, comfortable furniture, arranged in a way that is conducive to the development of a good therapeutic alliance, set within an organization that is sympathetic to the practice of counselling or psychotherapy.

The theoretical frame which underpins the practitioner's understanding of human growth and development and provides a paradigm for the facilitation of change in client work will vary considerably between one theoretical orientation and another. To be competent the therapist will need to be very clear about the paradigm within which she is working. Integration between the various models of psychological therapy is possible, but not without a great deal of thought about the complexities of the differences. The therapist needs the security of a thorough training in the core theoretical model within which she works to give her confidence that theory supports practice. Similarly there will be skills and interventions that fit with the theoretical background with respect to which the practitioner must be comfortable to work. A conceptual frame describes the synthesis of theoretical knowledge and the material presented by the client which then informs the therapeutic strategy.

Finally the code of ethics to which the practitioner adheres will vary according to the professional organization to which they subscribe. The code of ethics provides the competent therapist with a set of rules and guidelines to ensure that clients are not exploited and that the help that they receive is delivered in a way that safeguards their confidentiality and well being. At first sight, a code of ethics such as the BAC *Code of Ethics and Practice for Counsellors* (1996a) may seem quite straightforward, but when behaviour is challenged it soon becomes apparent that interpretations can differ. Bond (1993) has at last clarified some complex ethical and legal issues for counsellors and his book is probably a necessity for the bookshelves of all therapists. Issues such as disclosure of child sexual abuse, intention to commit suicide and confession of crime can be challenging and his work provides helpful guidance in negotiating tortuous situations.

Environment

Competent counsellors or psychotherapists need to be worldly wise. Not only do they need to have thought about themselves, be able to listen to their clients, form a relationship and have some knowledge about human growth and development and counselling or psychotherapy theory, but they also need to be aware of the social, political, cultural, economic and geographical environment in which they and their clients are living or may have lived. The influence of the external world of the client needs to be recognized alongside the intrapsychic processes that may be present.

There is a political dimension to psychological therapy. Careful thought sometimes has to be given to the origin of a client's difficulties and where responsibility for the solution lies. For instance, the assessment of an unemployed, working-class, single parent mother, living on minimum social security benefits in poor housing, who presents for counselling suffering from depression, might conclude that her mental health is affected as much, if not more, by her environment than by her internal dynamics. She may need practical help alongside any counselling work that can be done. Similarly, the assessment of a homosexual teenager, who has recently 'come out' and is facing harassment from his peers at school, may recommend counselling support to help him face a hostile environment, but may also include some intervention on the part of his school. In a different arena, a company executive with high aspirations who is made redundant from his job after fifteen years in post will need help not only in coming to terms with his changed self-image as an unemployed person, but may also need help to come to terms with the changing environment of industry in which job security is rare.

Therapist training is often organized to focus on work with individuals, implying that there are individual solutions to life problems. In some cultures collective responsibility by a family, village or community is seen as more important than individual concerns. Individual therapy would not be seen as viable by that community but there may be people within it who espouse Western values and choose to try to find an individual solution. This sometimes happens within Asian communities in Britain when a daughter or son, raised in Britain, is unhappy with their marriage arrangements. The individual solution has to be carefully weighed up against the needs, wishes and expectations of the family or community.

Hence competent therapists need to be well informed about cultural affairs and modern society. They need to keep abreast of local, national and world news which may have an impact on some clients. They need to have some knowledge of cultures other than their own and be open minded about alternative lifestyles. It is not often that foreign travel is on the syllabus of counselling or psychotherapy courses, but it could be a beneficial adjunct to training. First-hand experience in an alien culture can teach us a lot about being a minority, managing change, customs and interpersonal behaviour and alternative value systems, as well as how other societies organize themselves. Perhaps a recommendation for a competent therapist that will be well received is more holidays.

Achieving competence

Having looked at a model of what makes a good counsellor or therapist, consideration is now given to the need to achieve competence, to feel valued and accepted as a competent practitioner through assessment and finally to maintain competence throughout professional working life.

I believe that to achieve competence the need for a comprehensive training that includes theory, practice, personal development and supervision is beyond dispute. However, it is also crucial that the person who sets out on the path to becoming a therapist has the potential to use the learning experience substantially to increase their sensitivity and understanding of themselves and others. Training is often sought as a result of a positive therapy experience or as a substitute for therapy. While therapists' own psychic wounds are not necessarily a negative indicator of their ability to help others, careful self-assessment is a prerequisite for embarking on a counselling or psychotherapy career.

One question concerns how much suffering the person's own psyche can bear. Regrettably it is often the students who are the least able to recognize their own blocks to learning that are the most difficult to dissuade from a career in counselling or psychotherapy. Projecting one's own distress into others and adopting the more attractive role as healer is a valuable and robust defence as a short-term strategy for survival. The compulsion to become a therapist can be strong and powerful. As a solution to both emotional turmoil and economic necessity the drive for therapy training holds great appeal. The reality of the demanding nature of training and psychotherapeutic work cannot always be foreseen.

Therapy training courses are offered in a wide range of institutions throughout Britain. There is often competition between institutions for students as each needs to fill its places in order to make financial ends meet. Truly competent trainers understand the importance of careful selection procedures to ensure that only those who are psychically robust and have the potential to withstand the pressures of training are chosen. There is considerable anecdotal evidence that applicants refused a place on one training course are accepted by another. While there may be good reasons why this happens, for example, if a candidate is more suited to a training in one particular orientation rather than another, surely there are times when selection decisions are made for economic reasons rather than for the benefit of the therapeutic counselling profession. As long as counselling and psychotherapy are unregulated and training courses proliferate, this situation is unlikely to change. For the aspiring therapist careful thought and investigation must be given to their personal suitability to take on this role. Feedback from others, although at times painful and hard to hear, can be invaluable when making a decision that will have a potent impact on their lives and the lives of others.

Training courses vary enormously. Some are run by competent professional psychotherapists or counsellors with many years of experience as practitioners, and others by academics who have read the books but have a paucity of experience. Some are run with the background of a core theoretical model that is well documented and coherent. Others offer a mishmash of theory and practice that reflects nothing but a lack of coherence in the training team or a lack of in-depth training, which leaves trainers regurgitating the essence of several theories because their experience has given them nothing else. There are some excellent integrative training courses to be found, where considerable skill and experience has been used to produce a training that is comprehensive and coherent. While it may be some years before the majority of counsellor courses are ready to submit an application for BAC Course Accreditation (BAC, 1996b), the accreditation scheme has set standards for counsellor training that provide a template for the structure and delivery of a course that is reputable and through which students can achieve competence. Wheeler (1994) discusses some of the pitfalls of choosing a training course that potential students may find helpful.

The UKCP (1996) has adopted a different system for recognizing psychotherapy training schemes. Organizations providing psychotherapy and/or training are invited into organizational membership of UKCP through the relevant section. Sections include analytical psychology, behavioural and cognitive psychotherapy, humanistic and integrative psychotherapy, psychoanalytic and psychodynamic psychotherapy. Each section defines minimum criteria required for psychotherapy training appropriate to the theoretical model it represents. Member organizations are responsible for training and individuals who successfully complete the training become professional members of their training organization and are then eligible for UKCP registration.

Assessment of competence

It will be important to most counsellors and psychotherapists to receive some external validation of their competence, just as it is important for the general public to have some recognizable symbol of competence to look for when choosing a therapist. Since 1996 there has been in existence a National Register of Counsellors. Counsellors may apply for registration as individuals or as members of an organization that is registered. As individuals, they need to have achieved BAC accredited status (BAC, 1995). Members of registered organizations can only be registered to practise within that organization. Hence for counsellors who practise privately or within an agency that is not eligible for registration, BAC accreditation provides a benchmark of competence. A counsellor awarded accreditation will have a minimum of 450 hours of counselling practice under supervision, 450 hours of training in theory and skills (or its equivalent in practice time and supervision), 40 hours of self-development or personal therapy, ongoing arrangements for supervision and professional development, and the ability to describe the core theoretical model they use in their work as part of their philosophy of counselling. They will need to demonstrate competence through two case studies as well as providing evidence of other accreditation requirements. Applications are scrutinized by a team of assessors who are rigorous in their judgement of suitability for accreditation.

Some practitioners are trained through psychotherapy courses or agencies and will seek United Kingdom Council for Psychotherapy (UKCP) registration rather than BAC accreditation. The UKCP accredits training agencies and therapists are registered when they achieve professional status, usually when their training is successfully completed, within the organization they have worked with. Other practitioners are accredited as Counselling Psychologists by the British Psychological Society (BPS) when they successfully complete the prescribed counselling psychology training course and practice requirements.

Most practitioners currently achieve their qualifications through counsellor or psychotherapy training courses, but there may be a change in this pattern with the advent of NVQs (National Vocational Qualifications). It has been estimated that 10 per cent of the UK workforce, about 2 million people (HMSO, 1993) are involved in either paid or voluntary work involving advice, guidance or counselling. In 1992, the Advice, Guidance, and Counselling Lead Body (later psychotherapy was added to this title to form AGC&PLB), was established to develop NVQs for the identified population. The aim of the Lead Body is to identify competencies required to perform discrete tasks broadly related to counselling and psychotherapy and to produce competency statements for each task or aspect of a therapeutic interaction. One set of competencies has the title 'Assuring the quality of professional practice'. The set is made up of five units which include 'Making the most of supervision', 'Maintain and enhance professional competence', 'Contract with clients', 'Operate referral procedures' and 'Manage professional practice'. Each unit has several elements. For example, the unit 'Maintain and enhance professional competence' has three elements, 'Operate within a formal Code of Ethics', 'Evaluate own practice', 'Engage in continuous professional development'. Each element gives performance criteria described in terms of outcome, a range statement, describing a spectrum of conditions in which the performance criteria are met, knowledge specification, topics that candidates should be familiar with, and finally evidence requirements, ways in which counsellors and psychotherapists might demonstrate their competence.

Qualifications will be offered by organizations such as City and Guilds and the Open University. Qualifications will be offered between Level 1 and Level 5, and will be awarded upon completion of a discrete set of units as defined by the awarding body. Candidates will be able to present themselves for assessment for individual units. Some assessment may take place in the therapist's place of work and other candidates will attend an assessment centre. The scheme is designed to enable candidates to achieve counselling or psychotherapy qualifications through on-the-job experience, without necessarily having had a formal training. Needless to say, despite many professional therapists having given hundreds of hours to the development of the scheme it is viewed with considerable scepticism. Frankland questions 'whether what counsellors are engaged in is an activity that is really amenable to a reductionist analysis' (1996: 31) and sees the description of counselling as a series of identifiable and measurable behaviours as fundamentally flawed. Nonetheless, the advent of NVQs in counselling and psychotherapy and their impact on training, accreditation and competence have yet to be witnessed and evaluated.

Maintaining competence

There are many things that can affect the competent practice of counselling and psychotherapy, including life events, mental and physical health, employment opportunities as well as environmental factors. Therapists can take control of some aspects of competence maintenance by having regular supervision, attending professional development events, reading, and taking care of themselves mentally and physically through diet and exercise and using support systems. Life events, employment and environmental factors have to be managed as they occur rather than are controlled.

The BAC reaccreditation scheme reassesses competence five years after initial accreditation and subsequent reaccreditation. Accredited counsellors are required to demonstrate that during the five years they have seen clients for a minimum of 150 counselling hours per annum, that they have had supervision for a minimum of one and a half hours per month with an appropriately qualified, non line management supervisor, that they have not had a break from counselling for more than six months and that they have engaged in some form of professional development. Their competence is reassessed through a further case study. It could be argued that hours of counselling say little about competence and considerable weight is given to the supervisor's report. UKCP does not reassess competence to practise, although member organizations may have their own rules and regulations.

In Britain, as in the USA and Canada, clinical supervision is a requirement for all counsellors, clinical psychologists and psychotherapists in training. Upon qualification or registration, the requirements differ. For counsellors who adhere to the BAC Code of Ethics (1996a), supervision is an ongoing professional requirement. Some psychotherapists may be required by their professional body to continue with supervision, but for many therapists and clinical psychologists supervision is optional.

Supervision can be a vital clinical and personal support to therapists as well as affording some protection for clients. Some therapists will have regular personal therapy but this is unlikely to be in place throughout their career, whereas supervision may be ongoing. It can be particularly helpful when the therapist faces a crisis in response to life events or other internal upheaval. Competence is at risk when the counsellor or psychotherapist is preoccupied by feelings in response to marital breakdown, death or illness in the family or other stimulus. It may be that the supervisor can help with the assessment of ability to practise during a crisis by encouraging time out or personal therapy when they are too stressed to recognize their own needs. It is at these times when therapists are particularly vulnerable that mistakes or errors of judgement may occur.

Another dimension of maintaining competence is through monitoring and evaluation of performance. For some practitioners working in organizations, evaluation of service provision will be part of the culture. 'In a climate of increased accountability and limited resources it is critical for service agencies to prove their worth in order to survive wholesale cuts, and there are strong indications that funding may increasingly become contingent on proven effectiveness' (Mellor-Clark and Barkham, 1996: 81). Counsellors and psychotherapists working independently may have to work harder and be more creative to evaluate their own work. Evaluation may be perceived as an aspect of research (which it is), an activity which practitioners often eschew (Hicks and Wheeler, 1994). However, even therapists in private practice could adopt fairly simple measures to evaluate the service they provide, which might include short questionnaires to clients at the beginning and end of therapy, to determine whether their expectations have been met. They could initiate an annual review with supervisors to illicit feedback on their performance. Some agencies such as employee assistance programmes collect their own evaluation information about client satisfaction, which can be sought from the company by individual counsellors. Similarly other agencies or individuals such as GPs, who regularly make referrals, could be consulted about their perceptions of the service provided. Peer support groups or supervision groups could dedicate time to peer review when feedback can be given and received.

There is some criticism of the need for any check on the maintenance of competence after graduation through a scheme of assessment. Feltham (1996) is scathing about the need for supervision to continue throughout a counsellor's professional working life as required by the BAC Code of Ethics, suggesting that it can easily become a collusive relationship in which shared beliefs, common core theoretical model and familiarity preclude real evaluation of performance and inhibit critical feedback. He prefers something like a professional troubleshooting hot line, that offers expert and tailored consultancy when a counsellor experiences difficulty with a specific client. It is the view of Bond (1993), Syme (1995) and others that vigilance and continued monitoring of performance are crucial, particularly in this increasingly litigious society which makes all professionals vulnerable to complaints launched through the legal system or their own professional associations. Counsellors and psychotherapists need to behave competently at all times, for their own benefit as well as that of their clients.

Conclusion

This chapter has briefly described some aspects of what a counsellor or psychotherapist needs in order to perform competently. This has included a discussion of the elements of psychotherapeutic competence and some nationally recognized schemes for assessing competence. The route to acquiring competence, achieving recognition and maintaining competence has been addressed. Therapy and counselling are regularly under attack from the media. Weldon (1997) decries 'therapism', likening it to a religion that worships individuality, and predicts that it will not last. There appears to be no evidence to support her prediction given the demand for counselling and therapy and the development of the profession. What is clear, however, is the demand for accreditation and accountability. Counsellors and psychotherapists will be expected to demonstrate their competence to gain accreditation and to maintain it. The profession is in the spotlight and it is the responsibility of each individual practitioner to see that standards of competence are upheld.

References

AGC&PLB (1995) *First Release of Standards*. Welwyn: Advice, Guidance, Counselling and Psychotherapy Lead Body Secretariat.

BAC (1995) *Counselling Accreditation. Accreditation Criteria*. Rugby: British Association for Counselling.

BAC (1996a) *Code of Ethics and Practice for Counsellors*. Rugby: British Association for Counselling.

BAC (1996b) *The Recognition of Counsellor Training Courses*. Rugby: British Association for Counselling.

Barnett, R. (1994) *The Limits of Competence*. Buckingham: Open University Press.

Bond, T. (1993) *Standards and Ethics for Counselling in Action*. London: Sage.

Clarkson, P. (1994) The psychotherapeutic relationship, in P. Clarkson and M. Pokorny, *The Handbook of Psychotherapy*. London: Routledge.

Cushway, D. (1996) New directions in stress, in R. Bayne, I. Horton and J. Bimrose, *New Directions in Counselling*. London: Routledge.

Feltham, C. (1996) Beyond denial, myth and superstition in the counselling profession, in R. Bayne, I. Horton and J. Bimrose, *New Directions in Counselling*. London: Routledge.

Fowler, H.W. and Fowler, F.G. (1964) *The Concise Oxford Dictionary*. Oxford: Clarendon Press.

Frankland, A. (1996) Accreditation and registration, in R. Bayne, I. Horton and J. Bimrose, *New Directions in Counselling*. London: Routledge.

Grimes, W.R. and Murdock, N.L. (1989) Social influence revisited: effects of counselor influence on outcome variables, *Psychotherapy*, 26: 469–74.

Guy, J.D. (1987) *The Personal Life of a Psychotherapist*. Chichester: John Wiley.

Harper Collins (1987) *Collins Gem Thesaurus*. Glasgow: Harper Collins.

Hicks, C.M. and Wheeler, S.J. (1994) Research: an essential foundation for counselling, training and practice, *Counselling*, 5 (1): 38–40.

HMSO (1993) Realising our potential: a strategy for science, engineering and technology. London: HMSO.

Johns, H. (1996) *Personal Development in Counsellor Training*. London: Cassell.

LaCrosse, M.B. (1980) Perceived counselor influence and counseling outcomes, *Journal of Counseling Psychology*, 31: 363–70.

Luborsky, L. (1976) Helping alliances in psychotherapy, in J.L. Claghorn (ed.), *Successful Psychotherapy*. New York: Brunner/Mazel. pp. 92–116.

McLeod, J. (1992) What do we know about how best to assess counsellor competence?, *Counselling Psychology Quarterly*, 5 (4): 359–72.

McLeod, J. (1993) *Introduction to Counselling*. Buckingham: Open University Press.

Mellor-Clark, J. and Barkham, M. (1996) Evaluating counselling, in R. Bayne, I. Horton and J. Bimrose, *New Directions in Counselling*. London: Routledge.

NCVQ (1995) *NVQ Criteria and Guidance*. London: National Council for Vocational Qualifications.

Rogers, C.R. (1951) *Client Centred Therapy*. London: Constable.

Rogers, C.R. (1957) The necessary and sufficient conditions of therapeutic personality change, *Journal of Consulting Psychology*, 21: 95–103.

Schon, D. (1987) *Educating the Reflective Practitioner*. London: Jossey-Bass.

Strong, S.R. (1968) Counselling: a social influence process, *Journal of Counseling Psychology*, 15: 215–24.

Syme, G. (1995) *Counselling in Private Practice*. London: Routledge.

UKCP (1996) *General Information*. London: United Kingdom Council for Psycotherapy.

Weldon, F. (1997) Mind at the end of its tether: once we believed in God, then the state, now we've turned it on ourselves seeking understanding, *The Guardian*, 11 January: 6.

Wheeler, S.J. (1994) Choosing a course: all that glitters is not gold, *Counselling*, 5 (3): 210–12.

Wheeler, S.J. (1996) *Training Counsellors: The Assessment of Competence*. London: Cassell.

9

Clinical Supervision: Luxury or Necessity?

Michael Carroll

Supervision has become a topical subject. The fall of the prestigious Barings Bank in 1993 was blamed on 'poor supervision'. A position paper (Faugier, undated) has called for a system of non-managerial supervision for nurses and employees in the health service. The Prison Service has established supervision training for the managers of its sex offenders treatment programme. There has been call for a counselling and supervision system, as well as a code of ethics and practice, for priests and ministers within both the Church of England and the Catholic Church (Doyle, 1996; Mann, 1996).

The last ten years have witnessed an amazing growth of publications on supervision in Britain. Before 1985 there was not a single book on counselling/psychotherapy supervision for a British audience: since then at least eight books have been published on the subject (Carroll, 1996a). Alongside this burgeoning in publication have come training courses for supervisors; a recent count put these at 43 (private communication, Irene Short). An accreditation scheme for counselling supervisors (through the British Association for Counselling, BAC) has been established since 1988, a *Code of Ethics and Practice for Supervisors* (first published 1988, revised 1995), and a spate of research projects on the subject (at least two doctoral dissertations and a number of Masters projects) further attest to the increasing popularity of supervision. Supervision has moved from the periphery of counselling and psychotherapy training to its heart – recent books on training in counselling (Connor, 1994; Dryden and Feltham, 1994; Dryden et al., 1995) recognize the need for supervision as a crucial ingredient of counsellor training. Through the effective use of supervision, theory is translated into practice, reflection on client work brings new insights, and the 'normative, formative and restorative' (Proctor, 1986) dimensions of supervision support and challenge the learning of trainees.

From this brief overview of the past ten years it is clear that supervision has become central to competent and ethical practice in a number of professions. No longer is it an optional extra or a luxury to be indulged in by the few; rather it is need for both training and qualified practitioners. Why is there such an upsurge in both the theory and practice of supervision?

This chapter will define supervision and outline its history as a back-cloth to understanding its need within counselling and psychotherapy today. It will then suggest four reasons to explain why supervision is needed:

1   To ensure the welfare of clients.
2   To enhance the personal and professional development of supervisees.
3   To gatekeep and monitor the profession itself.
4   To facilitate ongoing reflexivity that results in a better quality service.

Throughout the chapter the terms counselling, therapy, counselling psychology and psychotherapy will be used interchangeably.

What is supervision?

Even though our awareness of the need for supervision has increased enormously, there are still no agreed definitions and descriptions of what it means in practice. While it is accepted that supervision is a valuable contribution and a definite need for professional practice, there is nowhere the same agreement on what is meant by the practice of supervision. Supervisors, by and large, have their unique styles in supervising, some of which are tied into theoretical orientations (Holloway et al., 1989; Carroll, 1995) and many of which have particular foci for supervision (Hawkins and Shohet, 1989). The demarcation line between supervision and therapy is still unclear, even though supervisees are adamant that they do not want their supervisors to become their therapists. Some supervisors view evaluation of supervisees as a key aspect of their supervisory work. Others consider evaluation as detrimental to the supervisory relationship and refuse to furnish evaluation reports. We are still some way off applying supervision in different contexts, for example, counsellors in organizational settings (Carroll, 1996b).

Despite the differences there is general agreement that supervision is the forum where counsellors reflect on their work with clients and learn from that reflection through their interaction with an experienced counsellor who takes on the role of supervisor. Supervision is a process where clients are presented and therapists' work with them is monitored, considered, reviewed, dissected and learning brought forth. Lambert (1980: 425) saw supervision as 'that part of the overall training . . . that deals with modifying their (professionals) actual in-therapy behaviours'. Holloway stressed the modelling aspects of supervision where supervisees 'capture the essence of the therapeutic process as it is articulated and modelled by the supervisor' (1992: 177). Bernard and Goodyear (1992) view the acquisition of skills as at the heart of supervision. From a compilation of the various views and a reading of the supervisory literature it seems to me supervision comprises the following components:

(a) a trainee who is training in counselling/psychotherapy/counselling psychology and is a member of an organized training course;
(b) a supervisor who is an experienced counsellor/psychotherapist/ counselling psychologist and who, hopefully, has had some training in becoming a supervisor; and
(c) an arrangement whereby they meet, either as a dyad, or with other supervisees, to review and reflect on the therapeutic work of the trainee/ s. The two main purposes of this relationship are the professional development of supervisees and the welfare of clients. (Carroll, 1996a)

Of course the above description of supervision focuses on trainee supervision, that is, where supervision is part of an initial training in counselling. There is also a process of consultative supervision where both participants, supervisor and supervisee, are qualified practitioners. While details of these relationships differ, for example, how evaluation is used, what they have in common is that both arrangements have as their focus the welfare of clients and the personal and professional development of supervisees. It must be said that counselling is one of the few professions that considers ongoing supervision for qualified practitioners essential for ethical practice. Here a distinction needs to be made between counselling, psychotherapy and counselling psychology. After qualifying, counsellors are mandated to be in some form of supervision. The BAC *Code of Ethics for Counsellors* is clear: 'It is a breach of the ethical requirement for counsellors to practise without regular counselling supervision/consultative support' (1992: B3.1). However, it seems to be only the British profession that makes such a demand. In North America and Europe supervision becomes optional when training is complete (Bond, 1993). The United Kingdom Council for Psychotherapy (UKCP), while insisting on 'close supervision' for trainees, makes a rather vague statement about those qualified: 'Psychotherapists are required to maintain their ability to perform competently and take necessary steps to do so' (undated: Section 2.9). The British Psychological Society (BPS, 1995) requires a ratio of 1:5 hours of supervision (one hour supervision for every five clients seen) for trainees on the Diploma in Counselling Psychology but again has no requirement for ongoing supervision/consultation after formal training has ended.

In brief, there is some discrepancy in ethical demands about whether or not qualified practitioners should be in supervision/consultation for their client work, with the BAC as the only professional body demanding it and other bodies recommending ongoing support but not specifying the details of that arrangement. There does seem to be movement towards more and more helpers setting up supervision for experienced practitioners and more and more arguments being forwarded to recommend it (Bond, 1993: 156–7).

History of supervision

Doyle (1996) has traced the roots of supervision to biblical times and viewed the early relationship between God and humankind as including a supervisory element. For him God oversees the work of his creation, walking with Adam in the 'cool of the evening' and supervising his work, watching over Abraham on his journeys and consulting regularly with Moses and the Israelites as they travel towards their promised land. Jesus carries on this supervisory role, discussing his work with his companions, asking them for feedback on what he is doing and how he is perceived, requesting support when needed, and closely monitoring the work of his disciples when he sends them out to spread his message. Throughout this era, and subsequently in the history of the Church, Doyle has suggested that the ongoing request to take time to reflect on what is being done, to review one's own motivation for being involved in the work and continually to increase awareness of new needs, is at the very heart of pastoral ministry. Reflexivity (what Neufeldt et al., 1996 call 'focused contemplation') becomes the cornerstone of ministry and is the basis for renewed action and for quality of service. This is not just a Western idea: the concept of mentoring originated from Homer's Odyssey where Mentor was appointed as teacher and overseer to Odyssey's son, a sort of supervisor. Throughout the history of Eastern spirituality, guides and directors (supervisors in a sense) were appointed to help those on spiritual journeys, for example, Sufi leaders.

Whether or not we can see supervision as a key element in the life of Judaism and/or Christianity, what is clear is that it has been an integral part of the helping professions since the latter part of the last century. Certainly social work training and teacher development had well-established systems of supervision by the early 1900s. Both of these used apprenticeship models of supervision where fledging novices were guided and supported as they increased in ability to work with clients and pupils. An experienced practitioner either watched them at work or listened to their account of what happened. The strength of this way of introducing candidates to the profession was its ability to monitor the work at first hand and to help students to learn from doing. Watching experienced others perform, as well as being watched as the first tentative steps are taken, provides a safe environment in which to practise the skills needed for the tasks.

This awareness for the need of a supervisor became part of the psychotherapy scene in the early 1920s. Before that, there had been informal groups of professionals who met to discuss aspects of client work (Freud set up such a group in Vienna), but for trainees the individual who conducted personal analysis also oversaw the client work of the trainee. In 1922, with the advent of formal training in psychoanalysis, the Institute in Vienna suggested that the two tasks, personal analysis and supervision (control analysis), would best be performed by two different people. Their rationale for this distinction was interesting: they saw supervision as more akin to teaching while personal analysis was obviously therapy. The need to draw this distinction was the beginning of supervision being seen as a task/role in its own right. This side of the education of psychotherapists took its place alongside the formal teaching and personal analysis. Trainees would learn from their work with clients while supervisors would monitor their work to ensure that clients were safe and that the professional development of the trainee was being enhanced. Implicit in this new arrangement (it was by no means accepted throughout the psycho-analytic world of the day) is the idea that effective psychotherapists need more than formal knowledge and personal analysis. They need to work with clients in an environment that helps them to learn from that experience and build skills based on that work.

With the arrival of other counselling and psychotherapy orientations and with the advance of technology came further adaptations of personal supervision. Audiovisual facilities allowed supervisors access into actual counselling sessions and group and peer supervision were seen as adding to individual supervision (group supervision was started in social work as a reaction to the need for permanent one-to-one supervision that many saw kept the worker dependent on an expert).

With the advent of the developmental and social work models of supervision the first dent was made in the apprenticeship model. These two models of supervision focused on several areas that changed the concept of supervision itself.

First, they brought the focus of supervision back on to the supervisee and away from the supervisor. Hitherto the apprentice joined the master-practitioner, watched, learned, tried out the work, was given feedback on how it should be done, practised and learned more. Power, the right way to do the job and how this was taught, resided in the hands of the supervisor. Developmental models of supervision reversed the process. What became important was the learning of supervisees. Education was concerned with the management of learning, with supervisors managing the learning of supervisees. At what stage are supervisees in their education, how do they best learn, what learning objectives are the focus of supervision time, how are they integrating the various components of counselling? These are the questions asked of supervision rather than what the supervisor has to offer as an expert in the field.

Second, they emphasized the need for supervisees to learn to do and be a therapist in their own way. Developmental models of supervision realize that there is no objective way of being a counsellor (as there is in being a carpenter, plumber or goldsmith, professions from which the apprenticeship models emerged). Trainees learn their way of doing it. Supervision is needed so that individuals can forge their own identity within the overall boundaries of the profession. Training is not about learning to do it as the supervisor does but about learning an individual and unique way of interacting with clients.

Third, they recognize that supervisees go through stages on their journey to becoming expert practitioners. If these stages can be designated then supervisors can pitch their supervision to that stage. Social role models of supervision have outlined the various tasks performed by supervisors as they work with supervisees. If these tasks can be geared to the developmental stage of supervisees then learning can be better managed and seen as cumulative.

Finally, developmental and social role models also stress the needs of clients and how the learning of supervisees can be geared to the client work they do. It is sensible and ethical to ask: (a) which clients are suitable for this supervisee at this level of development with the experience they already possess; (b) whether clients are getting the service they need and require; (c) whether referral is necessary.

The history of clinical supervision traces developments in the understanding and application of supervision. In brief it brings out several learning issues:

1   The need to look to other professions to help therapists understand and learn about their work, for example, education, psychology. Therapy-bound models of supervision (those that kept rigid links with their core theoretical orientations and supervision) were seen as rather parochial in their application, for example, person-centred supervisors do not teach formally or evaluate; psychoanalytic supervisors were reluctant to use experiential learning or audiovisual work.

2   The need for supervisors to have a range of teaching methods available for the learning of supervisees. Supervisors were being asked to involve themselves in a number of roles with supervisees: teachers, evaluators, monitors, models, counsellors, consultants, etc.

3   The need to understand how learning takes place within an overall training programme and how best to manage that learning as it evolves through various stages.

Importance of supervision

There is no doubt that supervisees find supervision valuable. Pruitt et al. (1986) conducted research with psychiatrists who had trained at the

Menninger Foundation between 1946 and 1954 around the training experiences which meant the most to them in later years and most affected their functioning. They discovered that supervision was rated as more influential than lectures, case conferences and personal reading.

It is not just its obligatory nature that makes supervision more in demand. Supervisees indicate that they find both their supervision and supervisors effective. Carroll (1995) reports that trainees over two years of their courses rate their supervision and their supervisors very positively (giving supervision a six out of ten in year one and a seven out of ten in year two; and giving their supervisors a six and a half in year one and a seven in year two).

The importance of supervision is further attested by the increasing amount of time supervisors are being asked to contribute to their professions. Robiner and Schofield (1990: 297), speaking from the USA, have pointed out that 'more than two thirds of counseling psychologists provide clinical supervision'. Hess (1987) found that 55 per cent of clinicians spend between 10 per cent and 29 per cent of their time in supervision and another 7 per cent claim to spend over 30 per cent of their time as supervisors. Hess and Hess (1983) discovered that supervisory staff spend an average of 3.76 hours per week on supervision. There is no similar research in the British context to indicate how important supervision is viewed or the amount of time spent by either supervisors and/or supervisees. If the increasing number of courses in training supervisors can be taken as a guideline of the importance of supervision, and if the impression is that there is a dearth of supervisors around, then there is every reason to believe that the demand for supervision is increasing rapidly.

Ensuring the welfare of clients

The first reason for the need for supervision is the welfare of clients. Since in many instances supervisees are trainees, it is imperative that their work is overseen by competent and experienced practitioners. This provides some guarantee that clients are not being harmed and that practitioners are working within their competencies. In some instances (for example, in the USA) a supervisor has 'vicarious responsibility' for clients. Cormier and Bernard (1982: 488) define this term as 'the doctrine [where] someone in a position of authority or responsibility, such as a supervisor, is responsible for acts of his or her trainees or assistants. Stated another way, supervisors are ultimately responsible for the welfare of clients counselled by their supervisees.' The British legal system is different from the American system in that all actors are deemed responsible for their own actions (Carroll, 1988). However, whether legal responsibility is the order of the day or not, moral responsibility rests with the supervisor to ascertain that, at worst, clients are not being harmed, and at best they are receiving the optimum service from this counsellor.

Ensuring the welfare of the client means that supervisors monitor the work of supervisees in ways that assure them, and can assure others, that clients are not being harmed as trainees work with them. Obviously, different supervisors have different methods of monitoring their work with supervisees. Some use live supervision, observing the counselling session as it takes place and intervening in the actual session should that be necessary. Other supervisors require audio or video tapes of actual counselling sessions as a way of monitoring the counselling work. Some rely solely on reports from supervisees and/or their own relationship with them as the central feature of accountability. These ways of presenting within supervision, as well as different supervision formats, for example, individual, group, peer, team, all have their own strengths and weaknesses (Carroll, 1996a). Supervisees need to be helped to discover what is best for them at the current stage of their professional development (Skovholt and Ronnestad, 1992). Whichever method is used to monitor client work, what is important is that the client is cared for, looked after and getting a good service. Therapeutic work is not about experimenting with clients for the learning of trainees, but about supervisees beginning to work with clients and using that work as a way of learning how to become better counsellors. The task of supervisors is to ensure that supervisees are not working beyond their capabilities and are being referred clients who are appropriate for them to see (Carroll, 1993).

With qualified therapists, supervision also plays an accountability role in respect of clients. Effective supervisors monitor the counselling work not just to ensure that clients are being cared for in an ethical and professional way, but also that the therapist is working as effectively as possible. This may mean reviewing client case loads, personal and professional demands, as well as time management and the management of therapy provision. Qualified practitioners all too easily fall into routines where they forget to ensure that their own learning is updated, that they are able to monitor and meet their own changing needs as persons and as therapists, and that they are working effectively to care for themselves as well as their clients. However, this is still an area of supervision that is not well developed, although there are some signs that the needs of experienced practitioners are being considered. Morrison (1996) has focused on the supervisory needs of qualified therapists. She suggests five tasks for this kind of consultant supervision:

1 To negotiate and maintain a collaborative relationship between supervisee and consultant supervisor.
2 To work together to give a voice to the 'unthought known' influencing work with clients. The 'unthought known' is a term coined to

illustrate the need to put into language that which is known but not yet thought or thought through.

3   To be able to refer the supervisee to professional resources needed personally or professionally.
4   To monitor the administrative/organizational aspects of the therapeutic work.
5   To monitor professional/ethical issues as they arise within client work, as well as the supervisory work.

Ultimately supervision, either for trainees or experienced practitioners, is for the welfare of clients and to ensure the quality of the service clients receive.

Personal and professional development of supervisees

The personal and professional development of supervisees, which facilitates the process whereby they move from being novices towards what Stoltenberg and Delworth (1987) call 'master-practitioners', is a key purpose of supervision. They offer three areas where this movement takes place:

1   Autonomy, where the counsellor has a progressive awareness of being able to function as a professional in an increasingly independent way. However, independence does not mean that practitioners do not need support and challenge as they work with clients. The kind of supervision will probably change as supervisees progress in their experience and many qualified personnel use peer group supervision as their learning forum.
2   Motivation, which outlines a movement towards more realistic reasons for working with clients and a realization of the hazards involved.
3   Self- and other-awareness, where therapists become more alert to themselves, clients and the relationships involved.

However, there is no overall agreement on what the professional development of practitioners means. This confusion is seen most clearly in the array of training courses for counsellors/counselling psychologists and psychotherapists where there may be some agreement at the early levels of training (diploma) but almost none at later levels. At higher degree level (Masters courses in counselling, counselling psychology, psychotherapy) there is very little agreement on what constitutes a basic curriculum. Some recent attempts have been made to standardize counselling training (BAC, 1990; Connor, 1994; Dryden et al., 1995; BPS, 1996).

To gatekeep and monitor the profession

The third need for supervision is the monitoring and welfare of the profession itself. Supervisors, whether they like it or not, are entrusted with being gatekeepers of their profession. It is they who will assess whether or not trainees are ready to work as practitioners, with which clients and in what contexts, and in particular whether they are able to work ethically and professionally. Supervisors' responsibilities to their profession revolve around three major areas:

1   Assessing supervisees for practice as professionals.
2   Ensuring that supervisees know and practise ethically.
3   Working with the organizational aspects of placements and training courses.

Assessment of supervisees is done mostly through evaluation of practice. While the majority of supervisors and supervisees accept that evaluation and assessment is part of supervision, many agree that it is probably the most difficult aspect. Evaluation, especially formal evaluation, introduces the judgement (good/bad, examination, assessment) element into the supervisory relationship. Evaluation is particularly difficult where one or other of the participants is seen as lacking.

Evaluation is part of all stages of supervision and should be an ongoing process that characterizes the work together. It is both formal and informal, the latter characterizing the ongoing feedback that is integral to each session. With trainees there may be a report written for the training course which requires a formal evaluation.

There is feedback from both participants on their work, their view of each other's work and on their relationship. Obviously this feedback and how it is delivered are key factors in learning. Supervisees learn by doing, by reflecting on that doing and by listening to others comment on their work. It is important not just to give feedback but to set up the environment in which feedback can be best used. A number of authors have commented on the skills and qualities involved in giving and receiving feedback (Borders and Leddick, 1987; Hawkins and Shohet, 1989; Inskipp and Proctor, 1993; Page and Wosket, 1994).

The second way in which evaluation takes place in supervision is formal, when time is set aside explicitly to evaluate supervision, the supervisee, the supervisor. This evaluation may be needed for the training course on which the supervisee is a participant, for membership of certain organizations (for example, BAC accreditation, BPS equivalency statements), or for an agency in which supervisees see clients. Whatever its purpose, it must be recognized that formal evaluation raises many issues for supervisors and supervisees. Supervisees are anxious that they will not live up to the standards required and often think they are not good enough. Even more seriously, they fantasize that evaluation will be used to interrupt their training or advise them to leave their chosen profession. Often supervisees hear the negatives and forget the positives. A supervisee put it well when he said, 'One negative evaluation equals twenty positives in supervision.'

Supervisors too are anxious about formal evaluation. They may be found wanting in meeting the needs of the supervisee, they may be very unsure of the criteria by which they are evaluating, and they may not want to disturb the positive quality of the relationship they have with their supervisees.

Supervision is needed because assessment of counsellors is required through evaluation processes that ensure they (trainees) are capable of practising professionally and ethically with clients. In this regard, supervisors need to be sure that supervisees:

1   know ethical codes (Feltham and Dryden, 1994, recommend discussing the BAC Code of Ethics with supervisees);
2   have a method of making ethical decisions;
3   belong to relevant professional bodies, and subscribe to appropriate codes of ethics and practice for counsellors/counselling psychologists/psychotherapists;
4   are not overworking, have reasonable case loads and are looking after themselves. Inskipp and Proctor describe this very well:

> It is your ethical responsibility to your clients, and your human right for yourself, to nurture and maintain your physical, emotional, intellectual and spiritual well-being.
> Counselling can be demanding and can be stressful in different ways at different stages of your development.
> Supervision is one major resource: it cannot fulfil all your needs for support and development.
> You may surprise yourself by realising how many opportunities you already use for replenishment – and how many more there are to use. (1993: 34)

5   have adequate insurance (Mearns, 1993);
6   are able to reflect critically on their interventions with clients;
7   are free to bring their 'bad' work to supervision;
8   are aware of ways in which they can abuse clients (Feltham and Dryden, 1994);
9   are aware of the stresses of their life and work at different stages of their development as practitioners.

In brief, supervisors need to be aware of their ethical responsibilities for supervisees and to their profession. As therapists are accountable for their work with clients, so supervisors are accountable for their work with supervisees.

A third way in which supervisors are responsible to their professions is in working with the organizational aspects of placements and training courses. The need for supervision extends to working with the agencies in which trainees see clients and with the training courses that organize the formal educational part of the course. Together these three systems, supervisors, training courses and placement agencies, work together so that graduates are seen to be well qualified to work effectively with clients.

Carr summarizes some of the issues that can arise within the training course which affect the supervisory relationship:

> The training organization is a powerful, ever present force influencing the relationship between supervisor and supervisee. Both can feel judged in different ways, with their work in supervision, not only the work of the supervisee under examination. The supervisee can feel there is a strong bond between his supervisor and the training body, and he is excluded from this like a child is excluded from relationships between the adults. Difficulties can sometimes arise between supervisee and the training body, in which the supervisee can seek to involve the supervisor in a collusive relationship against the training body. Supervisors can over-identify with their students and perhaps we are familiar with the supervisor, all of whose geese are swans. (Carr, 1989: 2–3)

All the more reason for having unity between the three main aspects of counsellor training: training, supervision and placement agency – together they ensure good practitioners for the profession.

Similar organizational issues arise with experienced practitioners. Close monitoring of the impact of organizations on therapy provision is necessary if it is to be effective. Carroll (1996a: 122) has suggested five areas to be considered by qualified professionals who work within an organization. These are:

1   Enabling supervisees to live and work within the organization.
2   Helping supervisees to control the flow of information within the organization.
3   Helping supervisees to manage the delivery of their service.
4   Working with supervisees at the interface between the individual and the organization.
5   Ensuring that supervisees look after themselves while working within an organizational setting.

Ongoing reflexivity for quality service

Perhaps the most important preparatory skill in helping supervisees to make effective use of supervision is the skill of reflexivity. Reflexivity has been described as 'focused contemplation' where the events of client sessions are followed by reflection, both personally and in supervision, to lead to new therapeutic behaviours. Reflexivity is a decision-making process whereby events in client work are dissected so that under-standing of what happened can be the basis of personal and professional development. Taking and maintaining a stance of critical inquiry on one's work enables supervisees to learn about that work. Neufeldt et al. (1996) asked five experts to illustrate the issues of reflexivity and the following were some statements which emerged from their interviews. Interviewees used statements such as: 'a search towards a more profound understanding of something'; 'it is directed to the therapist's own actions, emotions, and thoughts in the counselling session'; 'things are happening, things are popping up, you're getting signals, you're trying to figure out the meaning of them as you're interacting there', 'I think fairly strongly that . . . maintaining that position of not knowing is an extremely important aspect of the process'. From the study above four dimensions emerged that characterize a reflective stance: intention (reviewing the purpose of the event), active inquiry, openness, and vulnerability (taking a humble approach). These four dimensions can result in giving meaning to what happened and they can be used to learn and create new ways of working as a counsellor. Neufeldt et al. summarize the process:

> The reflective process itself is a search for understanding of the phenomena of the counselling session, with attention to therapist actions, emotions, and thoughts, as well as to the interaction between the therapist and client. The intent to understand what has occurred, active inquiry, openness to that understanding, and vulnerability and risk-taking rather than defensive self-protection characterise the stance of the reflective supervisee. Supervisees use theory, their prior personal and professional experience, and the experience of themselves in the counselling session as sources of understanding. . . . To complete the sequence, reflectivity in supervision leads to changes in perception, changes in counselling practice, and an increased capacity to make meaning of their experiences. (Neufeldt et al., 1996: 20)

In helping supervisees to create a reflective position, supervisors first help them to learn how to learn. Knowing and watching their own processes of learning can be an initial help in creating an environment of learning and an understanding of personal dynamics within that process. Allowing awareness to surface without defensiveness can be difficult for beginning supervisees who are afraid of getting it wrong. Inskipp and Proctor (1993) have talked about developing a 'fair witness' to client work. Four elements appear here of benefit to supervisees:

1 Learning how to learn.
2 Creating awareness of what is happening.
3 Openness to 'fair witness'.
4 Developing the 'helicopter ability', that is, the skill of seeing the problems of clients in wider and wider contexts.

This reflective stance, for both trainee and qualified therapists, ensures better quality and better thought through work for clients. By its very nature, it should increase the quality of client work, keeping practitioners in touch with themselves, with their interventions and allowing them to change what needs changing for the sake of quality in their therapeutic relationships. One supervisee, Naomi, recounts how she prepares for supervision:

> My preparation for supervision is a continuous process which begins as I leave the previous supervision session. I am already formulating goals for working with individual clients and with the organization. Ethical issues have a priority on my agenda. In working with organizations these seem to arise much more frequently. I am aware that there is no ethical code covering this area of counselling work. I also anticipate supervision by preparing anything I have to write for the organization – reports, policies, statements. I bring any communications with the organization for monitoring and evaluation. My own professional development is always on the agenda. With the greater multiplicity of variables in organizational counselling, preparation for supervision has increasingly to be about reflection and openness about myself, including my values and vulnerabilities. (Carroll, 1996b: 207)

Effective supervision depends on good preparation by supervisees and supervisors and in turn this depends on supervisees' ability to reflect on the work they do and use that reflection to prepare an agenda for their supervision time.

Assumptions about supervision

Having reviewed the need for supervision from four perspectives – the welfare needs of clients, the personal and professional development of supervisees, the needs of the counselling/psychotherapy profession and the value of ongoing reflection as part of therapeutic work – it is now possible to summarize some of the basic tenets of a modern effective supervisory system. The following statements (Carroll, 1996a) are assumptions that underlie how effective supervision can best meet these four areas above as well as being reasons why supervision is needed today:

1 Supervision is now an essential requirement of training and no longer an optional extra.
2 Supervision is a formal, professional relationship between supervisees and supervisors.
3 The purposes of supervision are the professional development of supervisees and the welfare of clients.
4 Supervision is not counselling or psychotherapy.
5 Supervision is primarily an educational process focused on the learning of supervisees.
6 Good therapists do not necessarily make good supervisors.
7 Supervisors require training in supervision.
8 Supervision is moving towards being a profession in its own right.

9 Supervisors enable supervisees find their way of being therapists.
10 Evaluation (formal and informal) is a crucial part of supervision.
11 Contracting and negotiating in supervision are essential.
12 The roles and responsibilities of supervisors and supervisees ought to be clear to all participants in supervision.
13 Bad/poor supervision exists.
14 There is a number of forms of supervision; all have strengths and weaknesses.
15 The relationship in supervision is made up of a number of roles, not one, and good supervisors are able to provide supervisees with a multiplicity of roles.
16 Issues of gender, race/culture and power play large parts in supervision and need to be addressed.
17 Supervision is a lifelong commitment for practitioners.
18 Ideally, supervisors should have a forum where they can discuss their supervision.
19 Supervisors and supervisees ought to be aware of the Ethical Codes for Supervision.
20 Supervisees have a right to expect help in taking on the roles of supervisee and be assisted in preparing for supervision.
21 Supervision works best when both parties are allowed the choice to work together and supervisees are not always best served by being assigned to a supervisor, either individually or in groups.
22 The learning process in supervision emerges from the client work of supervisees. Supervision is not about formal teaching, skills training, learning ethical codes, dealing with personal issues that are unconnected to the work being done with clients.

Conclusion

While the need for supervision, both in training and as a qualified practitioner, has been recognized for some time within counselling and psychotherapy, it is only latterly that other professions are beginning to realize its importance for the quality of their work. It would seem that the future will see more instances of supervision at the very heart of 'people work' and that wherever individuals interact with others in a helping role, be it welfare, social work, medical, educational and/or occupational, there will be a need for supervision. To answer the question posed in the title: supervision is both a luxury and a necessity.

References

BAC (1988, 1995) *Code of Ethics and Practice for Supervisors*. Rugby: British Association for Counselling.

BAC (1990) *The Recognition of Counsellor Training Courses*, 2nd edn. Rugby: British Association for Counselling.
BAC (1992) *Code of Ethics and Practice for Counsellors*. Rugby: British Association for Counselling.
Bernard, J. and Goodyear, R. (1992) *Fundamentals of Clinical Supervision*. New York: Allyn Bacon.
Bond, T. (1993) *Standards and Ethics for Counselling in Action*. London: Sage.
Borders, D. and Leddick, G. (1987) *The Handbook of Counseling Supervision*. Virginia: Association for Counselor Education and Supervision.
BPS (1996) *Regulations and Syllabus for the Diploma in Counselling Psychology*. Leicester: British Psychological Society.
Carr, J. (1989) A model of clinical supervision, in *Clinical Supervision: Issues and Techniques*, papers from the public conference: April 1988: The Jungian Training Committee. London: J.C. Press.
Carroll, M. (1988) Counselling supervision: the British context, *Counselling Psychology Quarterly*, 1 (4): 387–96.
Carroll, M. (1993) Trainee counsellors' clients, in W. Dryden (ed.), *Questions and Answers in Counselling in Action*. London: Sage. pp. 57–61.
Carroll, M. (1995) The generic tasks of supervision. Unpublished PhD dissertation, University of Surrey.
Carroll, M. (1996a) *Counselling Supervision: Theory, Skills and Practice*. London: Cassell.
Carroll, M. (1996b) *Workplace Counselling: A Systematic Approach to Employee Care*. London: Sage.
Connor, M. (1994) *Training the Counsellor*. London: Routledge.
Cormier, S. and Bernard, J. (1982) Ethical and legal responsibilities of clinical supervisors, *Personnel and Guidance Journal*, 60: 486–91.
Doyle, M. (1996) Pastoral supervision of priests: caring for the carers, *The Month*, 2nd New Series, 29, 8: 312–16.
Dryden, W. and Feltham, C. (1994) *Developing Counsellor Training*. London: Sage.
Dryden, W., Horton, I. and Mearns, D. (1995) *Issues in Professional Counsellor Training*. London: Cassell.
Faugier, J. (undated) Clinical supervision: a position paper. Manchester: University of Manchester.
Feltham, C. and Dryden, W. (1994) *Developing Counsellor Supervision*. London: Sage.
Hawkins, P. and Shohet, R. (1989) *Supervision in the Helping Professions*. Milton Keynes: Open University Press.
Hess, A.K. (1987) Psychotherapy supervision: stages, Buber, and a theory of relationships, *Professional Psychology*, 18 (3): 251–9.
Hess, A.K. and Hess, K.A. (1983) Psychotherapy supervision: a survey of internship training practices, *Professional Psychology, Research and Practice*, 18: 251–9.
Holloway, E. (1992) Supervision: a way of teaching and learning, in S. Brown and R. Lent (eds), *The Handbook of Counseling Psychology*, 2nd edn. New York: John Wiley.
Holloway, E., Freund, R.D., Gardner, S.L., Nelson, M.L. and Walker, B.R. (1989) Relationship of power and involvement to theoretical orientation in supervision: an analysis of discourse, *Journal of Counseling Psychology*, 36 (1): 88–102.
Inskipp, F. and Proctor, B. (1993) *Making the Most of Supervision*. Middlesex: Cascade.
Lambert, M.J. (1980) Research and the supervisory process, in A.K. Hess (ed.), *Psychotherapy Supervision: Theory, Research and Practice*. New York: John Wiley. pp. 423–50.
Mann, E. (1996) The organizational issues of setting up counselling and supervision systems in the church. DPsych research proposal, City University.
Mearns, D. (1993) Against indemnity insurance, in W. Dryden (ed.), *Questions and Answers in Counselling in Action*. London: Sage. pp. 161–4.
Morrison, J. (1996) The forum of consultative supervision: room for discovering the unthought known. Dissertation for the Diploma in Supervision, Metanoia Institute.

Neufeldt, S.A., Karno, M.P. and Nelson, M.L. (1996) Experts conceptualization of supervisee reflexivity, *Journal of Counseling Psychology*, 41 (1): 3–9.

Page, S. and Wosket, V. (1994) *Supervising the Counsellor: A Cyclical Model*. London: Routledge.

Proctor, B. (1986) Supervision: a co-operative exercise in accountability, in M. Marken and M. Payne (eds), *Enabling and Ensuring: Supervision in Practice*. Leicester: National Youth Bureau.

Pruitt, D., McColgan, E.B., Pugh, R.L. and Kiser, L.J. (1986) Approaches to psychotherapy supervision, *Journal of Psychiatric Education*, 10 (2): 129–47.

Robiner, W.N. and Schofield, W. (1990) References on supervision in clinical and counseling psychology, *Professional Psychology: Research and Practice*, 21 (4): 297–312.

Skovholt, T.M. and Ronnestad, M. (1992) *The Evolving Professional Self: Stages and Themes in Therapist and Counselor Development*. New York: John Wiley.

Stoltenberg, C.D. and Delworth, U. (1987) *Supervising Counselors and Therapists*. London: Jossey-Bass.

UKCP (undated) *Ethical Guidelines*. London: United Kingdom Council for Psychotherapy.

10

Reading, Writing and Research

John McLeod

It would appear that counsellors and psychotherapists tend to read a lot. The evolution and success of counselling as a profession has been more than matched by an expansion in the number, scope and variety of publications of different kinds within this field. Most large bookshops contain a section specifically devoted to counselling and psychotherapy books, sometimes with separate sections assigned to different approaches or areas of application. In parallel, the 1980s and 1990s have seen a steady increase in the number of counselling and psychotherapy research and professional journals. Finally, the birth of the Internet has been accompanied by a flourishing set of therapy interest group websites.

But what is the significance of the therapy literature? Do therapists really need to keep in touch with this growing mass of published work? How meaningful is all this? After all, few if any counsellors would consult a textbook during an actual session. It could well be argued that the fundamental attributes of the effective therapist – the capacity to form a productive therapeutic relationship, the ability to empathize, the possession of a secure sense of self – owe little or nothing to breadth of reading or familiarity with the professional literature. Indeed there is plentiful evidence (for example, Strupp and Hadley, 1979; Berman and Norton, 1985) that people with minimal training who have read virtually nothing about counselling or psychotherapy can operate competently in a therapeutic role. So, although the literature exists and continues to proliferate, there has been little discussion of the functions of reading, writing and allied activities such as carrying out research in contributing to good quality services to those who seek counselling or psychotherapy.

The aim of this chapter is to explore the place of the literature within the working lives of counsellors and psychotherapists and to consider the different functions that it fulfils. The chapter will begin by mapping the contours of the literature, before moving to a consideration of the place of reading and writing in aiding conceptualization, the development of professional identity, and the ability to learn from others. The direct use of literary skills in therapy will also be examined. This will be a critical discussion. It is by no means obvious that all forms of reading and writing are equally valuable or necessary, or that the literature we have is the one we need.

Mapping the literature

A literature is a body of written knowledge pertaining to a particular topic area. It comprises a structuring of information and experience that exceeds and transcends the ability to know of any one individual. Written materials of this kind function as a kind of massive external memory and problem-solving device, a kind of collective intelligence. For example, if I want to grow cabbages in my garden I can look up a gardening book, which will tell me what to do. If my child runs a high temperature in the middle of the night, I can consult a childcare manual. If I want to know about nineteenth-century relationships and morals, I can read a Jane Austen novel. These are all domains within a general literature that is widely available through libraries and bookshops. But it is clear that there are alternative literatures on each of these topics. There are competing childcare manuals and family health advice columns in popular newspapers. There are medical journals and textbooks devoted to child health. Similarly, the counselling and psychotherapy literature is structured and differentiated in complex ways.

A rather rough and preliminary categorization of the psychological therapy literature is presented in Table 10.1. There is perhaps no one equipped to explore all the different regions of this territory. In many areas of the literature, reading and understanding require specific technical skills. To decipher the language and rhetoric of a classic psychoanalytic case study or a statistically dense research paper is no easy matter. All published writing necessarily builds upon taken for granted assumptions that the writer must make concerning the prior knowledge and interest of the readers. The counselling literature is further structured into various subdomains, such as student counselling, AIDS counselling, etc.

Another source of complexity within the literature arises from the fact that it is historically sedimented, with contemporary writings building upon what has gone before. Often, to gain a true understanding of what is implied by using a particular approach to counselling or psychotherapy, it is necessary to return to material that was originally written thirty, forty or more years ago. There can be problems in gaining access to such primary sources. Many training courses operate in colleges or independent institutes that cannot afford to maintain adequate library stocks. Even when early seminal writings can be tracked down, however, it can be difficult to make sense of them in the absence of an appreciation of the historical circumstances under which they were originally produced.

Whose voices are heard within this literature? There can be no doubt, based on a scan of authors' names and biographies, that the dominant voice is male, white, heterosexual, able bodied. It is also a confident, hopeful voice, very positive about the benefits of therapy. It is a logical, rational voice, one that seldom lapses into poetry or musicality. It is

Table 10.1   *A preliminary map of the therapy literature*

Foundational 'how to do it' primary sources: books and articles by key figures such as Freud, Jung, Rogers, Wolpe, Berne.

Post-foundational 'how to do it' primary sources by members of mainstream schools of therapy.

'How to do it' books written by therapists who cannot be classified as belonging to a particular approach or school of thought, for example, Scott Peck, Sheldon Kopp.

Professional writings concerned with issues of training, ethics, accreditation, etc.

Textbooks offering an overview or review of different approaches and issues.

Technical reports of research studies into counselling process or outcome.

Books or articles written by consumers of therapy.

Items written by external observers of therapy – philosophers, sociologists, anthropologists, journalists, cartoonists.

Limited circulation pieces, for example, case studies written by trainees, annual reports of counselling agencies.

Portrayals of therapy in novels and plays.

predominantly the voice of the master therapist rather than that of the person in therapy; less confused, hesitant, stumbling, and more knowing and certain. Curiously, the pain and despair which are so much a part of counselling practice are generally found only around the edges of the literature. It is important to acknowledge that the literature that is available is not in any simple sense a mirror of what is happening within the counselling and psychotherapy community. Instead, the literature is constructed by those with the authority and power to put into tangible print form their views of things. It is of some interest that within medicine, an occupation with a much longer history as a profession, there has emerged a tradition, in at least some medical schools, of giving students opportunities to explore the potential of poetry and novels to represent experiences of doubt, despair, pain and joy not captured in the formal, scientific literature. Knights (1995) has developed a similar approach within counselling and psychotherapy training.

Conceptualizing and a sense of inquiry

Mapping the literature gives a sense of the abstractness of much that is written about counselling and psychotherapy. For instance, through Carl Rogers' reflections on his work with people, he arrived at a formulation of the basis of his practice as comprising a commitment to engage in a therapeutic relationship characterized by empathy, acceptance and genuineness. He initially wrote about this in the 1950s and 1960s. Other people then wrote books and articles discussing what Rogers meant, whether it was valid, how it compared with competing ideas about therapy. Still other people carried out research to test these notions. Yet more people reviewed all this, and so on. Increasingly, the discourse becomes 'experience–distant'. Although in his earliest writings Rogers stuck fairly close to his description of what he felt was happening in therapy (see, for example, Rogers, 1951: Chapter 3), as the literature on his ideas gained momentum this 'experience-near' form of communication gave way to a more abstract, experience-distant mode of writing.

Paradoxically, perhaps, the abstractness of much of the literature can be seen as serving a highly useful purpose for counsellors and psychotherapists. People come to see therapists for many reasons, but often because they are enmeshed in the difficult, stuck, concrete realities of their lives. They cannot 'see beyond' their immediate dilemma, anxiety or bereavement. While it is essential for the counsellor or psychotherapist to be able to meet the person in his or her pain, it is also important that he or she should be able to maintain, at the same time, a broader perspective. This ability to 'see beyond' the immediate specific situation is greatly assisted by an ability to conceptualize, to apply ideas that make links across different situations or pieces of information. Research into expertise in many fields of activity (Glaser and Chi, 1988) suggests that the people who are most effective in their profession or occupation are those who are best able to employ concepts, who see the bigger picture. There is some evidence that this is true also for counsellors (Combs, 1989). It could be argued, then, that familiarity with the literature may provide counsellors and psychotherapists with training in thinking conceptually about the problems they meet in their work.

The capacity to make conceptual links can, therefore, be helpful in the therapy room, in allowing the therapist a sense of perspective on matters. Much of the time, therapists may be able to get by without drawing on such a capacity. After all, the person being helped possesses his or her own ability to make sense, and the more they exercise this ability the better.

Conceptualizing is perhaps even more essential in the area of communication with colleagues. It is hard to imagine a conversation between a psychotherapist and a supervisor, or between a trainer and trainee, or a group of counsellors engaged in a team meeting, that did not rely upon an ability to discuss things in a way that goes beyond specific instances or cases. It is hard to see how a therapist could reflect on his or her performance without relating concrete memories and events to abstract principles.

A genuine engagement with the psychological counselling and therapy literature not only promotes a facility in constructing a conceptual framework within which to make sense of the therapeutic process, but also reinforces the sense of inquiry of the practitioner. It is not possible to read widely without gaining an appreciation of the uncertainty, ambiguity and limitations of what is known. Whiteley et al. (1967) have shown that cognitive flexibility, defined as a tolerance for ambiguity and uncertainty, can be associated with effectiveness as a therapist. I would suggest that breadth of reading is a practice that can help to develop appropriate levels of cognitive flexibility. The process of reading widely is also a way of demonstrating a sense of enquiry, a realization that there is always more that can be known. Again, this unwillingness to be dogmatic, or to take for granted how things seem to be, constitutes an essential element of counselling and psychotherapy practice.

What is being suggested here is that ongoing immersion in the psychotherapy literature not only provides the reader with useful content (for example, information and ideas) but also develops and reinforces the use of important higher level cognitive skills that play a significant role in therapy practice. It is of course necessary to recognize that the relationship between reading the literature and the acquisition of cognitive skills relevant to counselling and psychotherapy is not a simple one. For example, it is easy to see that some therapists may read too much, with the result that they come to adopt to an over-theorized approach to the person, or become so taken up with the ambiguity and multiple meaning of any statement that they become almost unable to communicate in a direct manner.

Developing a professional identity

There is, understandably, a major emphasis within the counselling and psychotherapy literature on the practicalities of doing therapy. However, looked at from a different angle, the literature taken as a whole serves the function of describing and defining what it means to be a counsellor. In other words, the literature is an expression of the professional identity of counselling and counsellors. We are now moving to a discussion of the role in counselling and psychotherapy of *writing* rather than reading. Everything that therapists write has the effect of defining the profession. There are three distinct aspects to professional identity: the way the profession identifies itself to itself, the set of relationships between counselling/psychotherapy and other allied professions, and, finally, the sense of work role identity experienced by the individual practitioner.

The first of these aspects of professional identity relates to the way that a group of people carrying out a particular type of work becomes a profession. Studies of the sociology of the professions (Macdonald, 1995) suggest that one of the key characteristics of any of the traditional professions (such as law or medicine) is the possession of its own body of specialized knowledge. The literature can be seen as the repository of this knowledge, although it is important to point out that the knowledge base of a profession comprises not only the knowing that is found in books and journals, but also a rich repertoire of practical knowing how imparted through professional socialization and training. If counselling and psychotherapy are to be regarded as professions, it is therefore essential that they are able to support a comprehensive and suitably differentiated literature.

It is also the case that if a profession is marked by the possession of a specialized body of knowledge, then to a large extent the credibility or legitimacy of that profession is evaluated in terms of how other allied professions view that literature. The territory inhabited by counselling has been a disputed territory, with counter-claims to the same kind of work having been made in the past by colleagues in psychotherapy, clinical psychology, social work, and psychiatric nursing. The firming up of the counselling literature in recent years has helped counsellors to define the appropriate domain for their activities. It is therefore important for practitioners of therapy to continue to document in writing the type of work they carry out, if to communicate no more to other professional colleagues than the simple message 'this is what a counsellor or psychotherapist can do'.

The literature also reflects aspects of potential tensions between adjacent professions. For example, in the field of research there is a strong expectation and tradition in clinical psychology and psychiatry that valid research studies are usually quantitative and 'scientific' in nature. By contrast, many counselling and psychotherapy researchers are more drawn toward qualitative, case study investigations. The distinctive values and professional identity of counselling and psychotherapy can be expressed not only through the type of research which counsellors and psychotherapists choose to do, but also in the ways that they engage in debate with more quantitatively oriented researchers from these other disciplines. Another example of interprofessional tension lies in the strong emphasis placed in social work on anti-oppressive practice, compared to the relative neglect of this issue in counselling and psychotherapy. This is a sphere in which it would be valuable for therapists to be engaged more actively in dialogue, opening the psychotherapeutic knowledge base and literature to what has been learned by social work colleagues.

A final dimension of professional identity concerns the development of a 'professional self' (Skovholt and Ronnestad, 1993) in the individual practitioner. Again, engagement with the literature has an important role to play in this process. At early stages of professional socialization it is inevitable that counsellors and psychotherapists in training will seek to identify with mythic pioneers such as Carl Rogers, Melanie Klein or Albert Ellis. However, later professional development requires that the practitioner finds his or her own 'voice'. It is essential that counsellors and psychotherapists who grow into mature leadership roles in the profession are willing to claim their own authority and to 'profess' their own position on issues. One of the ways in which this can be achieved is through contributing to the professional literature. The process of writing for publication in itself can help to clarify and crystallize ideas, and the ensuing feedback from professional colleagues can be usefully challenging as well as affirming. The significance of writing for colleagues can be contrasted with the implications of not engaging in such writing. Experienced practitioners with something to say who do not write are not only excluding others from learning from them, but are also taking the risk of enclosing their own insights within a self-contained idiosyncratic system of thought.

Using research to support practice

The relationship between research and practice in counselling and psychotherapy has been widely explored in recent years. In two key papers, Morrow-Bradley and Elliott (1986) and Cohen et al. (1986) reported on surveys carried out with psychotherapists in the USA, examining the use that these clinicians made of research findings in their work with service users. These were all practitioners who had at an earlier point in their careers received significant research training as part of Masters or Doctoral courses. Nevertheless, despite this strong background in research, the majority reported that they perceived research as having relatively limited use with respect to their actual practice. Table 10.2 summarizes the views of the therapists surveyed in the Morrow-Bradley and Elliott (1986) study. It can be seen that these practitioners strongly favoured oral forms of knowledge transmission and learning (through, for example, relationships with clients, colleagues and their own therapist) in preference to written modes of learning (reading books and journals). A similar result was also reported by Cohen et al. (1986), who found that the therapists in their sample gave 'discussions of clinical cases with colleagues' an average rating of 6.67 on a 7-point rating scale of usefulness (where 7 indicated 'provides very useful information for delivery of services'). By contrast, 'empirical research articles on clinical practice' gained an average rating of 3.43 on the same scale.

The clinicians who took part in these surveys claimed that the way that research was carried out, with large samples and statistical generalizations, made it impossible to apply findings to individual cases, and that the questions being asked by researchers were not sufficiently in tune with the needs of clinicians. The conclusions of these surveys initiated a debate over the role of research in counselling and psychotherapy. Writers such as Rennie (1994) have argued that qualitative research is more likely to yield results and new understandings that are of value for practitioners. Dryden (1996) has compiled an edited collection in which leading researchers explain the practical relevance of their studies for clinical work. There is an emerging trend for counselling and psychotherapy textbooks to contain chapters on research (McLeod, 1993;

Table 10.2 *Sources of information considered 'most useful'*
by 278 therapists in the USA

Source of information	%
Ongoing experience with clients	48
Theoretical/practical books/articles	10
Experience of being a client	8
Supervision or consultation with others	7
Workshops/conferences not based on psychotherapy research	7
Psychotherapy research presentations	6
Discussion with colleagues	5
Psychotherapy research books/articles	4
Doing psychotherapy research	3
Other	1

Source: Morrow-Bradley and Elliott, 1986

Woolfe and Dryden, 1996), so that practitioners are exposed to research ideas from the beginning of their careers. Despite this debate and these initiatives, it is nevertheless true that few counsellors pay much attention to what is published in research journals and relatively few training courses include a substantive research component.

The lack of interest in research findings is regrettable, because research journals contain information that is potentially of great value for practitioners. The overemphasis on quantitative, experimental research designs is being replaced by an openness to qualitative and case study methods, and a general acceptance of a 'pluralist' approach to methodology (see McLeod, 1994). The neglect by practitioners of contemporary research publications is perhaps attributable to three factors that prevent counsellors and psychotherapists from making full use of this resource: accessibility, understandability and applicability.

Many practitioners find it hard to gain access to research journals. The expense of this type of publication means that a therapist may, at best, subscribe to only one title, which will inevitably carry only a limited range of articles. Relatively few established practitioners have access to university libraries, and in any case there are only a few universities that carry a full range of counselling and psychotherapy publications. There is a real need for a service that will publish abstracts of counselling and psychotherapy research articles, ideally linked to a facility for ordering full copies of relevant papers.

However, even when they find pertinent research papers, some people have difficulty in understanding what these papers have to say. As mentioned earlier, deciphering research papers is a skill that requires practice. Getting the most out of the research literature demands reading regularly, to keep in touch with the development of areas of research, as well as to keep these skills alive.

Finally, some readers of research papers are deterred by their inability to see how the outcomes of research investigations can be applied in practice. In fact very few counselling or psychotherapy research studies generate knowledge that can be immediately put to tangible use. Therapy research is not like medical research where, for example, a GP may read an article that demonstrates the efficacy of using a particular drug, which he or she is then able to begin prescribing to appropriate patients. On the whole, research into counselling and psychotherapy contributes instead to the development of frameworks for understanding, through which the practitioner can gain a more differentiated appreciation of the possible implications of certain decisions or courses of action. The limitations of research knowledge in relation to actual clinical practice are further constrained by the reality that, since few counsellors read research, it is very seldom that research findings are cited in supervision or case discussion situations. Practitioners therefore have very limited practice and experience in applying research perspectives in their work.

Counsellors and psychotherapists who do have an appreciation of the research literature almost always owe this capacity to their experience of actually carrying out their own research study. The process of defining and refining a set of questions about counselling or psychotherapy, discovering a means of gathering evidence relevant to these questions and analysing the pattern and meaning within these data, can provide a surprisingly (for many) meaningful learning experience. The research process forces a counsellor/psychotherapist to be explicit about his or her assumptions or 'model', and there can be a great sense of achievement about creating a new piece of knowledge, however small. Where research is motivated by a genuine spirit of inquiry, it can help to open up a realization that less is known about counselling and psychotherapy than might be imagined, that there are endless creative possibilities for working effectively with people. Again, this is a type of learning that can reinforce the flexibility and lack of dogmatism that were discussed earlier. Many counsellors and psychotherapists are critical of the move towards Masters and Doctoral qualifications in counselling and psychotherapy, on the grounds that they diminish the importance of the experiential and practical elements that are essential in training. These experiential elements are indispensable, but equally important is the ability to reflect critically on practice, an ability that can be facilitated through the experience of carrying out a research thesis.

Reading and writing as therapeutic interventions

For the most part, counselling and psychotherapy are carried out through the medium of spoken dialogue, of conversation. Therapists are taught to listen and to encourage therapeutic talk. However, in the last few years there has been increasing interest shown in the therapeutic potential of the written word. Perhaps the most influential theorists and practitioners in this arena have been White and Epston (1990). Their argument is that written communications have two powerful advantages in therapy. First, a written statement conveys a sense of authority, is more convincing and 'definitional' than an equivalent spoken statement. This is because, in our culture, we are accustomed to being defined through official written documents such as referral letters and case files. Second, written documents are more permanent than the spoken word. A person in counselling can look again and again at a written statement, can use it to remind himself or herself of some hard-learned experiential truths. If merely spoken, these truths might have a transient impact, but are more likely to fade, become distorted, be forgotten or denied.

White and Epston developed the practice of writing to the people with whom they were working, in the form of letters and certificates of achievement. Many other therapists have also evolved their own versions of this type of technique (see, for example, Burton, 1965; Yalom et al., 1975; Aveline, 1986). From a different therapeutic tradition, Ryle and his colleagues, who were responsible for the creation of Cognitive-Analytic Therapy (CAT), arrived at the idea of presenting their case formulation to the person being helped in the form of a letter (Ryle, 1990). Research has confirmed the value of this type of intervention (Ryle, 1995).

The valuable therapeutic tools developed by White and Epston, Ryle and others depend on the therapist's ability and willingness to commit his or her thoughts and feelings to paper, and therefore call upon at least some degree of literary confidence or skill. In a parallel set of developments, other therapists have been encouraging people seeking help to write about their problems and experiences. Pennebaker (1988, 1993a,b), for instance, has carried out an intriguing set of research studies which have demonstrated the therapeutic benefits of writing about trauma. Greening (1977) and Birren and Birren (1996) have identified the therapeutic benefits of writing an autobiography. Lange (1994, 1996) is one of many therapists who has adopted the practice of asking people to write letters to express their feelings about significant others. For example, Lange (1996) refers to a man who had always felt that his wife had underestimated his capacity to cope. Lange invited this man to write a series of open and honest letters to his wife, sitting down at the same time each day at the same desk. These letters were not sent, but enabled him to externalize and acknowledge the depth and extent of his feelings about this matter. Eventually, he was able to write a final considered letter to his wife, which formed the basis for new negotiations of aspects of their relationship. Recently, Bacigalupe (1996) has described his practice of writing with the people who come to him for therapy. The concept of writing alongside the person captures well the way that therapeutic writing about problems takes place. When a person in therapy engages in a writing task, the therapist, at least implicitly, takes on the role of audience or witness. To be involved effectively in such a role draws on the counsellor's sensitivity to the dynamics and nuances of the written word. Omer (1993) has argued that such sensitivity should be part of the repertoire of competencies developed by all effective therapists.

The literature as a place of danger

So far, the discussion has focused mainly on the advantages for counsellors and psychotherapists of viewing reading, writing and involvement in the literature as activities that are beneficial to psychotherapeutic practice. However, there exist forceful arguments in the opposite direction. The literature can be a place of irrelevance, illusion, even of danger.

As has already been mentioned, the counselling and therapy literature largely reproduces a particular kind of writing: logical, rational, linear, scientific. The author, in predominantly using the third person, conveys a 'God's eye' mastery or all-seeing knowledge. These characteristics can be seen very clearly in the case studies of Sigmund Freud. These studies represent the foundations of psychodynamic counselling, and, to some extent, of all contemporary therapy. With benefit of hindsight and historical perspective, it is possible to detect and deconstruct the rhetorical devices through which Freud convinces readers of the validity of his arguments. Typically, toward the beginning of a case study, Freud would convey his scientific credentials by placing the patient within certain diagnostic categories, sometimes drawing upon neurological evidence or analogies to reinforce his point. Then, in the main part of the case, Freud would invite the reader to participate in a quest, a detective story search through myriad clues for the ultimate answer to the patient's current distress. This answer would inevitably take the form of a childhood sexual 'crime', but this revelation could only be revealed after the master detective has dealt with innumerable false trails and denials of the truth. Spence (1987) has drawn attention to the way that Freud structured his case presentations within the genre of detective fiction.

The point here is not to minimize the enormous contribution made to counselling and psychotherapy by Freud and his followers. The issue is, basically, that any piece of writing about therapy necessarily structures the experience and process of therapy within a particular genre. The lived reality of therapy is complex, changing, multilayered and open to different interpretations. In attempting to capture this complexity within a written report a writer, any writer, must impose a simplifying structure. Spence (1986) uses the term 'smoothing' to describe the transformation that takes place between participation in a therapy session and writing a report about it. But the act of smoothing is itself shaped by the dominant cultural metaphors within which the writer operates. Thus, Freud constructs an account of therapy as if he was a detective; many cognitive-behavioural writers produce accounts written as if they were primarily scientists, and so on. The potential danger here is that the genre gets mistaken for the actuality. Consumers of the therapy literature need to learn how to deconstruct what they are reading, to see the assumptions and values implicit in the way a book or paper is written.

Conclusion: the importance of the oral tradition

The critical tension that exists in the relationship between counsellors and therapists and the professional literature is the division between spoken, oral communication, and writing. Despite the examples of uses of writing in therapy described earlier, therapy practice is to an over-whelming extent an oral activity. However, we live in a culture in which the written word is privileged, has authority. The significance of this can be exposed by considering some of the psychological differences between written and spoken modes of communication. Speaking, for example, in the context of a conversation, is intrinsically personal and relational, it involves the hearing sense organ. What is conveyed in speech is open ended and available for negotiation between speaker and listener. Speech draws on musicality and the capacity for poetry. In the quality of the voice there is always information about emotion, self and status. Written communication, by contrast, is more logical and complete in itself. Reading is a visual, distanced experience, usually carried out alone. The style of most therapy literature is impersonal, as if written from an all-seeing, all-knowing, omniscient 'God's eye' vantage point on the world. Written text allows the possibility of backward scanning, which minimizes inconsistency and ambiguity. These and other differences between orality and literacy are reviewed in detail by Ong (1982).

It is my belief that it is in the contrast between speech and writing that the pros and cons of the counselling and psychotherapy literature are most clearly apparent. The lived experience of therapy is trans-formed by being written down. Writing or reading about therapy is so different from actually doing it that reading a book or article always has the potential to enable the experience to be understood in a new way. This is partly what is meant by the earlier discussion of the relationship between reading and the ability to conceptualize. We have all, no doubt, had occasions where a confused, muddled or chaotic experience is illuminated by reading. The trick of linear prose is to sort raw experi-ence into categories and to link up what goes with what. This is why reading and writing can sometimes be exciting: things are falling into place. Writing, in this sense, is a form of organized thinking and problem solving. The mistake is then to impose the clarity and logic of the written word on to the flow of therapy. Doing therapy is not a literary experience.

References

Aveline, M.O. (1986) The use of written reports in brief group psychotherapy training, *International Journal of Group Psychotherapy*, 36: 477–82.
Bacigalupe, G. (1996) Writing in therapy: a participatory approach, *Journal of Family Therapy*, 18: 361–73.
Berman, J.S. and Norton, N.C. (1985) Does professional training make a therapist more effective?, *Psychological Bulletin*, 98: 401–7.
Birren, J.E. and Birren, B.A. (1996) Autobiography: exploring the self and encouraging development, in J.E. Birren, G.M. Kenyon, J-K. Ruth, J.J.F. Schroots and T. Svensson (eds), *Aging and Biography: Explorations in Adult Development*. New York: Springer. pp. 283–99.
Burton, A. (1965) The use of written productions in psychotherapy, in L. Pearson (ed.), *Written Communications in Psychotherapy*, Springs, Ill: Thomas.
Cohen, L.H., Sargent, M.M. and Sechrest, L.B. (1986) Use of psychotherapy research by professional psychologists, *American Psychologist*, 41 (2): 198–206.
Combs, A.W. (1989) *A Theory of Therapy: Guidelines for Counselling Practice*. London: Sage.
Dryden, W. (ed.) (1996) *Research in Counselling and Psychotherapy: Practical Applications*. London: Sage.
Glaser, R. and Chi, M. (1988) An overview, in M. Chi, R. Glaser and M. Farr (eds), *The Nature of Expertise*. Hillsdale, NJ: Lawrence Erlbaum.
Greening, T.C. (1977) The uses of autobiography, in W. Anderson (ed.), *Therapy and the Arts: Tools of Consciousness*. New York: Harper and Row.
Knights, B. (1995) *The Listening Reader: Fiction and Poetry for Counsellors and Psychotherapists*. London: Jessica Kingsley.
Lange, A. (1994) Writing assignments in the treatment of grief and traumas from the past, in J. Zeig (ed.), *Ericksonian Methods: The Essence of the Story*. New York: Brunner/Mazel. pp. 377–92.
Lange, A. (1996) Using writing assignments with families managing legacies of extreme trauma, *Journal of Family Therapy*, 18: 375–88.
Macdonald, K.M. (1995) *The Sociology of the Professions*. London: Sage.
McLeod, J. (1993) *An Introduction to Counselling*. Buckingham: Open University Press.
McLeod, J. (1994) *Doing Counselling Research*. London: Sage.
Morrow-Bradley, C. and Elliott, R. (1986) Utilization of psychotherapy research by practicing psychotherapists, *American Psychologist*, 41 (2): 188–97.
Omer, H. (1993) Quasi-literary elements in psychotherapy, *Psychotherapy*, 30: 59–66.
Ong, W.J. (1982) *Orality and Literacy: The Technologizing of the Word*. London: Routledge.
Pennebaker, J.W. (1988) Confiding traumatic experiences and health, in S. Fisher and J. Reason (eds), *Handbook of Life Stress, Cognition and Health*. Chichester: John Wiley.
Pennebaker, J.W. (1993a) Putting stress into words: health, linguistic and therapeutic implications, *Behaviour Research and Therapy*, 31: 539–48.
Pennebaker, J.W. (1993b) Social mechanisms of constraint, in D.W. Wegner and J.W. Pennebaker (eds), *Handbook of Mental Control*. Englewood Cliffs, NJ: Prentice-Hall. pp. 200–19.
Rennie, D.R. (1994) Human science and counselling psychology: closing the gap between research and practice, *Counselling Psychology Quarterly*, 7: 235–50.
Rogers, C.R. (1951) *Client-centered Therapy: Its Current Practice, Implications and Theory*. London: Constable.

Ryle, A. (1990) *Cognitive-Analytic Therapy: Active Participation in Change: A New Integration in Brief Psychotherapy*. Chichester: John Wiley.

Ryle, A. (1995) Research relating to CAT, in A. Ryle (ed.), *Cognitive-Analytic Therapy: Developments in Theory and Practice*. Chichester: John Wiley. pp. 175–91.

Skovholt, T.M. and Ronnestad, M.H. (1993) *The Evolving Professional Self: Stages and Themes in Therapist and Counsellor Professional Development*. Chichester: John Wiley.

Spence, D.P. (1982) *Narrative Truth and Historical Truth: Meaning and Interpretation in Psychoanalysis*. New York: W.W. Norton.

Spence, D.P. (1986) Narrative smoothing and clinical wisdom, in T.R. Sarbin (ed.), *Narrative Psychology: The Storied Nature of Human Conduct*. New York: Praeger. pp. 211–32.

Spence, D.P. (1987) *The Freudian Metaphor: Toward Paradigm Change in Psychoanalysis*. New York: W.W. Norton.

Strupp, H.H. and Hadley, S.W. (1979) Specific vs. nonspecific factors in psychotherapy: a controlled study of outcome, *Archives of General Psychiatry*, 36: 1125–36.

White, M. and Epston, D. (1990) *Narrative Means to Therapeutic Ends*. New York: W.W. Norton.

Whiteley, J.M., Sprinthall, N.A., Mosher, R.L. and Donaghy, R.T. (1967) Selection and evaluation of counselor effectiveness, *Journal of Counseling Psychology*, 14: 226–34.

Woolfe, R. and Dryden, W. (eds) (1996) *Handbook of Counselling Psychology*. London: Sage.

Yalom, I.D., Brown, S. and Bloch, S. (1975) The written summary as a group psychotherapy technique, *Archives of General Psychiatry*, 36: 605–13.

11

Evaluating Effectiveness: Needs, Problems and Potential Benefits

John Mellor-Clark and Michael Barkham

To address the needs, problems and potential benefits of evaluating effectiveness requires some initial orientation, context and structure for the reader. For orientation, two points are worth noting at the outset. First, it would appear that the specific need to evaluate effectiveness has not been comprehensively addressed in any previous text. Consequently, the first section of this chapter attempts to fill an important gap in the literature. This has necessarily required us to prioritize breadth at the expense of depth, although we direct the reader towards more detailed literature where it is available. Second, as the focus of this chapter will hopefully be of both interest and utility to the full range of psychological therapy providers, where appropriate, the more generic term practitioner has been adopted rather than using the terms counsellors and psychotherapists interchangeably.

For context, we have previously suggested that many practitioners hold the view that either the need to evaluate effectiveness is unnecessary or that the task itself is impossible (Mellor-Clark and Barkham, 1996). For those practitioners attempting to implement evaluation in their own service settings, it is not unusual to meet with significant reluctance and resistance. Often, effectiveness evaluation is considered unnecessary because practitioners 'believe' themselves to be effective. Such a belief is apparently supported by particular client behaviours. These include: attending regularly, rarely complaining, completing satisfaction surveys positively, and even recommending the service to friends (Shipton, 1994; Mellor-Clark and Shapiro, 1995). Additionally, effectiveness evaluation can also be considered impossible for the following reasons: the tendency for evaluation to slip down the list of priorities in the face of pressures to maintain service provision (Barker et al., 1994; Tyndall, 1994); the lack of technical expertise (Barker et al., 1994); or the lack of appropriate measures (Heisler, 1977; McLeod, 1994; Strupp, 1996). The objective of this chapter is to address this reluctance and resistance by helping practitioners to understand the needs, problems and potential benefits of effectiveness evaluation. To accomplish this, the structure of the chapter addresses three questions. Why do practitioners

need to evaluate effectiveness? What problems can practitioners anticipate (and how can researchers help solve them)? What are the potential
benefits of evaluation?

Why do practitioners need to evaluate effectiveness?

This section outlines the momentum behind the need for practitioners to
evaluate effectiveness and considers: the increase in counselling provision and scrutiny; definitions of effectiveness and efficacy; the efficacy
base of psychotherapy and the limitations of the psychotherapy efficacy
base to practice; the gap between research and practice; a new research
paradigm.

The increase in counselling provision and scrutiny

In recent years there has been a substantial increase in the number of
practitioners of psychological therapy. In counselling alone, membership
of the British Association of Counselling (BAC) has risen from 1,300 to
14,000 in the last twenty years, and organizations affiliated to BAC have
risen from 76 to 790 in the last ten years. One specialist division of BAC
showing considerable growth is Counselling in Medical Settings (CMS),
where current membership exceeds 2,000 practitioners. The rise in membership of the CMS division reflects the escalating numbers of practitioners being employed to provide counselling in primary healthcare. In
the past three years, surveys on the employment of counsellors in fund-
holding general practice estimate provision to have doubled, increasing
from 31 per cent (Sibbald et al., 1993) to 65 per cent (Curtis Jenkins, 1996).
Concomitantly, as 'supply' has increased, 'demand' also appears considerable from both potential users and purchasers. For potential users,
85 per cent of respondents to a recent MORI poll survey considered
'counselling' to be the treatment of choice for depression (MORI, 1995),
and for potential purchasers, the survey conducted by Sibbald et al.
(1993) reported that of those general practices not providing a counselling
service, 80 per cent expressed a wish to do so.

This increase in both supply and demand has led to significant scrutiny
by a range of interested parties in counselling provision. Academics (for
example, Wesley, 1996), professional groups (for example, Illman, 1993;
Blakey, 1996); litigation enquiries (for example, Derby City Council, 1996)
and the media are increasingly calling for urgent change to the ad hoc
development of counselling practice. In the most part, the call is for an
increase in the quality of service provision through appropriate utility
and increased accountability. This takes place in a context in which public
sector practitioners are under pressure to demonstrate 'evidence-based
practice' and 'promote clinical effectiveness' (NHSE, 1996). Similarly,
voluntary sector practitioners are under pressure to demonstrate their
effectiveness to address contingent funding demands (Hicks and

Wheeler, 1994), while private practitioners are beginning to share a growing belief that effectiveness evaluation is both fundamental to ethical practice (for example, Watkins and Schneider, 1991) and, more pragmatically, recognizing that those who do not have effectiveness information may increasingly lose clients to those who do (Nezu, 1996). But what is meant by effectiveness and whose responsibility is it to demonstrate it?

Effectiveness and efficacy

To address effectiveness requires us to distinguish the term effectiveness from that of efficacy. Within the research literature, these two terms are used to identify very different forms of research inquiry, and hence evidence. The accepted distinction is that 'efficacy demonstrates achievable results in the setting of a research trial, whilst effectiveness demonstrates the outcomes of treatment in routine practice' (Roth and Fonagy, 1996: 13). Consequently while efficacy research can identify potentially useful interventions, it does not address the question of how effective such interventions are in actual practice. This is a crucial distinction, requiring not only consideration of the relative contributions of the efficacy and effectiveness base for psychological therapy practice, but also consideration of the relationship between research and practice.

The efficacy base of psychotherapy

The efficacy base of psychotherapy has derived from successive generations of research employing experimental designs which have placed a premium on the construct of internal validity. That is, the research endeavour has prioritized establishing cause–effect relations within the context of controlling for extraneous variables. The move towards specificity in psychotherapy research was encapsulated in Paul's (1967) litany of what treatment, delivered by whom, is most effective for what individual with what specific condition, under which set of circumstances? This led to a tradition of psychotherapy research adopting the randomized controlled trial (RCT) as the methodology of choice for scientific investigation, and has resulted in a vast body of evidence attesting to the fact that psychotherapy is more effective than a placebo treatment which, in turn, is more effective than a no treatment condition. Lambert and Bergin reviewed the extensive literature on psychotherapy outcome and concluded that there is now 'little doubt that psychological treatments are, overall and in general, beneficial, although it remains equally true that not everyone benefits to a satisfactory degree' (1994: 144).

More recently, Roth and Fonagy (1996) have provided an extensive review of the evidence for the efficacy of specific psychological treatments in relation to specific diagnostic categories. The foreword to this text maintains that the positive yield of fifty years of research on the outcomes of psychotherapy is that there is more, and better quality, scientific evidence to support psychotherapy than for many other interventions in healthcare today. However, such a statement raises a crucial question. In light of the distinction between efficacy and effectiveness, can the positive yield of clinical trials be utilized as an evidence base for psychotherapy in practice? Furthermore are efficacy findings generalizable to the wider field of psychological therapy practice?

The limitations of the psychotherapy efficacy base to practice

In addition to RCTs producing clear evidence for the efficacy of psychotherapy, such studies have provided archival data for subsequent meta-analytic reviews evaluating the effectiveness of psychological interventions (for example, Lipsey and Wilson, 1993), as well as providing source material for systematic reviews (for example, Cochrane Centre). However, while the sophistication of analytic procedures continues within this research paradigm, there appears a growing recognition in the literature that clinical trials or RCTs are limited as the sole evidence base for psychological therapies in routine practice (for example, Aveline et al., 1995; Black, 1996; DOH, 1996).

One of the most coherent arguments suggests that RCTs may be premature, uninformative and unrepresentative in the absence of a broader range of investigative methods (Aveline et al., 1995). The suggestion is that RCTs may be premature in advance of more pluralistic inquiry representing and profiling routine practice, uninformative because paradoxically the rigour imposed by the design dilutes the informativeness for routine practice; and unrepresentative in that they concentrate on a set of 'purified' treatments, patients, providers and problem characteristics seldom seen in routine practice. Thus, the distinctions between efficacy and effectiveness suggest that we cannot consider the yield of the RCTs to be an appropriate evidence base for the effectiveness of practice in the absence of other methods of inquiry. At best, the yield of RCTs can address what works for whom in the most ideal set of circumstances, delivered by the most ideal practitioners, to the most ideal patients, with the most ideal specificity and severity of problem.

The difficulty in applying findings from such a research paradigm to practice settings is apparent when we consider the following. First, it has been estimated that the range of therapies provided in practice probably exceeds 400 (Fonagy, 1995). Second, the percentage of eclectic therapists (those mixing treatment methods) has been estimated to be between 30 to 68 per cent of practitioners (Garfield and Begin, 1994). The effort involved in devising, implementing and funding RCTs to test over 400 therapies would be immense, and even then, would be unlikely to correspond with individual therapists' mixing of treatment methods.

Therefore, RCTs, with their tight scientific rigour and manualization of treatment, may be potentially incongruent with practice for their lack of applicability.

McLeod (1995) takes a similar stance in considering the applicability of the psychotherapy efficacy base for counselling. He concludes that it is largely uninformative for counselling practice for the following reasons: (a) there is a diverse array of professionals acting as practitioners in practice; (b) the therapists that take part in RCTs are almost always psychiatrists or clinical psychologists; (c) most RCTs are conducted in a few elite research institutions; (d) traditional counselling services operating an open-door policy of seeing people at the point of crises are undertaking a more 'front line' activity; (e) traditional counselling services do not have the same service structures as professionals in the NHS (that is lengthy waiting lists, careful screening and assessment).

Taken together these considerations present a sound basis from which to question the appropriateness of utilizing the efficacy base derived from RCTs as the evidence base for the practice of psychotherapists and counsellors. Not only do psychotherapy researchers themselves consider the applicability of trial evidence to be limited as an evidence base of effectiveness, but also those representing the wider field of practice see it as inappropriate and inapplicable. Why is there such a divide between research and practice?

The research practice gap

It has been recognized for some time that a considerable gap has developed between research and practice, despite the efforts of researchers to communicate with practitioners (for example, Elliott, 1983; Strupp, 1989). In a survey carried out in the USA, practitioners were found to be critical of psychotherapy research for being too uninformative about practice and service development (Morrow-Bradley and Elliott, 1986). The survey found that ongoing experience with clients, supervision, personal therapy and practical therapy books were all considered more valuable than research. Again, such a view also appears to have substantial support in counselling in both the USA and UK. In the USA, Watkins and Schneider (1991) cite numerous studies showing counsellors not to engage in research and to hold negative views about it. In the UK, a BAC membership survey (BAC, 1993) found only 20 per cent of counsellors had been involved in research and of these only 14 per cent had published their work (that is, less than 3 per cent of total responders).

There appear two interrelated reasons for the gap developing between research and practice. First, because the traditional empirical approach to the efficacy question cannot address the complexity of actual practice, practitioners often complain that research fails to take account of the unique 'puzzles' which individual clients present. Diagnosis, psychological characteristics and social circumstances all interact to present practitioners with a complex decision-making problem (Roth and Fonagy, 1996). Thus, each client presents as a unique constellation of facets, rendering the dictates of research oversimplistic for application to practice. In short, research is criticized for ignoring actual practice dynamics, rendering the applicability of research as implicit, indirect and diffuse (McLeod, 1994).

Second, we should not be surprised at this lack of applicability. The emphases of researchers and practitioners are very different. Researchers focus on enhancing our understanding of the particular phenomenon under investigation and primarily address their findings to the scientific community. Invariably, a priority is placed on aggregate data and tests of statistical significance. In short, researchers research researchers' problems (Nezu, 1996), and while the practitioner requires information which can be applied to a specific client, research can dismiss the contri-bution of practitioners' case histories as subjective and anecdotal (Hansen, 1984). This has led to the recent proposal that research and practice are necessarily divided and should remain so (Fensterheim and Raw, 1996). But is there some common ground? Can research and practice collaborate to be mutually informative, and can such a collaboration cut across the barriers of psychotherapy and counselling?

A new research paradigm: closing the research–practice gap

Interestingly, the domains of psychotherapy research and counselling research would appear to be converging. McLeod (1995) has proposed that the effectiveness agenda for counselling, in the absence of stan-dardized and readily accessible measures, requires counsellors to evalu-ate single case studies utilizing descriptive accounts supplemented with standardized, regularly applied rating measures demonstrating what is possible in practice. This approach appears highly congruent with research practitioners in psychotherapy. Howard et al. (1996) propose 'patient-focused research' – empirically monitoring an individual client's progress over the course of therapy and feeding back to other prac-titioners, supervisors and/or case managers. In short, it appears that the time is right for a new emphasis in psychological therapy research that involves an active collaboration between researchers and practitioners relating research to practice and in turn to the individual client. The burgeoning increase in practitioners and practice, the changes in health and social care policy emphasizing demonstrated effectiveness, and the limitations of the efficacy base for practice offer both the appropriate 'push' and the 'prod' to bring research closer to practice. This is a change in emphasis that is happening both in the USA and UK and is highly pragmatic in its search for an evidence-base on which to justify funding, develop services, and hopefully increase resources. The following examples help to exemplify the current position.

In the USA, Speer and Newman (1996) maintain that it is in the best interest of providers and ultimately the public to obtain, analyse and report outcome information about the recipients of their services. In the UK, Parry (1995) maintains that while psychotherapy research can identify potentially useful interventions, it can say little about how effectively therapies are implemented in any particular setting – local data collection concerning effectiveness is crucial to answer this question. For clinical and counselling psychology, Barker et al. (1994) argue that evaluation should be a routine part of applied psychology. Too much clinical and counselling work is based on custom and practice rather than any formal (empirical) knowledge base. Evaluating practice is a way of seeing whether or not it lives up to its claimed benefits. For counselling, McLeod (1995) argues that outcome research is a neglected area which is important to restore it to a high place on the counselling research agenda at a time when funding bodies are making increasing demands for accountability. Hicks and Wheeler (1994) support this view, advocating that in a climate of increased accountability and limited resources it is critical for counselling agencies to prove their worth. The process of organizing and delivering counselling services should not be based on information derived from intuition and gut feeling, but from systematic evaluation of the facts. Finally, Nezu (1996) maintains that all practitioners, including those in private practice, need to engage in evaluation as an essential ingredient of their professional portfolio.

Collectively, this consensus on the need to evaluate psychological therapy provision helps demonstrate the urgency for research to direct resources to help practitioners to gather and feed empirical data into practice in a form that enhances and justifies their work. Currently, in the UK and USA there appears a plethora of interest and concern about outcome evaluation. This is manifesting not only in an ever-increasing number of commentaries on its importance, but also numerous work- shops on outcome evaluation methods. However, there is a bind. At the present time, research funding for psychological therapy research remains heavily in favour of efficacy research and there appears a reluctance to rationalize the expense of large-scale naturalistic service evaluations. Despite the increasing observation of the poor cost–benefit ratio of the efficacy research tradition for practice, it is near impossible to obtain research funds to support observational methods while funders view them as having little or no value. For the present, this position withstands views contesting that such denigration is unjustified and limits our potential to evaluate and hence improve the scientific basis of how we treat individuals and how we organize services (Black, 1996).

So in the absence of funding, how might research and practice converge to address and operationalize the task of marshalling and assisting practitioners to demonstrate their effectiveness? The second part of our chapter considers this question. Drawing primarily from experience, we begin to map out a way for science-based researchers to help practitioners become practice-based evaluators in service of providing 'evidence-based practice' (statutory sector practice), responding to 'contingent funding demands' (voluntary sector practice), and maintaining 'private revenue' (private sector practice).

What problems should practitioners anticipate and how can researchers help solve them?

This section identifies four problems facing practitioners who are motivated or pressurized to evaluate their effectiveness. These include: the lack of guiding materials; the reluctance and resistance of practitioners; the process of implementation; the choice of measures. These problems are considered in turn, with the conclusions to each, suggesting ways in which researchers can help.

The lack of guiding materials

One of the central problems for practitioners in evaluating effectiveness is the lack of guiding materials in both texts and journals. Few texts have concentrated on the topic in detail. Those that do exist tend to be either on related areas such as audit (for example, Firth-Cozens, 1993), or research (for example, Barker et al., 1994; McLeod, 1994), or otherwise be short 'pepper-shot chapters' within texts of broad scope (for example, Barkham, 1993; Barkham and Barker, 1996; Hardy, 1995; Mellor-Clark and Barkham, 1996; Parry, 1996). To date, no comprehensive text is available to 'tool-up' practitioners wishing to evaluate their practice. Journal articles too are limited in providing insight into the content and process of evaluation, tending to reflect the empirical work of trials, rather than more practice-based experiential and utility accounts. Two sources exemplify this. Speer and Newman (1996) conducted a review of journal papers published between 1989 and 1995, identifying 583 relating to 'outcome'. However, utilizing criteria weighted towards the more naturalistic studies, only 9 (1.5 per cent) were found to focus on services for adults with mental health difficulties. These were largely formative evaluations of innovative services rather than summative evaluations of more traditional service configurations. Similarly, McLeod (1995) in a smaller scale review of three mainstream counselling journals found 254 outcome studies reported within a two-year period of which only 17 (7 per cent) were focused on counselling. He also found no papers reporting on the effectiveness of relationship counselling, employee counselling or counselling in medical settings (McLeod, 1995). Therefore, in the absence of guiding materials, one of the first ways in which researchers can begin to help practitioners to evaluate effectiveness is by sharing their experience of contracted evaluation research through dissemination (in both texts and journals) not only of experience but, more importantly, the methods and tools utilized.

Reluctance and resistance revisited

In the introduction, the reluctance and resistance of practitioners to engage in effectiveness evaluation was framed in the context of literature suggesting it can be seen as either unnecessary or impossible. We have attempted to demonstrate that evaluation, far from being unnecessary, is increasingly becoming a prerequisite for current practice. We now suggest that effectiveness evaluation is both possible and eminently feasible if appropriate time and consideration are given to the rationale, process and content of this procedure. We consider these in turn, linking the final issue to the choice of measures.

In order to highlight the need to appropriately consider the rationale for effectiveness evaluation, Table 11.1 summarizes some of the reactions of practitioners involved in the implementation of contracted evaluation. These are presented in the form of 'hopes' and 'fears', addressing the potential positive and negative impacts on clients, practitioners and service development. While fears offer typical expressions of resistance and reluctance, hopes offer converse expressions of engagement and enthusiasm, clearly demonstrating the inherent juxtaposition of effectiveness evaluation. This serves to illustrate the rationale of evaluation by highlighting the potential positive impact that it can offer for clients, practitioners and service development. Thus, a second way in which researchers can help practitioners to evaluate effectiveness is by sharing their experience of implementing contracted evaluation and highlighting the rationale through the potential benefits exemplified in the 'hopes' of practitioners. The methods by which such potential benefits might be realized (and fears mitigated), moves us on to consider the process of implementation.

The process of implementation

In a previous text we outlined an implementation model of service evaluation highlighting some of the benefits of undertaking 'hopes' and 'fears' workshops with practitioners in order to address and arrest anxieties at the outset of implementation and harness and secure enthusiasm and potential benefit (see Mellor-Clark and Barkham, 1996). The experiences of these workshops have offered invaluable insights into some of the problems inherent to service or practitioner evaluation. The task is to mitigate the negative threats and realize the positive opportunities. Our experience is that the requisite service evaluation skills to accomplish this task are analogous to both therapeutic skills and processes, and therefore at the heart of practitioners' skills repertoire.

Table 11.1   *Practitioner 'hopes' and 'fears' for effectiveness evaluation*

Impact point	Hopes	Fears
Clients	Evaluation could enhance clients' perceptions of the credibility of the service if they feel that their comments are taken seriously.	Clients could be unhappy and objectionable, experiencing evaluative questionnaires as intimidating and intrusive resulting in an increase in attrition.
	Evaluation could reinforce the very ethos of therapy through collaborating in an endeavour which empowers the client.	The administration of evaluation questionnaires could be insensitive to the distressed client and/or may revive painful issues for clients and thus be disempowering.
Practitioners	Evaluation could enhance practitioners' personal and professional development via detailed personal feedback of effectiveness.	Effectiveness evaluation criteria may not capture important aspects of service delivery.
	Evaluation could identify personal training needs.	Evaluation could reinforce the fear of finding out that one isn't as effective as one thought.
	Evaluation could be energizing through specific feedback on particular interventions or particular client groups.	Evaluation could be de-energizing by creating an oppressive sense of scrutiny and a fear that the data will be misused by others.
	Evaluation could be unifying, creating a culture of openness and sharing.	Evaluation could be divisive, seeding a competitive culture and fuelling anxieties about scrutiny.
Service development	Evaluation could positively enhance service planning by reducing waiting times through enhanced allocation and referral.	Evaluation could test confidentiality, reinforce paranoia and shift the emphasis from the delivery of therapy to the administration of evaluation.
	Evaluation could demonstrate to funders that the service is cost effective, thereby satisfying purchasers and possibly even leading to an increase in funding.	Evaluation could lead to a decrease or cut in funding by not capturing the profound changes in clients.

Hopes and fears need to be identified and worked through within a collaborative, empathic and trusting relationship. Implementation requires those responsible to establish rapport and trust, to listen and to respond non-defensively to weaknesses and threats (fears), and reinforce the potential strengths and opportunities (hopes). Practitioner training offers good grounding in these areas, and practitioners can use the specific 'tool bag' of researchers to build on them. Person-centred counselling theory maintains that people will collaborate more effectively when a relationship is established which is characterized by the core conditions of empathy, acceptance and congruence (McLeod, 1995). Practitioners have all the appropriate process skills for implementing evaluation: the methods, models and experience of researchers merely need help to guide them. Therefore, third, perhaps the most appropriate extension of the contribution of researchers over experiential dissemination is to act as consultant guides to practitioners charged with co-ordinating evaluation. This relationship would not only provide the much needed implementation methods, models and experiential anecdotes to address process, but also the technical expertise in one of the most problematic areas – the content of measures.

The choice of measures

The principle tools of the science-based researchers are the measures used to determine efficacy in clinical trials. Froyd, Lambert and Froyd (1996) reviewed 334 outcome studies published in 21 selected journals from 1983 to 1988 and found 1,430 outcome measures of which 851 (i.e. 58%) were used a single time. Clearly, there is a dilemma for any practitioner wishing to choose measures for the evaluation and demonstration of their effectiveness and some guidelines for selection criteria are crucial. McLeod (1995) maintains that few counsellors have access to or can afford the sorts of measures used in psychotherapy research. Many are too long for use in front-line agencies where clients may object to completing questionnaires or there may be space difficulties. McLeod further argues that the priority for counselling outcome research is the development of a set of tools that can be understood and applied by counsellors: 'The lack of purpose-designed, user-friendly techniques for assessing the effects of counselling reflects the low power and status of counselling in relation to psychiatry and clinical psychology' (McLeod, 1995: 198).

There are many issues to consider in relation to measures. Here we consider just five of them. First, whose 'perspective' should one use? Usually the choice is between the client's or the counsellor's, although there is also the option of obtaining a third party's view (for example, spouse or partner). On balance, if only one perspective can be sampled, it is better to take that of the client. This may then be used, for example, in conjunction with the counsellor's judgement, to inform decisions about treatment termination.

Second, how many measures are needed? Obviously one is the minimum but there are clear advantages in administering more than one measure. If only one measure is used, then the practitioner is wholly dependent on that single measure to detect change in multiple domains of personal functioning. Often one measure will show considerable change while another will not. This may be due, among other factors, to the actual domains measured, or the intrinsic error built into any measure. If only one measure is used it becomes difficult to tease out these aspects.

Third, and related to this, how long does it take to complete outcome measures? If, as likely, the practitioner does not want a client to spend more than 5–10 minutes completing an evaluation questionnaire, there is a choice between selecting a highly refined measure (fidelity) which may tap a single domain, or sampling a range of domains (bandwidth). It is probable that the latter will have greater utility given its emphasis on pragmatics rather than high quality research.

Fourth, will the outcomes of one client be able to be compared with another? The important distinction here is between nomothetic and idiographic measures. Nomothetic measures enable outcomes to be standardized to specific populations (for example, non-distressed or distressed) so that the practitioner can make statements about the probability of a client belonging to one or other population. Examples of nomothetic measures include the Symptom CheckList-90-R (SCL-90-R; Derogatis, 1983) and the Beck Depression Inventory (BDI; Beck et al., 1988). However, these measures have been developed in the USA and there is a dearth of information on UK norms. On the other hand, there are measures such as the General Health Questionnaire (GHQ; Goldberg and Williams, 1988) which have been developed in the UK but carry different problems (for example, the GHQ is not a change measure). By contrast, idiographic measures employ the unique statements and concerns presented by individual clients and therefore provide an invaluable balance to nomothetic measures.

Fifth, how often does a measure need to be administered? All too often, a measure is administered at the beginning of therapy and never again. If information is to be gained about outcome, then a pre–post administration is the minimum required. However, if service planning is to have an empirical basis, then measures need to be administered throughout the duration of client/practitioner contact. This provides both an adjunct to practitioners' judgements as well as information on the temporal course of therapy. Keep in mind that if only a pre- and a post-therapy measure is administered, then graphically all one can do is draw a straight line between the two points. Whether that line portrays improvement, deterioration, or a plateau (no change), it seems unlikely that the course of an individual's counselling or psychotherapy is best summarized by a linear function.

Table 11.2 presents an example of a comprehensive effectiveness evaluation exemplifying the above considerations within a single protocol. This is a client completed protocol, utilizing both quantitative nomothetic items (marked [n]) alongside qualitative idiographic items (marked [i]), delivered over four time points relating to therapy: pre-therapy, in-therapy, post-therapy and follow-up. Pre–post measures are

Table 11.2   *An example of an effectiveness evaluation protocol*

Pre-therapy	In-therapy	Post-therapy and follow-up
Biographic data		
Age		
Ethnicity		
Employment status	⟶	Employment status
Occupation	⟶	Occupation
Living arrangements	⟶	Living arrangements
Service use		
Previous therapy		
Recent GP visits	⟶	Recent GP visits
Recent medication	⟶	Recent medication
Presenting problems		
Client self-reported difficulties to be helped by therapy [i]	⟶	Client self-reported difficulties met by therapy [i]
Inventory of interpersonal problems [n]	⟶	Inventory of interpersonal problems [n]
Emotional functioning [n]	Emotional functioning [n]	
Social roles [n]	Social roles [n]	
Mental health [n]	Mental health [n]	
Anticipated benefits of therapy	Benefits of therapy	
Symptoms		
Brief symptoms inventory [n]	⟶	Brief symptoms inventory [n]
		Overall impact
		Helpful aspects of therapy [i]

[n] nomothetic items
[i] idiographic items

indicated by the arrows between pre-therapy and post-therapy items. Naturally, it is not anticipated that practitioners would utilize all the measures applied by researchers undertaking contract evaluation, but Table 11.2 does highlight the challenges inherent in evaluation by illustrating some of the measurement options and choices faced by practitioners.

One initiative which will go some way to remedying the measurement options and choices faced by practitioners is a 'core outcome system', currently in development under Mental Health Foundation funding. In brief, these will be short, single-sheet measures comprising 'core' items which tap a broad range of personal functioning, administered regularly across the course of therapy (if so desired), utilizing minimal completion time and on which there would be UK normative data (Connell et al., 1997). Importantly, these core measures would be effectively in the public domain and therefore free. In addition, these core measures could be expanded by administering one or more instruments from a battery of 'reference' measures on which there would be UK normative data. This initiative reflects researchers prioritizing practitioner need within acceptable bounds of scientific rigour, providing the fourth and final way in which researchers can (and are) beginning to help solve some of the problems of practitioners faced with effectiveness evaluation. It is a move very much representing the ethos presented in this chapter. Logic and pragmatism are the driving forces devising 'standardized' methods and measures widely applicable across the various domains of practice to address practitioner need. With services using core methods and measures much can be gained. The concluding section attempts to illustrate some of the potential benefits to all stakeholders associated with the provision of psychological therapy.

What are the potential benefits of evaluation?

There is currently a serious problem in the organization of psychological therapy services which we believe only the collaboration between practitioners and researchers in effectiveness evaluation has the potential to solve:

> Someone in need of psychological therapy cannot yet rely on the NHS to deliver the right intervention at the right time in the right place. Services are fragmented . . . whether you end up having an outpatient appointment with a psychiatrist, primary care counsellor, a clinical psychologist . . . seems alarmingly arbitrary. On which shore you wash up is not generally determined by who is able to offer the most appropriate help for your problem. It depends as much on which GP you see, who happens to know whom, or where you live. (Parry, 1995: 164–5)

The *raison d'être* of effectiveness evaluation should be to address this problem by ultimately improving the 'quality' of practice. Table 11.3 idealizes the capacity for effectiveness evaluation to accomplish this, hypothesizing the potential benefits for the range of stakeholders associated with psychological therapy practice. Table 11.3 sequentially addresses the following: intra-service stakeholders (clients, practitioners, supervisors, service managers); inter-service stakeholders (referrers, purchasers, planners and policy-makers); and those responsible for serving and informing practice (trainers and researchers).

In conclusion, there appears much to be gained from practitioners and services engaging in effectiveness evaluation. Active collaboration between researchers and practitioners could help address the pragmatic needs of practice through the use of models, methods and tools in service of not only helping to demonstrate the effectiveness of actual practice, but ultimately to help define, reflect and maintain 'best practice'. If counsellors and psychotherapists can begin to see effectiveness evaluation as necessary and possible, then much can be realized.

Table 11.3   *The potential benefits of effectiveness evaluation for psychological therapy stakeholders*

Stakeholder	Potential benefits
Clients	Clients will benefit from the receipt of evidence-based, validated therapies within quality-led, accountable services delivering appropriate interventions for appropriate durations following optimally efficient waiting times.
Practitioners	Practitioners will benefit from enhanced satisfaction and professional development gained from the empirical demonstration of personal effectiveness, identified training and supervision needs and the security of appropriate referrals.
Supervisors	Supervisors will benefit from enhanced supervision practice through empirical data to support case reviews/discussion, and the monitoring of treatment planning and goal attainment.
Service managers	Service managers will benefit from the availability of empirical data to assist rationalized service development, resource allocation, and cost containment. This will help promote an accountable public image, enhance marketing and potentially securing increases in resourcing through the empirical demonstration of potential inadequacies in existing provision, practice and procedures.
Referrers	Referrers will benefit from both empirically informed guidelines improving the appropriateness of referral and standardized progress and outcomes information for referred clients.
Purchasers	Purchasers will benefit from the receipt of empirical data to justify expenditure through the demonstrated cost-effectiveness of provision.
Policy-makers and planners	Policy-makers and planners will benefit from the receipt of empirical data to improve ad hoc decision-making identifying what outcomes, processes and cost-containment standards are feasible for each category of consumer, for each domain of service.
Trainers	Trainers will benefit from the receipt of empirical data to enhance the integration of practice into teaching, testing the application of methods, models and theories of therapy in practice.
Researchers	Researchers will benefit from the utilization of practice-based empirical data to enhance the informativeness of research, leading to more generalizable research designs and the potential to help services develop realistic practice guidelines to aid service planning and development.

References

Aveline, M., Shapiro, D.A., Parry, G. and Freeman, C. (1995) Building research foundations for psychotherapy practice, in M. Aveline and D.A. Shapiro (eds), *Research Foundations for Psychotherapy Practice*. Chichester: John Wiley. pp. 301–22.

BAC (1993) *Survey of the Membership*. Rugby: British Association for Counselling.

Barker, C., Pistrang, N. and Elliott, R. (eds) (1994) *Research Methods in Clinical and Counselling Psychology*. Chichester: John Wiley.

Barkham, M. (1993) Understanding, implementing and presenting counselling evaluation, in R. Bayne and P. Nicholson (eds), *Counselling and Psychology for Health Professionals*. London: Chapman and Hall. pp. 63–83.

Barkham, M. and Barker, C. (1996) 'Evaluating counselling psychology practice', in R. Woolfe and W. Dryden (eds), *Handbook of Counselling Psychology*. London: Sage. pp. 87–110.

Beck, A.T., Steer, R.A. and Gabin, M.G. (1988) Psychometric properties of the Beck Depression Inventory: twenty-five years of evaluation, *Clinical Psychology Review*, 8: 77–100.

Black, N. (1996) Why we need observational studies to evaluate the effectiveness of health care, *British Medical Journal*, 312: 1215–18.

Blakey, R. (1996) Some thoughts on the development of clinical psychology in primary care, *Clinical Psychology Forum*, 97: 37–9.

Connell, J., Barkham, M., Evans, C., Margison, F., McGrath, G. and Milne, D. (1997) The Clinical Outcomes in Routine Evaluation (CORE) outcome measure: guidelines for use – Full version (1.0). PTRC Memo 333. Psychological Therapies Research Centre, University of Leeds.

Curtis Jenkins, G. (1996) The cost of counselling in primary care – or the lack of it: who pays the price? Paper presented at Leeds Mind Conference, Leeds.

Department of Health (1996) *NHS Psychotherapy Services in England: Review of Strategic Policy*. London: NHS Executive.

Derby City Council (1996) *Report into the Case of Anthony Smith*. Independent inquiry by Derby City Council and Derbyshire Health Authority.

Derogatis, L.R. (1983) *SCL-90-R: Administration, Scoring and Procedures*, 3rd edn. Minneapolis: National Computer Systems, Inc.

Elliott, R. (1983) Fitting process research to the practising psychotherapist, *Psychotherapy*, 20: 47–55.

Fensterheim, H. and Raw, S.D. (1996) Psychotherapy research is not psychotherapy practice, *Clinical Psychology: Science and Practice*, 3: 168–71.

Firth-Cozens, J. (1993) *Audit in Mental Health Services*. Hove: Lawrence Erlbaum.

Fonagy, P. (1995) Is there an answer to the outcome research question? – waiting for Godot, *Changes*, 13: 168–77.

Froyd, J.E., Lambert, M.J. and Froyd, J.D. (1996) A review of practices of psychotherapy outcome measurement. *Journal of Mental Health*, 5: 11–15.

Garfield, S.L. and Bergin, A.E. (1994) Introduction and historical overview, in A.E. Bergin and S.L. Garfield (eds), *Handbook of Psychotherapy and Behavior Research*, 4th edn. New York: John Wiley. pp. 3–18.

Goldberg, D. and Williams, P. (1988) *A User Guide to the General Health Questionnaire*. Windsor: NFER-Nelson.

Hansen, G. (1984) Research utilization in rehabilitation counseling practice, *Journal of Applied Rehabilitation Counseling*, 15: 39–42.

Hardy, G.E. (1995) Organisational issues: making research happen, in M. Aveline and D.A. Shapiro (eds), *Research Foundations for Psychotherapy Practice*. Chichester: John Wiley. pp. 97–116.

Heisler, J. (1977) Client–counsellor interaction, *Marriage Guidance*, January–February: 233–8.

Hicks, C. and Wheeler, S. (1994) Research: an essential foundation for counselling, training and practice, *Journal for the British Association for Counselling*, 5 (1): 38–40.

Howard, K., Moras, K., Brill, P.L., Martinovich, Z. and Lutz, W. (1996) Evaluation of psychotherapy: efficacy, effectiveness, and patient progress, *American Psychologist*, 51: 1059–64.

Illman, J. (1993) Are counsellors any use at all?, *GP Life and Leisure*, 21 May.

Lambert, M. and Bergin, A.E. (1994) The effectiveness of psychotherapy, in A.E. Bergin and

S.L. Garfield (eds), *Handbook of Psychotherapy and Behavior Research*, 4th edn. New York: John Wiley. pp. 143–89.

Lipsey, M.W. and Wilson, D.B. (1993) The efficacy of psychological, educational, and behavioral treatment: confirmation from meta-analysis, *American Psychologist*, 48: 1181–209.

McLeod, J. (1994) *Doing Counselling Research*. London: Sage.

McLeod, J. (1995) Evaluating the effectiveness of counselling: what we don't know, *Changes*, 13: 192–9.

Mellor-Clark, J. and Barkham. M. (1996) Evaluating counselling, in R. Bayne, I. Horton and J. Brimrose (eds), *New Directions in Counselling*. London: Routledge. pp. 79–93.

Mellor-Clark, J. and Shapiro, D. (1995) It's not what you do . . . it's the way that you do it: the inception of an evaluative research culture in Relate marriage guidance, *Changes*, 3: 201–7.

MORI (1995) *Attitudes Towards Depression*. Research study conducted for the Defeat Depression Campaign. London: Royal College of Psychiatry.

Morrow-Bradley, C. and Elliott, R. (1986) Utilization of psychotherapy research by practising psychotherapists, *American Psychologist*, 41: 188–97.

Nezu, A. (1996) What are we doing to our patients and should we care if anyone else knows, *Clinical Psychology: Science and Practice*, 3: 160–3.

NHSE (1996) *Promoting Clinical Effectiveness: A Framework for Action in and through the NHS*. Leeds: NHS Executive.

Parry, G. (1995) Bambi fights back: psychotherapy research and service improvement, *Changes*, 13: 164–7.

Parry, G. (1996) Service evaluation and audit methods, in G. Parry and F.N. Watts (eds), *Behavioural and Mental Health Research*, 2nd edn. London: Erlbaum. pp. 423–49.

Paul, G.L. (1967) Strategy of outcome research in psychotherapy, *Journal of Consulting Psychology*, 31: 109–18.

Roth, P. and Fonagy, A. (1996) *What Works for Whom? A Critical Review of Psychotherapy Research*. New York: Guilford Press.

Shipton, G. (1994) Swords into ploughshares: working with resistance to research, *Journal of the British Association for Counselling*, 5 (1): 38–40.

Sibbald, B., Addington-Hall, J., Brenneman, D. and Freeling, B. (1993) Counsellors in English and Welsh general practices, *British Medical Journal*, 306: 29–33.

Speer, D.C. and Newman, F.L. (1996) Mental health services outcome research, *Clinical Psychology: Science and Practice*, 3: 105–29.

Strupp, H.H. (1989) Psychotherapy: can the practitioner learn from the researcher?, *American Psychologist*, 44: 717–24.

Strupp, H.H. (1996) The tripartite model and the consumer report study, *American Psychologist*, 51: 1017–24.

Tyndall, N. (1994) *Counselling in the Voluntary Sector*. Milton Keynes: Open University Press.

Watkins, C.E. and Schneider, L.J. (eds) (1991) *Research in Counselling*. Hillsdale, NJ: Erlbaum.

Wesley, S. (1996) The rise of counselling and the return of alienism, *British Medical Journal*, 313(7050): 158–60.

12

Survival

Rowan Bayne

Counsellors and psychotherapists face many perils in their work. Several are summarized well, if bleakly, by Brady et al. (1995), and to these can be added 'hidden' motives for being a counsellor, as speculated about by Hawkins and Shohet (1989) and others. These perils or potential perils are discussed briefly in the first two sections. Then I will focus on how best each counsellor can increase her or his chances of surviving and surviving well, first by noticing early signs of too much or too little stress and second by choosing effective strategies. Aspects of two strategies for survival are covered in detail – physical activity and writing – and particular attention is paid to how to implement them. For example, a key practical question about physical activity is what is the minimum amount needed to maintain a particular level and kind of fitness.

I chose physical activity (new term for exercise) because of some recent information about it and because it is part of looking after our bodies: it seems possible that counsellors and psychotherapists as a group (with the obvious exceptions of Reichians, Gestaltists, etc.) attend more to minds than bodies. I realize that some people have no wish to look after their bodies and that they survive well without doing so. The section on physical activity is for those who are not happy in this respect. I also recognize that there can be deeper, motivational problems and I have assumed that counsellors and psychotherapists already have well-developed views on these and what to do about them. I chose writing, again because of some new information, but also because it emphasizes emotional self-care and, unlike physical activity, it tends to be ignored in texts on stress management. There are discussions of other strategies – some likely to be familiar, others strange – in numerous sources, for example, Bond (1986), Rosenthal (1993), Palmer and Dryden (1995) and Bayne (in press).

Ideas and findings about actually using survival strategies can be very interesting and practical. For example, physical relaxation seems an obvious way of coping with stress, both short-term, at the level of managing symptoms, and long-term: two ten-minute sessions of progressive relaxation a day seem to have a beneficial and cumulative effect (Seligman, 1995). However, Lazarus and Mayne (1990) argued that it has some serious limitations, for example, competing too hard with others or yourself and being afraid of losing control. In addition, considerable patience and persistence are required, which come more easily to some people than to others.

A main theme throughout the chapter is the central role of self-awareness, in the sense of awareness of one's own thoughts, emotions, feelings, sensations, intuitions, intentions, fantasies, etc. The final section is the most explicit in this respect: it relates Myers' theory of psychological type (Myers, 1980; Bayne, 1995) to what each 'kind of person' is likely to find most stressful, and to which strategies for managing stress are most likely to be effective and enjoyable.

Perils Part 1

The subheadings for this section are five of the seven 'broad, overlapping burdens' for counsellors distinguished by Brady et al. (1995). Of the other two burdens, I see 'emotional depletion' as more a result of too much stress than a primary cause, and I have included 'physical isolation' under 'working conditions'.

The burdens may make painful reading, even in summary form: 'Mental health professionals are regularly engulfed by their clients' pain and disability, are routinely confronted by conscious and unconscious hostility' (Brady et al., 1995: 21–2). Such views may raise the question who would want to be a counsellor. However, Brady et al. do also recognize that most counsellors feel 'enriched, nourished and privileged' by their work.

Client behaviours

Several behaviours are discussed by Brady et al. (1995). Perhaps the most obviously stressful are suicidal clients whose counsellors or therapists can be terrified of the client actually killing him or herself. Other particularly stressful 'client behaviours' include depression, aggression, lying, dependence and talking about abuse. Moreover, relatively minor rejections and losses, for example, clients ending their counselling abruptly, can have a cumulative effect.

Guidelines have been suggested for responding to particular sources of stress (for example, Corey and Corey, 1993; Bayne et al., 1994; Dryden, 1995), as well as general strategies like those discussed later in this chapter. Reading about other counsellors' experience of 'failure' may also be helpful (for example, Yalom, 1989; Mearns, 1990).

Working conditions

Some of the working conditions that can cause too much stress are 'organizational politics, excessive paperwork, demanding workloads and professional conflicts' (Brady et al., 1995: 5). Counsellors in private practice will avoid some of these but are more likely to face others, for example, 'financial instability' (Feltham, 1993, 1995; Syme, 1994). 'Physical isolation' applies most to counsellors in private practice or those who see many clients 'in the same small room, hour after hour' (Brady et al., 1995: 10). Again, the underlying cause – too many clients – is obvious, unless of course there is a deeper underlying cause (as discussed in the section on motives). Too many clients seems to me a basic problem in the sense that if it can be managed well then other potential sources of stress are also reduced.

Psychic isolation

In the therapeutic relationship, the client's needs and interests come first. In most approaches the counsellor's self-disclosure is limited or non-existent. However, sometimes counsellors and therapists behave in the same way in their personal relationships: too much listening and 'eventually losing a clear sense of self' (Brady et al., 1995: 13). Moreover, confidentiality may get in the way of seeking emotional support from friends, family and colleagues, who in turn may resent being shut out. As a further layer here, Brady et al. (1995) cite a study reporting that 60 per cent of psychotherapists in a survey said they had few friends at school and felt 'somewhat isolated' there. Again, the 'solution' is, in theory, obvious. Counsellors too need close human contact and support.

Therapeutic relationships

Brady et al. (1995: 15–16) write: 'We alternate between sleepless nights fraught with recollections of hostility and anxiety incurred from characterologically impaired patients, and fleeting moments of realization that we have genuinely assisted a fellow human being.' I do not feel sympathetic about this statement. I see it as unhelpfully dramatic and I think counsellors need realistic expectations of therapist efficacy and perhaps some clients who are untangling problems of life as well as those who are 'characterologically impaired'. I realize that variety of clients in this sense is not always practical, but I think there are times when we should try to make it practical.

Personal disruptions

Upsetting life events can reduce a therapist's effectiveness at work and, conversely, being a therapist can disrupt personal life, for example, spouses and children feeling neglected. Storr (1990) referred to an exhaustion which leaves little emotional energy to spare. One effect of this on him was that he lost interest in reading novels. A particularly stressful aspect here of course is being calm and professional with clients who are talking about problems which are related to your own.

Perils   Part 2

This section touches on ideas about the hidden motives of counsellors and psychotherapists as a source of stress – only touches on because the evidence for the ideas, especially if they are applied widely, is limited (Cushway, 1996). Trying to avoid loneliness was mentioned earlier. Other possible motives for being a helper are seeking praise, to relieve 'buried disturbance', to have power over others, and fear of power-lessness and intimacy. Hawkins and Shohet refer to these as 'the shadow side of helping' (1989: 10). They tend to be hidden motives and it is their denial which is costly rather than the motives themselves. Hawkins and Shohet also recognize a need to care and heal as a fundamental motive. The useful general principle here is to examine our motives for helping – through supervision, personal therapy, writing, etc. – to be as clear about them as we can, and to take appropriate action. For example, Bond (1986) recommends assertiveness as a way to avoid exhaustion from compulsive helping. A new set of fears may then come to the fore: fears about needing support and receiving help and about the impossibility of systematically using self-care skills on oneself.

Managing stress

This section outlines an approach to managing stress which I hope you will use to review your own current approach and perhaps refine or revise it. The first step is to recognize when you are stressed. How do you as an individual experience too much or too little stress and, in particular, what are the early signs? The early signs are important because it is easier and healthier to take action then and because the source(s) of our reaction may be more apparent and more readily dealt with.

Table 12.1 lists a few of the more common effects or signs of too much or too little stress. It is important to note that some of these indications may be caused by illness rather than stress and need medical attention. Several illnesses are also thought by most researchers in the area to be caused by chronic stress or made worse by it, for example, asthma, heart disease, headaches. Stress does alter immune function, through hor-mones and through depriving the immune system of energy.

You may already 'keep watch' on yourself and notice when you are becoming over-extended. However, improvement may be possible through asking others how they know when you are stressed and by self-observation (difficult though this is). You may, for example, find that a twitching eye (a sign of muscle tension) or a tight mouth are reliable early warnings for you, but that an observant colleague uses the way you speak as her main clue about you. Psychological type theory

Table 12.1   *Effects of stress*

On thoughts and emotions
- difficulty concentrating
- anxious
- tired
- bored
- depressed
- lonely

On the body
- tight throat
- sweating
- dry mouth
- tics
- frequent urination
- aches

On behaviour
- irritable
- critical
- accidents
- drugs
- difficulties in sleeping
- eat less/more

(discussed later) predicts that some people will be more skilful at observing such clues, but everyone can improve.

Two strategies

Table 12.2 lists some strategies for managing stress. There are many other classifications of strategies, for example, mind, emotions, body and 'spirit', and 'problem-focused' strategies versus 'emotion focused', with no agreement as yet on which, if any, is the most useful (see, for example, O'Driscoll and Cooper, 1996).

Four general points about choice of strategies are worth making. First, very little is known so far about matching personality and/or problem to strategy, or how useful this idea is. Much the same can be said of matching client personality to therapist personality, orientation or technique (Lazarus, 1989; Bayne, 1995). Finding the best strategies is therefore a matter of experimenting on yourself, perhaps with the help of psychological type theory. Second, too many changes, or changes which are too ambitious, are stressful in themselves. However, people of some psychological types are more comfortable with change (and more likely to cause it) than others. Third, and at first sight contradicting the previous point, variety of strategy is probably a good thing. Fourth, the most obvious strategies for counsellors are supervision (Chapter 9) and peer support groups (Nichols and Jenkinson, 1993). Supervision, perhaps

Table 12.2   *Some strategies for managing stress*

1   Reduce effects of stress
  • relaxation
  • play/fun
  • massage
  • exercise (short-term)
  • 'present awareness'
  • meditation
  • daydreams/guided fantasies
  • distractions, e.g. TV, music, gardening

2   Increase self-awareness (with a view to action)
  • talk/write to friends
  • peer support group
  • write a journal
  • counselling
  • uncover, challenge and replace irrational beliefs
  • clarify values
  • develop other assertive qualities and skills

3   Discover situational causes (and consider dealing with them directly or changing your attitude towards them)

4   Build up resistance: diet, exercise (long-term), sleep

of more than one kind at once, is frequently recommended by the contributors in Dryden (1995).

Physical activity

The first question about physical fitness is what do you want to be fit for? If it is for everyday life rather than a sport, only a comfortable level of physical activity is needed. The new recommendations from the Center for Disease Control, USA have changed from sweaty and out of breath for twenty minutes, three times a week, to more frequent, lower intensity activity like walking and climbing stairs, and aiming to accumulate about thirty minutes of this most days (Wimbush, 1994). The opposite question – how much exercise is too much? – seems to be a problem for only a few people (Cockerill and Riddington, 1996).

The main principle in physical activity is gradually and comfortably to be more active. Comfortably implies a judgement based on feeling, radically different from an external criterion like number of miles or minutes (Morehouse and Gross, 1977). Building up to thirty minutes, or maintaining it, can be done according to your own inner rhythm. Doing more, and more vigorous, exercise gives a reserve of fitness and probably more protection against some diseases, but is an extra rather than necessary (Wimbush, 1994; Seligman, 1995).

Thayer's research (1987, Thayer et al., 1994) on mild exercise and its effects on mood supports the effectiveness of fairly brisk ten-minute walks. They increase energy and reduce tension for the next two hours on average. Music was also reported as quite effective (so dancing might be particularly beneficial).

Counselling and psychotherapy usually involve lots of sitting so I have included an exercise for waists. It is from an old book (Morehouse and Gross, 1977) but I have checked with a physiotherapy lecturer that it is safe and consistent with current thinking. Sit-backs, according to Morehouse and Gross (1977), are an easier, safer and more effective way of strengthening stomach muscles than the better known sit-ups.

1   Sit on the floor with your feet held by someone or under a heavy piece of furniture and your knees bent and comfortably close to your chest.
2   Move your back towards the floor until you feel your stomach muscles working (this may be a few inches at first). Hold at this point for 15–20 seconds and return to the starting position and rest. Do this at your own rhythm for about 2 minutes. Rest with your arms on the floor or holding your knees.
3   If your muscles start to quiver you've gone too far back. Work towards 20 seconds before the quivering starts. Your body is telling you what it can comfortably do. Similarly, try one set of sit-backs a day at first and increase them at a comfortable rate.
4   Keep breathing as you do the sit-backs.
5   If you decide to go so far as to hold a sit-back for 20 seconds with your back brushing the floor, you may or may not wish to make it even more difficult by putting your arms behind your head, holding for longer or holding a weight on your chest.

A variation is to tighten your stomach muscles as you walk, starting with a few steps, then relaxing, and building up comfortably and gradually. For similar simple exercises – preventive and healing – for backs and necks, see McKenzie (1983, 1988). Both books are currently recommended to physiotherapy students at the University of East London, and I would like to have known about them long before I did. Check with a doctor, physiotherapist or osteopath first though.

Writing

The therapeutic effects of writing about stressful experiences have been studied by Pennebaker and his colleagues (for example, Pennebaker, 1993; Pennebaker et al., 1990; Spera et al., 1994). Pennebaker et al. (1990) divided students who had just started their first year into two random groups. The experimental group were asked to write for twenty minutes on three consecutive days about their 'very deepest thoughts and feelings about coming to college'. The control or comparison group wrote on what they had done since they woke up that day. In the first group, therefore, thoughts and feelings were emphasized, in the second behaviour. The main finding was that students in the experimental group showed better immune system function than those in the control group and went to the health centre less in the next six months. The basic finding and variations have been replicated several times, with some attention to explaining the positive effects of this form of writing on health.

In a related study (Spera et al., 1994), unemployed professionals either wrote about their reactions to redundancy (experimental group) or about relatively superficial matters (control group). Those in the experimental group found new jobs more quickly, although not because they applied for more jobs or wrote more letters. The most likely explanations are a gain in perspective and sense of control, and less energy used in suppressing troubling thoughts and emotions. Rumination – being preoccupied with an emotional upset, when it goes 'round and round' and dominates – seems to be particularly stressful (Roger and Hudson, 1995). Writing of the kind investigated by Pennebaker may also work through reducing rumination. A further explanation is that writing may help the writer to sort out what matters most and decide what can wait, be delegated or discarded. Back to autonomy and sense of control again.

The area of research and counselling called 'narrative therapy' (McLeod, 1996) is expanding rapidly. A basic assumption is that a defining characteristic of being human is 'telling stories'. A strategy which is consistent with Pennebaker's research is outlined below in five steps, followed by an example. The five steps ask you to take your inner experience seriously, but guard against becoming morbidly introspective or unduly passive by also emphasizing action.

Five steps

1 Choose a troubling 'event'.
2 Describe the event in a few words.
3 Write as freely as possible about it – not analysing at this point and not concerned with literary merit.
4 Analyse using one or more of the following questions or similar questions:
   (a) Might it be useful to be more specific about any aspects?
   (b) What is the evidence for any assertions, beliefs?
   (c) Are there any familiar feelings or patterns here?
   (d) Am I making any assumptions?
   (e) Do my reactions tell me anything about myself, for example, suggest important values or principles?
   (f) How realistic am I being?
   (g) What other ways (however unlikely) are there of looking at what happened and how I reacted?

5   Consider action:
   (a) Is there any action I want to take now ('action' includes changing an attitude or belief)?
   (b) Is there anything which I might do differently next time?

I have included an example to try to 'bring alive' this skeleton.

Steps 1 and 2   Given extra work to do. Reacted angrily to X.

Step 3: write freely   I was furious. How dare he give me more work and not ask me first. I've got too much to do already. But it was that half-smile and look away that really got to me. I think he knew exactly what he was doing. Perhaps he wants me to leave. Perhaps it's revenge or putting me in my place. Well he can sod off. I just won't do it and see what he does then.

Step 4: analysis   What I actually said to X was 'This sort of thing makes me feel like leaving.' I said it angrily but not abusively. I don't *know* what his motives were. I resent most being told what to do as if I was a servant. Autonomy is very important to me. He may have been embarrassed to ask me to do more when he doesn't ask Z. I'm glad I reacted spontaneously and strongly. Now I feel calmer the extra work has some positive possibilities (though I'd still much rather not do it).

Step 5: possible actions
Talk to A and B about it. Ask for their views.
Accept that it's not worth a fight – probably.
Nor is the insult – the 'servant' part. I don't trust X enough, at least at the moment. On the other hand, it doesn't take any trust to say something to him about consultation. Think about how to put it.
Think about what to put less effort into or postpone/cancel, in order to do the new work.
Check how realistic the positive possibilities are.
Note my characteristic reaction to being ordered about and talk/write about it.

Evaluation of the example   The steps have been followed fairly well. There is reasonable self-awareness, for example, of emotions. The writer shows some commitment to pursue related 'patterns' – is not just preoccupied by his immediate problem. The possible actions seem realistic but they could be stated more specifically, for example, when will the writer talk to A and B?

Final comments on writing   Rainer (1978) reviews a wide variety of other writing methods, for example, letters, lists, conversations. One I particularly like for its simplicity and focus is: At the end of a day, find one adjective to describe it and another for how you'd like the next day to be.

A general model of counselling and psychotherapy is embodied in the five steps: first, express and feel a 'problem'; second, analyse and think it through; third, consider action. The method and Pennebaker's excellent research on a variation of it, raise the question of what counsellors and therapists do which adds more (Freud and Horney both analysed themselves extensively). This may itself be a stressful idea. However, I suspect that only some clients would benefit more from writing (or being 'counselled' by a computer) than they would or do from therapy itself. On the other hand, writing as a form of self-therapy has several attractions: it is private, free and readily available.

Psychological type and stress

In Myers' theory of psychological type the central concepts are 'preference' and 'type'. Preference can be defined as 'feeling most natural and comfortable with'. Thus, behaving in the opposite way to your preference happens, but is usually less frequent and takes more effort. If you prefer introversion to extraversion, for example, then social events and doing things are likely to take more effort and energy than reading or 'just sitting', but most introverts can still actually be sociable.

This point probably makes sense to most people because it is about something very visible. Type theory gets more interesting when it says that if you prefer extraversion, then reading and reflecting are likely to be more effortful than social events. Introverts, certainly this introvert, may understand extraversion cognitively, but – according to type theory – will never really know what it is like experientially, or will know it at best fleetingly and in a pale, undeveloped form. In the same way, the theory assumes that extraverts never really know what it is like to be an introvert. The same notion applies to all the preferences and their combinations.

The theory assumes that people who do not behave like their types most of the time become 'frustrated, inferior copies of other people' (Myers, 1980: 189). A more gentle variation is that they are less happy and less effective than they would be as their true types. Finding or clarifying your true type, through therapy or other means, is reported to be like 'coming home'. Perhaps it is also worth adding that people of any of the psychological types can be good counsellors or psychotherapists.

At the basic level of type theory, four pairs of preferences are distinguished (Table 12.3). Their meaning is very briefly indicated by the following characteristics, which are behaviours that tend to be associated with the preferences rather than definitions of them. There are sixteen possible combinations of the preferences and these form the sixteen

Table 12.3 *The four pairs of preferences*

Extraversion (E)	or Introversion (I)
Sensing (S)	or Intuition (N)
Thinking (T)	or Feeling (F)
Judging (J)	or Perceiving (P)

types. Extraversion (E) is associated in part with being more outgoing and active, introversion (I) with being more reflective and reserved. People who prefer sensing (S) tend to be more comfortable with practical things and the familiar, and to be more aware of the present and what is actually happening, in contrast to those who prefer intuition (N) who tend to be more interested in possibilities, patterns, inspirations, and the future. People who prefer thinking (T) more easily analyse, criticize and use logic, in contrast to those who prefer feeling (F) who tend to decide on the basis of likes and dislikes more, and on how much something 'fits' or 'feels right'. Judging (J) and perceiving (P) are partly about two approaches to life: more organized and planning (J) versus more flexible and easygoing (P).

One of the great strengths of psychological type theory is that it is useful at its simplest levels and in this section I will discuss only aspects of the first two levels: the preferences and the temperaments. Five levels of type theory can be distinguished:

1 Each preference.
2 Combinations of preferences, in particular the four 'temperaments' and the sixteen types.
3 Type dynamics, in which one function (S, N, T or F) is seen as dominant, another as auxiliary and so on.
4 Type development.
5 Subscales for each preference (21 subscales so far).

Four temperaments are proposed by Keirsey and Bates (1978): SP, SJ, NT and NF. Each includes four types, for example, INTJ, ENTJ, INTP, ENTP are all NTs. The stick figures (Figure 12.1) summarize this part of the theory and can be used as a provisional or working self-assessment of temperament and therefore of part of type. Please note that the theory sees each person as a mixture of the temperaments, but with one predominant. Similarly, the descriptions of what is most stressful for each temperament and characteristic reactions (Tables 12.4 and 12.5) can be used for self-assessment (and often lead to a wry self-recognition). However, they have not yet been tested formally. Other methods of discovering and verifying one's type and temperament are discussed in Bayne (1995). The Myers–Briggs Type Indicator or MBTI (questionnaire), plus skilled feedback, is generally the most accurate method.

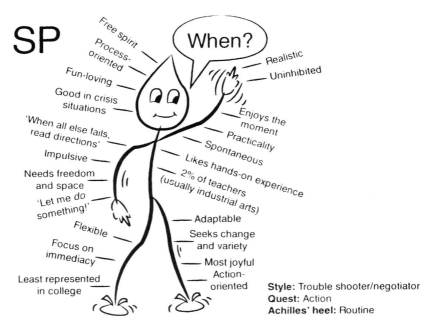

Typical SP characteristics (© Otto Kroeger Associates).

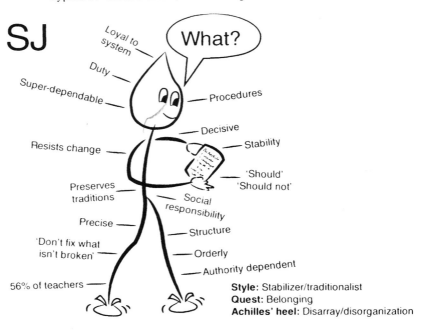

Typical SJ characteristics (© Otto Kroeger Associates).

Figure 12.1   *The temperaments. Reproduced from Bayne (1995) with permission from Chapman & Hall*

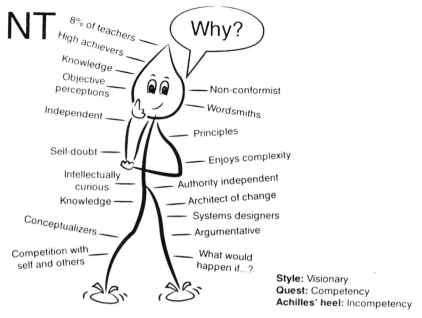

Typical NT characteristics (© Otto Kroeger Associates).

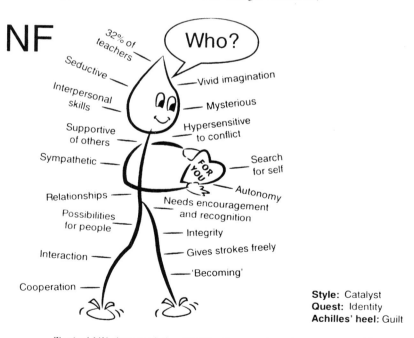

Typical NF characteristics (© Otto Kroeger Associates).

Table 12.4 *Temperament and what is most stressful*

SP	Not much happening. Lack of freedom.
SJ	Ambiguity. Changes of plan. Lack of control.
NT	Repetitive things. Bureaucracy.
NF	Conflict. Saying no. Criticism.

Sources: Bayne, 1995, adapted from unpublished material by Valerie Stewart; Keirsey and Bates, 1978

Table 12.5 *Temperament and reactions to stress*

SP	Frivolity, flight
SJ	Redefine objectives, more effort
NT	Fight, conform rebelliously, pedantic debate
NF	Self-sacrifice, hysteria, depression, cynicism

Sources: Bayne, 1995, adapted from unpublished material by Valerie Stewart; Keirsey and Bates, 1978

Table 12.6 *The preferences and having 'a good stretch'*

E	Take notes, write
I	Talk personally and spontaneously
S	Fantasize
N	Do something sensory
T	Empathize
F	Analyse
J	Abandon the schedule
P	Plan something and do it

Sources: Bayne, (1995), adapted from Kroeger with Thuesen, 1992

One suggestion for managing stress is to use our own preferences, for example, if we prefer S – a sensory activity; N – design something; T – analyse or critique something/someone; F – do something that involves decisions of like/dislike. This is the main strategy and can be refined further using type dynamics (Quenk, 1993; Bayne, 1995). However, Kroeger with Thuesen (1992: 247) suggest that sometimes the most effective strategy is *briefly* to use one of the *opposite* preferences to your type. They call this having 'a good stretch' and apply it to all the preferences (Table 12.6). There is a risk here of type theory trying to cover all the options and thus be unfalsifiable. However, progress is being made in theory and research towards clear specification of when each strategy is most likely to succeed (Bayne, 1995).

Conclusion

Self-care is a professional responsibility for all counsellors and psychotherapists (BAC, 1990; Cushway, 1996). This chapter has touched on some of the main obstacles – inner and outer – to surviving well as a counsellor or psychotherapist and has discussed some strategies for doing so. I hope I have helped to set the scene for improving our self-care rather than being taken to say, 'It's straightforward. All you need is . . .'. It is far from straightforward, but it is possible and involving.

Acknowledgements

I would like to thank Moya Armstrong, Jenny Bimrose, Alina Das Gupta, Philip Hayes, Ian Horton and Tony Merry for their helpful comments on a draft of this chapter or a section of it.

References

BAC (1990) *The Code of Ethics and Practice for Counsellors.* Rugby: British Association for Counselling.

Bayne, R. (1995) *The Myers–Briggs Type Indicator. A Critical Review and Practical Guide.* London: Chapman & Hall.

Bayne, R. (in press) Looking after yourself, in R. Bayne, P. Nicolson and I. Horton (eds), *Counselling and Communication in Health Care Settings.* Leicester: British Psychological Society.

Bayne, R., Horton, I., Merry, T. and Noyes, L. (1994) *The Counsellor's Handbook. A Practical A–Z Guide to Professional and Clinical Practice.* London: Chapman & Hall.

Bond, M. (1986) *Stress and Self-Awareness: A Guide for Nurses.* London: Heinemann.

Brady, J.L., Healy, F.C., Norcross, J.C. and Guy, J.D. (1995) Stress in counsellors: an integrative research review, in W. Dryden (ed.), *The Stresses of Counselling in Action.* London: Sage.

Cockerill, I.M. and Riddington, M.E. (1996) Exercise dependence and associated disorders: a review, *Counselling Psychology Quarterly,* 9 (2): 119–29.

Corey, M.S. and Corey, G. (1993) *Becoming a Helper,* 2nd edn. Pacific Grove, CA: Brooks/Cole.

Cushway, D. (1996) New directions in stress, in R. Bayne, I. Horton and J. Bimrose (eds), *New Directions in Counselling.* London: Routledge.

Dryden, W. (ed.) (1995) *The Stresses of Counselling in Action.* London: Sage.

Feltham, C. (1993) Making a living as a counsellor, in W. Dryden (ed.), *Questions and Answers on Counselling in Action.* London: Sage. pp. 165–70.

Feltham, C. (1995) The stresses of counselling in private practice, in W. Dryden (ed.), *The Stresses of Counselling in Action.* London: Sage.

Hawkins, P. and Shohet, R. (1989) *Supervision in the Helping Professions.* Buckingham: Open University Press.

Keirsey, D. and Bates, M. (1978) *Please Understand Me,* 3rd edn. Del Mar, CA: Prometheus Nemesis.

Kroeger, O. with Thuesen, J.M. (1992) *Type Talk at Work.* New York: Delacorte Press.

Lazarus, A.A. (1989) *The Practice of Multimodal Therapy.* Baltimore: Johns Hopkins University Press.

Lazarus, A.A. and Mayne, T.J. (1990) Relaxation: some limitations, side effects and proposed solutions, *Psychotherapy,* 27 (2): 261–6.

McKenzie, R. (1983) *Treat Your Own Neck.* Waikanae, NZ: Spinal Publications.

McKenzie, R. (1988) *Treat Your Own Back.* Waikanae, NZ: Spinal Publications.

McLeod, J. (1996) Working with narratives, in R. Bayne, I. Horton and J. Bimrose (eds), *New Directions in Counselling.* London: Routledge.

Mearns, D. (1990) The counsellor's experience of failure, in D. Mearns and W. Dryden (eds), *Experiences of Counselling in Action*. London: Sage.

Morehouse, L.E. and Gross, L. (1977) *Total Fitness in 30 Minutes a Week*. St. Albans: Mayflower.

Myers, I.B. (1980) *Gifts Differing*. Palo Alto, CA: Consulting Psychologists Press.

Nichols, K. and Jenkinson, J. (1991) *Leading a Support Group*. London: Chapman & Hall.

O'Driscoll, M. and Cooper, C.L. (1996) Sources and management of excessive job stress and burnout, in P. Warr (ed.), *Psychology at Work*. Harmondsworth: Penguin.

Palmer, S. and Dryden, W. (1995) *Counselling for Stress Problems*. London: Sage.

Pennebaker, J.W. (1993) Putting stress into words: health, linguistic and therapeutic implications, *Behaviour Research and Therapy*, 31: 539–48.

Pennebaker, J.W., Colder, M. and Sharp, L.K. (1990) Accelerating the coping process, *Journal of Personality and Social Psychology*, 58: 528–37.

Quenk, N.L. (1993) *Beside Myself: The Inferior Function in Everyday Life*. Palo Alto, CA: Consulting Psychologists Press.

Rainer, T. (1978) *The New Diary*. New York: St. Martin's Press.

Rakos, R.F. (1991) *Assertive Behaviour: Theory, Research and Training*. London: Routledge.

Roger, D. and Hudson, C. (1995) The role of emotion control and emotional rumination in stress management training, *International Journal of Stress Management*, 2 (3): 119–32.

Rosenthal, T. (1993) To soothe the savage breast, *Behaviour Research and Therapy*, 31 (5): 439–62.

Seligman, M.E.P. (1995) *What You Can Change and What You Can't*. New York: Ballantine Books.

Spera, S.P., Buhrfeind, E.D. and Pennebaker, J.W. (1994) Creative writing and coping with job loss, *Academy of Management Journal*, 37: 722–33.

Storr, A. (1990) *The Art of Psychotherapy*, 2nd edn. London: Heinemann/Secker & Warburg.

Syme, C. (1994) *Counselling in Independent Practice*. Buckingham: Open University Press.

Thayer, R.E. (1987) Energy, tiredness, and tension effects of a sugar snack versus moderate exercise, *Journal of Personality and Social Psychology*, 52 (1): 119–25.

Thayer, R.E., Newman J.R. and McClain, T.M. (1994) Self-regulation of mood: strategies for changing a bad mood, raising energy, and reducing tension, *Journal of Personality and Social Psychology*, 67 (5): 910–25.

Wimbush, E. (1994) A moderate approach to promoting physical activity: the evidence and implications, *Health Education Journal*, 53: 322–36.

Yalom, I.D. (1989) *Love's Executioner and Other Tales of Psychotherapy*. Harmondsworth: Penguin.

13

Spiritual Responsibility in a Secular Profession

Brian Thorne

The therapy explosion

The last twenty years have seen an astonishing increase in the UK and elsewhere of those seeking help (or in some cases inspiration) from counsellors and psychotherapists. At the same time, whether in response to a manifest need or as a further indication of it, the ranks of therapists have swollen exponentially and the schools of therapy have proliferated. Currently, too, our newspapers and popular journals are seldom devoid for long of stories about counselling and psychotherapy. Furthermore such journalistic interest often displays a remarkable polarization: therapists are portrayed both as demonic abusers and as compassionate healers of the emotionally wounded whom our culture seems consistently to spawn. The fact that counselling and therapy have now entered the mainstream of our national life is significantly demonstrated every time there is a major disaster. It is taken for granted that counsellors of some kind will be on hand to respond to those who have been caught up in a traumatic event and it is even considered appropriate that such help be extended to those whose very job it is to attend disasters – the police, the ambulance workers, the members of the fire brigade. Therapeutic help, it would seem, is for everyone no matter how apparently macho or resilient.

The clientele and the context of relationship

The increase in the numbers of those seeking therapeutic help is itself remarkable but in some ways the diversity of the clientele is more so. My own clinical experience spans higher education, private practice and counselling in the work place. In all three settings I am struck by the range of the clientele and of the concerns which they present. In my university context, for example, I am likely in any one week to see people varying in age from 18 to 70, drawn from many different countries and presenting problems as diverse as examination panic, sexual abuse and bereavement. In the consulting room where I offer counselling to members of a major insurance company, I am as likely to see a senior manager as a junior clerical worker. In private practice I have listened to the woes of the 'great and good' of the provincial capital where I live as well as to the pain of the unemployed or those for whom the psychiatric system has nothing further to offer. It is difficult to imagine a more 'catholic' clientele.

The fascination of this situation is such that it is easy to overlook one aspect of their behaviour which these multifarious clients have in common. They have all chosen to share their difficulties and concerns within the context of a relationship. It may be that they have not initially conceptualized it in this way; they may, for example, have decided to consult 'an expert' or to seek 'professional help'. Those who make it beyond the first session, however, will be in little doubt that they have crossed the threshold into a particular form of relationship and that this is the arena in which they will now explore their difficulties and seek an alleviation of their pain and confusion.

Again this may seem unremarkable enough until we reflect that it is perhaps a characteristic of what sociologists call our post-modern culture. It is not uncommon for older people to wonder – often ironically – what happened 'before all these counsellors were around'. The subtext to such comments is that in previous generations people showed more grit and determination and got on with their lives without whingeing and without indulging in continual self-analysis. Perhaps there is some truth in this assertion but it leaves out of account, I believe, a number of important factors. Not least is the undeniable change in the social fabric of our communal life in the second half of the twentieth century. The 'mobile society' has in many areas destroyed the geographical reality of the extended family and the changes in social mores have more recently threatened the shaky stability of the so-called nuclear family, which in itself is but poor protection against the vicissitudes of the economy and political fashions. But if the fabric of society has undergone profound changes, so too, have many of the prevalent attitudes which underpinned the old order. In no sphere is this more dramatic than in the attitude to religion and, more recently, to medicine.

The reasons behind these shifts in attitude are complex. They involve belief systems, changing responses to authority of all kinds and a growing scepticism about the efficacy and even the integrity of much conventional wisdom. The net result, however, is that for growing numbers in our society neither the priest nor the doctor any longer constitute trustworthy sources of knowledge or support. It is perhaps significant that as far as ministers of religion are concerned, those who do still command allegiance, usually of an extreme kind, are wedded to a highly dogmatic brand of belief which brooks no argument and can lead to punitive exclusion if the 'believer' deviates from the 'truth' or gives expression to doubt. Only absolute authority, it seems, remains appealing (for some) in a world of almost infinite relativity.

Past responses to emotional and psychological distress

It may be that previous generations were emotionally and psychologically more resilient than we are today. We shall never know, although there is plenty of evidence of the mental and physical suffering which ruined many lives in the past. The stories which are recounted by many older clients also explode the myth that emotional resilience was once universal and that we are now witnessing the emergence of a degenerate species which has lost its backbone. More relevant, I suspect, are the shifts in social structures and the changes in attitude to which reference has been made above. It is my fantasy that in the past the confidential sharing of pain and confusion (which is one way of defining the therapeutic activity) was more likely to take place within the family circle, in the vicar's study or in the 'family' doctor's surgery than it does today. It is also, I believe, a tenable hypothesis that a sense of continuity and of common reference points was a part of most people's framework of reality until well into the twentieth century, despite the advances of science and technology and the devastation of war. This aided the maintenance of individual identity and kept at bay some of the more poignant existential questions which characterize the distress of many of those who currently seek the help of therapists.

Today there is for most of us a sense of the inadequacy of many of the understandings and basic assumptions that were until comparatively recently operative in society. In his book *The Gutenberg Elegies*, the American critic, Sven Birkerts, puts it starkly and concisely: 'The maps no longer describe the terrain we inhabit. There is no clear path to the future. We trust that the species will blunder on, but we don't know where to. We feel imprisoned in a momentum that is not of our own making' (Birkerts, 1994: 20).

The therapist as family, doctor and priest

Counselling and psychotherapy have been described as the impossible profession and the description is apt enough if counsellors and therapists believe that they must satisfy the needs and yearnings of all their clients. The work is even more daunting when it is perceived within the context of the rapidly shifting sands which Birkerts graphically portrays. After all, therapists are themselves no more than struggling representatives of the species which 'blunders on' without direction and with an increasing sense of foreboding. Indeed the task is so evidently impossible that the temptation is to give up altogether or to redefine the therapeutic activity in strictly limited but perhaps more realistic terms. The cognitive-behavioural therapists have learned this lesson well. They are satisfied, for example, if they can enable a client to cope more effectively with a phobia or develop a more assertive stance towards an oppressive parent or employer. The establishment of well-defined and often short-term goals has become commonplace at the outset of many therapeutic 'contracts' and there is no doubt that this 'humble' approach often achieves results of a sort, preserves the therapist from *folie de grandeur* and presumably reduces somewhat the possibility of an embittered band of disillusioned clients. Settling for limited objectives would certainly seem a sensible policy and the therapist who wishes to sleep soundly at night might be well advised to pursue this path. It fits comfortably, too, with the current obsession to prove the efficacy of therapeutic interventions through the production of tangible and irrefutable results. Funding bodies and their affiliated researchers long to believe in the existence of a world where it is known that such and such a therapy will 'cure' panic attacks in four sessions or chronic depression in six. The truth of the matter, however, is that such neat solutions are rare and that even when they seem to apply there is no guarantee that the client has found anything more than a temporary alleviation of pain or a provisional move from what Freud described long ago as 'neurotic misery' to 'common unhappiness'.

I am unwilling to opt for the limited role, however 'sensible' and appealing. I confess to a desire to engage at a deeper and more influential level with my clients while knowing that such a desire may be the result of an inflated assessment of my own importance and capacity or an indication of an unconscious masochism which may end in exhaustion and burn-out. The implications of such possible folly are far-reaching. The starting point is a willingness to acknowledge the nature of the challenges which clients have been presenting to me for almost thirty years. Of course, there are those who need little more than a friendly companion to stay around for a while so that decisions can be made or complicated situations untangled. It is a privilege to be invited into such persons' lives for a space and to share in their deliberations and dilemmas. They seem to be saying to me: 'Be a committed attentive listener so that I may discover what I truly feel and think and need to do.' If my professional life were spent entirely with people of this kind, I have little doubt that I should feel useful and perhaps content even if in danger of courting complacency or occasional boredom.

The legacy of the last thirty years, however, is, very much more complex. Many clients who have entered my life have stayed a long time (some are there still) and I am changed as a result of them. There are times when they have driven me to the brink of despair or compelled me almost in spite of myself to examine honestly the belief system to which I subscribe. Their voices reverberate in my mind and even if they have never uttered the precise words I ascribe to them, I know I am not mistaken in my interpretation of their demands. Some say: 'Love me.' Others cry out: 'Heal me.' Others again plead: 'Give me meaning.' There are those who have demanded all three at different times.

The therapist as lover, healer and provider of meaning suggests the impossible profession to beat all impossible professions and yet my experience tells me that this is what has been asked of me by many persons for many years. What is more, such people are on the increase and it is ironical that their proliferation coincides with a time when the 'value for money' approach to healthcare means that, in the public sector, therapy, when it is available at all, is often restricted to short-term contracts with limited goals. It is unlikely that in such an ethos a client will be prompted to contract for love, healing and meaning to be delivered in six sessions. The therapist who accepted such a contract would in any case be guilty of the most irresponsible collusion with insane expectations.

My perception is perhaps simplistic but I am suggesting that as the family disintegrates, institutional religion declines and the medical profession loses some of its credibility and much of its authority, those who seek love, healing and meaning do not know where to turn. The counsellor and psychotherapist offer hope: here are the potential substitute family members, doctors and priests for an age where, to quote Birkerts again, 'our post-modern culture is a vast fabric of competing isms: we are leaderless and subject to the terrors, masked as the freedoms, of an absolute relativism' (1994). If we therapists accept that this is indeed the case and that a new and apparently impossible role has been thrust upon us, we are faced with an agonizing dilemma. Do we run away altogether from such a daunting prospect, do we reject the role and adopt another as our economic masters seem to require or do we refuse to submit to panic and look the unpalatable truth in the face? Interestingly enough, in a telling paragraph in his prophetic analysis of our plight, Sven Birkerts incites us to face what may be our new vocation. 'Where the Virgin was once the locus of spirit and care', he writes, 'the protectress of the interior life, the new site of power, now secular, is the office of the trained therapeutic specialist' (1994: 218).

The therapist as 'believer', in a disintegrating culture

I like the metaphor of the therapist as the protector of the interior life and as the locus of spirit and care. These are words with which I can identify. Such a person, it seems to me, does not cut an altogether foolish figure in the face of someone who yearns for love, or healing or meaning. Nor is he or she anything other than supremely important in a world which is increasingly cut off from beauty, simplicity, passion and the spiritual. Thus encouraged, I can look the unpalatable facts in the face and discover, as Carl Rogers once proposed, that perhaps they are friendly after all.

To brass tacks then. What does it mean to accept that as a therapist I shall be sought out by those who desire love, healing and meaning? How can I possibly equip myself for such encounters? These are the questions to which the rest of this chapter addresses itself in various ways. For the moment I offer some initial but fundamental reflections.

In the first place, I must rid myself of the grandiose idea that I can give love, healing or meaning to anyone, let alone that it is my professional duty to do so. Any gift, however precious, is ultimately useless unless it is treasured and received by the one to whom it is offered. I am dependent on the other to receive and this in turn will be determined by the quality of our relationship. Second, I must renounce any pretension I might entertain to be the sole or even principal provider or source of love, healing or meaning for another individual. However deep the yearning may be, if I set myself up as the ultimate response to it, I am likely to be the cause of disillusionment or, at worst, of abuse. What, then, can I do?

I would suggest that I can attend with the utmost seriousness to my own belovedness, to my own healing and to the meaning of my own life. If I do this I shall not be afraid in the presence of the other's yearnings and demands, nor shall I be tempted to use the other's needs as a means of filling my own emptiness. Attending to my own belovedness will entail an openness in my personal relationships which allows others to nourish me. It will also require of me a willingness to be cherished by the natural environment and by the spiritual forces which surround me. Attending to my own healing will entail a refusal to be anything other than my whole self, to insist on acknowledging my essential unity as body, mind and spirit and not to submit to fragmentation. Attending to the meaning of my own life will require a preparedness to stay closely in touch with the day-to-day pressures of my own living and to relate these to what I profess to believe about human beings and the nature of reality. It will also require a continual monitoring of my beliefs about the therapy I practise and a commitment to living them out in my work rather than simply mouthing them at professional conferences and seminars. If all this sounds like a stern discipline it should come as no surprise. How otherwise could it be possible to welcome into relationship those who yearn for love, healing or meaning without the fear of being eaten alive or of succumbing to an annihilating despair?

As our materialistic and increasingly electronic culture embraces a network of communications where the interior life is sacrificed on the altar of efficiency and to the shallowness of the instant response, so the counsellors and psychotherapists must commit themselves to a deeper level of experiencing. For my own part, without such commitment I have concluded that the only honest thing to do would be to trade in my professional diplomas and seek alternative employment.

The need for meaning

Spirituality, religion and psychology

One of the more intriguing developments among therapists in recent years has been the change of attitude towards notions of spirituality and the spiritual dimension of personality. Therapists who a decade or so ago would have scoffed at such preoccupations have now acknowledged their relevance and in many cases have been forced to review their own understanding of human nature and human destiny. This change is undoubtedly partly attributable to the manifest existential needs of clients referred to above and to the increasing willingness on the part of some to articulate their need for meaning and to insist on therapists engaging with them in this exploration. Although there are still therapists who tend to perceive spiritual concerns – especially if they touch on matters concerning life after death or unspecified spiritual forces – as evidence of neurosis or even incipient psychosis, such practitioners it would seem, are either on the decrease or have become much less vocal in their views. It would be wrong, however, to see this shift in attitude as being entirely client driven. There is I believe something of a sea change taking place within the fields of both psychology and theology which is resulting in a developing dialogue that would have been unthinkable until very recently. It is significant, for example, that a lectureship has been endowed (by a successful novelist specializing in spiritual matters) in the Faculty of Divinity of Cambridge University for the study of science and religion and that the first incumbent is a clinical psychologist who also happens to be an Anglican priest. In 1994, too, the respected journal *American Psychologist* carried a major article on psychology and religion. Its author, Dr Stanton Jones, had this to say: 'It seems that psychology is, in American society, filling the void created by the waning influence of religion in answering questions of ultimacy and providing moral guidance' (Jones, 1994: 192). Later in the same article he quotes an earlier writer, Browning, who observed: 'Traditional religion and modern (therapeutic) psychology stand in a special relation to one another because both of them provide concepts and technologies for the ordering of the interior life' (Browning, 1987).

The needs of clients, the signs of a tentative dialogue between religion and psychology and the ravages of competitive materialism all contribute to the creation of a climate where it is becoming increasingly difficult for the therapist to avoid adopting a stance towards spiritual experience. There would seem to be at least three possible positions to take up. He or she can deny the reality of spirituality and see so-called spiritual phenomena as ultimately explicable in psychological terms and therefore not requiring an alternative framework for their conceptualization. A second position is to acknowledge the validity of spiritual experience but to exclude it from the therapeutic arena on the score that counsellors and psychotherapists are not equipped to respond to it and have more pragmatic behavioural, cognitive and affective objectives to achieve. The third position is to accept spiritual experience as one of the 'givens' of being human and fully to engage with it. What is not possible any longer is for a therapist of integrity to duck the question altogether.

A parenthesis is required at this point in order to differentiate between spirituality and religion. The latter involves a set of beliefs or understandings which are held in common and attempt to explain, at least partially, the totality of human experience including those aspects which are not susceptible to empirical enquiry. In most cases, too, a religion will have an organizational or institutional structure to support its members in their belief and conduct. Clearly a religion can and often does serve the spiritual aspirations and development of its members but this is by no means invariably the case. All too often religions become so preoccupied with the minutiae of their belief systems or with the complexities of their organizational structures that the fostering of spirituality gives way to sterile dogmatic conflicts or hierarchical power-mongering. It is for these reasons among others that institutional religion in the UK is at such a low ebb and why many thousands of people have deserted or disregard the mainstream churches and seek to nourish their spirituality in new and often uncharted ways. For those for whom this is far too hazardous there may be a descent into apathy or cynicism or a flight into the dogmatic certainty of fundamentalism of one kind or another.

What, then, is this spirituality in the face of which I am suggesting all therapists are called to take a stance? I have battled with this question elsewhere and have lamented the inadequacy of language to do it justice (Thorne, 1993). The starting point is human nature itself. The concept of spirituality cannot be embraced half-heartedly: if it has meaning at all it must take as its basic assumption that the ultimate foundation of our being is spiritual and that it is in our spirituality that the source of identity is to be found. It follows from such a belief – and it is a belief and not a provable fact despite the wealth of evidence buttressing it – that the human spirit shares in the creative source of energy which reflects the moving force within the cosmos. To quote myself:

> It is because I am essentially a spiritual being that I am, whether I know it or not or whether I like it or not, indisputably linked to all that has been or will be. I am not an isolated entity but rather a unique part of the whole created order. What is more this spiritual essence of my being defines me in a way which goes far beyond my genetic inheritance, my conditioning and all the ramifications of my unconscious processes. . . . Spirit itself, unlike matter, is not subject to destruction which means that my fundamental self transcends the boundaries of time and space. (Thorne, 1993: 74)

If I regard myself in this way – as I do – it is self-evident that I must regard my clients in similar fashion, whatever they may believe or not believe about themselves. This is not to suggest that my belief will be articulated to my client (although it might be) but, insofar as I am in many ways the embodiment of what I believe, it goes without saying that my spirituality will be powerfully present in my therapeutic encounters. It is my contention that not only is this highly desirable given the enormity of the existential yearnings of so many clients but also that it places upon me and upon all those therapists who share a belief in the ultimate reality of spirit a responsibility with profound implications.

Therapy as a spiritual vocation

The word 'vocation' has an oddly old-fashioned ring about it. It sits uncomfortably in a world where young people are constantly encouraged to think in terms of 'improving their skills', or 'becoming flexible and adaptable' and are cautioned against the idea of 'a job for life'. On the contrary, they are told to prepare themselves for entry into a marketplace where it is likely they will change not only jobs but functions many times and where there can be no predictability beyond the present short-term contract. In such an environment the notion of 'being called' to a particular form of work and way of life seems anachronistic at best and foolish at worst. This being the case it is, I believe, striking that in my experience the vast majority of those who present themselves for counsellor training in the university where I practise and teach lay claim to precisely such a sense of vocation. What is more this seems to be true equally of those who are in their late twenties or younger and of those who have discovered their 'vocation' after many years of toil in other occupations or professions. I even receive letters these days from undergraduates and sixth-formers who express, often movingly and passionately, their conviction that they wish to devote their lives to therapeutic work. Such a conviction seems often to be the outcome of experiences which have confronted the individual with the essential vulnerability and mysteriousness of the human person and with the power of relationship for both good and ill. It is not too fanciful, I believe, to see this as the encounter with the spiritual in the seemingly wholly secular domain of human pain and interaction. This 'vocational' conviction in aspiring therapeutic trainees contrasts markedly with the dwindling number of those presenting themselves for ordination to the full-time priesthood or pastorate and with the disillusionment which is sending many general practitioners into early retirement and nurses into other occupational areas. It is also an open secret that many erstwhile clergy and medical personnel are to be found in the ranks of the therapists and that others seem to find the strength to continue part-time in their former roles from the enlivening injection provided by their therapeutic work.

Spiritual discipline and the place of faith

The therapist who is 'called' to exercise his or her vocation and willingly accepts the task of entering the spiritual dimension of experience is faced with an awesome responsibility. The danger, we have seen, of capitulating to despair or of assuming a guru-like grandiosity is great. Traditionally, in Britain at least, considerable emphasis is placed on the need for the therapist to undergo personal therapy or similar self-development experiences and for supervision to be a regular part of professional practice. Vital as these elements are, I doubt if they are sufficient to sustain and support the therapist who is committed to embracing his or her own spiritual yearnings and those of clients. I have attempted elsewhere to describe what it might mean for a therapist to develop a discipline which pays due regard to the spiritual dimension of his or her professional work (Thorne, 1994). For those who are nourished by the rituals and practices of a faith community this discipline will clearly be an extension of what may already be a well-developed rule of life, but for those who have no such allegiance the challenge is altogether more severe.

Recent research suggests, however, that no challenge is more relevant and that the well-being of many clients may depend on its successful accomplishment. Herbert Benson, Associate Professor of Medicine at Harvard Medical School and President of its Mind/Body Medical Institute, has published a book which no less an authority than M. Scott Peck has described as 'a gold mine of information about the integration of body, mind and soul' (Benson, 1996). Benson draws on numerous empirical research studies and concludes that human beings are literally programmed with a need for faith. What is more he demonstrates that the positive beliefs, particularly belief in a higher power, which we entertain as practitioners and as clients make a critical contribution to our physical health.

If we translate Benson's findings into the therapeutic arena it becomes clear that the therapist's belief system and his or her ability to have faith in the essentially positive forces at work in the cosmos have a profound contribution to make to the client's healing. Contrary to the often held view that therapy is an essentially value-free activity and that what matters is the therapist's competence and not his or her belief system, Benson's findings point to the central importance of what the therapist believes about the resources available to the client in his or her struggle for life. It goes without saying that the therapist who experiences daily that he or she is sustained by the powerful and loving forces of the cosmos is the more likely to become a beacon of hope and a channel of energy for the depressed and dysfunctional client. Hence the critical importance for the therapist of evolving and maintaining a spiritual discipline which ensures that his or her faith does not become depleted. Faith of this kind and its strengthening is not only an essential buttress against the therapist's own potential burn-out but, as Benson would have it, a matter of central importance for every client with whom he or she comes into relationship.

Faith in the relationship

The eternal now and the quality of presence

Benson's authoritative account of the overwhelming significance of the helper's faith and belief system serves as weighty and empirically based confirmation of studies undertaken in the 1960s and 1970s by Arthur Combs, the client-centred therapist and researcher and his colleagues. Reviewing the outcome of an original study in 1962 and of thirteen additional studies in the years following, Combs concluded that what makes a good helper is 'a direct outcome of the helper's perceptual organization or belief system' (Combs, 1986).

Furthermore, Combs and his associates went a long way towards identifying some of the major characteristics of the belief system which facilitates client movement. Foremost among these characteristics was the therapist's beliefs about himself or herself and about the people who formed the clientele. Combs discovered that effective helpers held a positive view of themselves, had confidence in their own abilities and professed a feeling of oneness with others. Not surprisingly, perhaps, they viewed the people who came to them for help as trustworthy, able, dependable and of great value. Another significant finding of the Combs inspired studies was the central importance of the therapist's beliefs about the ultimate purposes of society, of the helping activity and of human relationships. In short, meaning mattered for it determined purposes and priorities.

It is clear that if as a therapist I value myself and my client highly I shall also attach great importance to the relationship between us for it is in the context of the relationship that our essential worth is experienced and mutually reinforced. What is more, it is in the relationship that I shall experience my oneness with the other and shall discover that in our relating we transcend our normal limitations. It is my growing conviction that it is precisely because of the potential for transcendence which therapeutic relating offers if it is based on a deep valuing of self and the other, that both consciously and unconsciously people are increasingly turning to therapists for love, healing and meaning. The relationship itself is what matters for it can be the vehicle of transcendence and transformation and gives access to a spiritual apprehension of reality which endows suffering with meaning and offers hope.

If I believe – as I do – that it is in our relating that we unlock the door to our glory, I shall enter each therapeutic relationship with a sense of awe at what may unfold. I know that I cannot love another into being and that I cannot heal through my own will. Nor can I inject meaning into the life of a person who is tortured by meaninglessness and lack of purpose. What I can do, though, is be thoroughly present to the other with all that I believe about myself, about him or her, about our essential interconnectedness and about the infinite resources by which we are surrounded. I can be fully present to him or her with all that I believe about the arbitrary constraints of time and space and about eternity which is now. I need give voice to none of this for it is what I believe that matters, not what I articulate. It is what I believe that irradiates my presence and determines how I am, what I say and how I behave towards this other whose value is no less and no greater than my own. Carl Rogers towards the end of his life spoke of those 'transcendental' moments when 'simply my *presence* is releasing and helpful' and when 'my inner spirit has reached out and touched the inner spirit of the other' (Rogers, 1986: 198). I have no doubt that Rogers was writing here of precisely the experience for which countless people yearn who cross the therapist's threshold. This is the moment of healing, of knowing one's belovedness and of sensing the meaning which is inherent in being and becoming.

Different therapeutic orientations and the deposit of faith

The language of the previous paragraph is unashamedly mystical but I would claim that it is buttressed and inspired by the rigorous empiricism of the likes of Combs, Benson and Rogers. I do not feel myself to be wreathed in incense mist as I write of our 'glory' and of knowing our 'belovedness'. On the contrary, I see myself as solidly based in experience and simply facing facts. Indeed, I have reached the point where I sometimes think that it is precisely because the data are so obvious that they are no longer accessible to modern consciousness, caught up as it is in the seductive complexities of the electronic age and in the conveying of undifferentiated information which threatens to overload our feverish brains and drive us mad.

It is when I remember that I and those who share my beliefs about therapy and its task have a long and noble lineage that I draw comfort and cease to fret that not all therapists share, as yet, my convictions. I recognize that in past centuries the great religions of the world and particularly their finest and often most misunderstood luminaries have consistently proclaimed the essential value of humankind, the primacy of human relating and the ultimate claims of the transcendent. This, I recognize, is the deposit of faith which I jealously guard in the vocation to which I am called as a therapist. What is more, I am sometimes persuaded that because it is supremely in the relationship that I must witness to my faith there is less chance that I shall be able to conceal my lukewarmness or my lack of commitment. Therapeutic relationships are a more demanding test of belief, fidelity and authenticity than most of the public and liturgical arenas of religious practice could ever be.

The work of the psychological technician

I cannot pretend, of course, that all therapists and counsellors can and would wish to conceptualize themselves in the way that I do and there are certainly those who would disassociate themselves completely from what they would perceive as grandiosity or sheer delusion. As I have suggested earlier, there is much in me which both respects and somewhat envies those therapists who work with limited objectives and derive their satisfaction from the slight but significant shifts in their clients' behaviour or way of thinking. For me this is the work of the skilled psychological technician and I honour it as such. I know, too, that for many clients this is the kind of help they want and that their lives are the better for it. Yet I sometimes suspect that those who practise in this way are themselves also prompted primarily by a love for and a concern for their fellow human beings which they cannot openly acknowledge in the marketplace for fear of the ridicule of their fellow practitioners.

When my colleague at the University of East Anglia, David Howe, came to investigate the experience of clients in therapy he discovered that what mattered to them seemed to have little to do with their therapist's training, knowledge or even therapeutic skills. Instead, what seemed to make the difference was the quality of the relationship they experienced and the quality of the person with whom they were in relationship. It seemed not to matter in the least whether the therapist was an analyst, a behaviourist, a person-centred practitioner or a Gestaltist. For the clients what matters, it seems, is that those of us who call ourselves therapists are high quality human beings capable of relating to them in ways which enable them to face their pain, to give expression to it and to find meaning in it (Howe, 1993). For me those are the marks of a person who knows, whether he or she openly acknowledges it or not, that it is through the relating and the valuing of the other that healing forces are released. This is the private and covert faith, I would suggest, of many of those who would publicly refute such an apparently 'mystical' attribution.

The counsellor/therapist – a new priesthood for a new age?

I have argued that it is no longer possible for therapists to ignore the spiritual dimension and that those who choose to engage fully with it may be implicitly accepting the mantle which in the past belonged to the priest or pastor. There is, however, a significant difference. The priest was and remains the representative of a particular faith community and of its beliefs and practices. The therapist owes no such allegiance. Instead he or she is committed to the primacy of the spiritual in the sum total of human experience and to the faithful accompaniment of his or her fellow human beings in their quest for spiritual truth and enlightenment. There is no one road to be followed in such accompaniment but many and various paths to be explored in the sharing of the pains and joys, confusions and ecstasies, betrayals and fidelities of unique but interconnected human beings the world over.

This is not the irresponsible dabbling in a kind of spiritual anarchy as it is sometimes critically caricatured; it is rather an embracing of an exhilarating freedom which has its anchorage in the paradox of individual uniqueness and the corporate identity of the human family. Through his or her daily immersion in the intimacy of unpredictable relationships and through faith in their efficacy as the context for spiritual encounter, the therapist knows that 'I am because we are and we are because I am'. This is not spiritual anarchy but an acceptance of what it means to be fully human and a refusal to avoid responsibility by seeking refuge in a dogmatic formulation of spiritual reality.

Many religions have claimed and claim still to be 'open to the spirit'. The therapist who dares to offer his or her client spiritual accompaniment has no option but to embrace such openness if he or she is to be faithful to the task. It is my conviction that as the new millennium approaches the demand for such companions will intensify as the dire and dreadful outcomes of a disintegrating materialistic culture become more apparent. It may be that the old religions will be reinvigorated and will offer new inspiration, but for many it will be the therapists who will keep the vision alive of a way of being which does justice to the true stature of humankind. That is, if the therapists are able to accept as theirs the responsibility of so awesome a task.

Folie de grandeur and the prevention of inflation

Humility does not come from a denial of ability or of responsibility. It is rather the result of acceptance of self and a recognition of the need for interdependence. When I am tempted to think of myself as a prophet or seer and of therapists as the potential saviours of the human race, I tell myself at one and the same time not to be absurd and to take myself more seriously. It is then that I recognize that to follow a calling is to proceed in the faith that the resources for the task are to be found not in puffing myself up but in allowing myself to be the recipient of those very things which are demanded of me. The wheel comes full circle: if I am in some mysterious but planful way to be a source of love, healing and meaning for others, I have no option but to open myself to the love and healing that others offer me and in so doing to deepen the meaning of their lives and mine. Seen in these terms the role of the therapist, as I would have it, is no longer merely an awesome responsibility: it is the opportunity to accept wholeheartedly the privilege of hastening forward the evolution of the human spirit.

References

Benson, H. (1996) *Timeless Healing: The Power and Biology of Belief.* London: Simon and Schuster.
Birkerts, S. (1994) *The Gutenberg Elegies.* Boston: Faber and Faber.

Browning, D. (1987) *Religious Thought and the Modern Psychologies*. Philadelphia: Fortress.

Combs, A. (1986) What makes a good helper?, *Person-Centered Review*, 1 (1): 51–61.

Howe, D. (1993) *On Being a Client*. London: Sage.

Jones, S.L. (1994) A constructive relationship for religion with the science and profession of psychology, *American Psychologist*, 49 (3): 184–99.

Rogers, C.R. (1986) A client-centered/person-centered approach to therapy, in I.L. Kutash and A. Wolf (eds), *Psychotherapist's Casebook*. San Francisco: Jossey-Bass. pp. 197–208.

Thorne, B. (1993) Spirituality and the counsellor, in W. Dryden (ed.), *Questions and Answers on Counselling in Action*. London: Sage. pp. 71–6.

Thorne, B. (1994) Developing a spiritual discipline, in D. Mearns and B. Thorne, *Developing Person-Centred Counselling*. London: Sage. pp. 44–7.

14

Recognition and Professional Status

Judith Baron

Recognition and professional status for counsellors and psychotherapists do not necessarily go hand in hand. However, the latter certainly depends on the former. Both have the potential to benefit client and practitioner. The designation of professional status will, in addition to recognition, depend in any society on a number of normative, legal and fiscal factors relevant to the moment. The practitioner who wants to achieve professional status needs to have a mechanism in place through which to understand and work with such variables and this is most likely to be achieved by coming together in association.

Examples of different designations of 'professional' can be found in VATA (1983) for tax purposes and in the Monopolies and Mergers Commission paper (1970) for occupational groupings. The elements of such definitions are not necessarily similar, even when clearly defined, and after that the public may not necessarily accept the definitions. For example, they may not readily equate the business manager with the nutritionist, doctor or bishop, counsellor or psychotherapist. This explanation of positioning, influence and mediation with the public is not something that individual practitioners can readily undertake on their own. Practitioners need to come together to create a credible public voice to do all this and to ensure recognition is deserved and status not abused.

In any contractual relationship there has to be gain by both parties in order for work to move forward or both sides need to perceive the potential for gain. Counsellors and psychotherapists stand to gain a great deal from recognition and professional status. Power, authority and employment are just some gains to be named. The public with whom they interface needs to see a gain too. This is why measures of effectiveness, competence and client satisfaction are so important to the field. If they cannot be found, the practitioner aspiring to professional status and recognition might as well shut up shop and go home. However, they are being found and documented and are referred to elsewhere in this book.

This move to demonstrate effectiveness and quality assurance represents a cultural shift. We now live in the technological and contract culture age where such measures are the name of the game. Practitioners cannot ignore this and descriptions and definitions of any form of counselling and psychotherapy which rely on 'road to Damascus' conversion or enlightenment and which question the client's ability to access her or his own thought processes without manipulation by a knowing therapist will be doomed to failure and rejection in this current climate. However, a note of caution, for mysticism might return with any new cultural shift and by rejecting it entirely one may be throwing out something that will be valuable in the future. Opportunism might well be a justified criticism here.

Recognition

Counselling and psychotherapy, and those practising it, are now firmly placed in the eye and ear of the British public. Hardly a day goes by without a mention of some kind in the media. For example, on 5 January 1997 *The Sunday Times* devoted three pages of its magazine to counselling (White, 1997) and gave even more space to counselling in its main columns. The tenor of much of the media attention is not always favourable. However counsellors, psychotherapists and their clients are surviving the news-hungry and sensational onslaughts. This has been achieved mainly by careful preparation for the challenges of public scrutiny and by meeting client need.

The British Psychological Society (BPS) has kept a careful watch on the media and regularly reports media activities in its magazine *The Psychologist*. It keeps the public informed on its research findings and conference papers through the national press. The United Kingdom Council for Psychotherapy (UKCP) has an external relations officer. The British Association for Counselling (BAC) has had an active policy for public relations since 1987. This is a more interactive approach to the media. The timing for 'going public' was given careful consideration and its first paid public relations and media appointment was made in 1993. BAC had waited until it had members able to form media teams, undertake training, be available to journalists, had support to deal with enquiries and had an administrative infrastructure to support members. Co-operation from practitioners undertaking research and who could recount their findings was also essential and the input from the BAC Research Committee has been invaluable. BAC also had to be ready with standards of conduct and practice and methods of dealing with complaints. The process for all concerned has not been smooth and without pitfalls. Each individual practitioner needs to be aware of how easy it could be for them to jeopardize their peers, counselling and psychotherapy professions by poor practice and poor media relations.

Whatever the media may say or print, practitioners ultimately depend on clients for recognition and survival. The exact extent of take up of counselling and psychotherapy is unknown. However, it is known that there are extensive waiting lists for the free or subsidized services of such voluntary organizations as Relate and for help through the National Health Service. Brief therapeutic interventions are being explored and used as a way to overcome both funding and waiting list problems. The number of enquiries into one BAC service alone – Information and Publications – rose in total from 21,401 in 1995 to 22,130 in 1996. This included 5,981 enquiries from people seeking a counsellor in 1996. Thus to receive and to give counselling and psychotherapy is a need perceived, recognized and sought after by the public.

Recognition is given not only by the person voluntarily seeking help in the consulting room but also by the purchasers of counselling and psychotherapy services. Major institutions in the UK such as the NHS are putting money into the provision of counselling and psychotherapy services. In 1990 the Department of Health offered general practitioners between 70 and 100 per cent reimbursement of the costs of hiring counsellors and other ancillary staff in the provision of primary care. The NHS Executive *Review of NHS Psychotherapy Services in England* (NHS, 1996) refers repeatedly to psychological therapies, including counselling, which should be co-ordinated and used effectively across primary and secondary care and between different secondary care providers. This report also draws attention to and underlines the need for well-targeted treatments, research evidence on therapeutic outcomes and cost efficiency, along with the need for proper training and professional accountability. Recognition, registration and professional status and accountability are obvious needs for the practitioner who wishes to practise within this society institution, the NHS.

Other organizations in our society embrace counsellors and psychotherapists among their services. There are growing numbers of employee assistance programmes. A report from ICAS on *EAPs and Counselling Provision in UK Organizations* (Reddy, 1993) reported that over 80 per cent of companies were testing counselling as a means of employee support at that time. The National Lottery organizers, Camelot, offer a counselling service to those winning large amounts of money. The emergency services routinely offer debriefing and counselling to their officers.

Not only is there recognition by those who use counsellors and related services, but educational institutions recognize the occupational group by providing training. BAC received 4,740 enquiries about counsellor training in 1996 and had 467 entries in its training directory. The cynic could say that the institutions are jumping on to a lucrative bandwagon. However, the view of counselling and psychotherapy as occupations with academic standing and a knowledge base is one shared with the Advice, Guidance, Counselling and Psychotherapy Lead Body (AGC&PLB), originally under the wing of the Department of Employment and Education. The standards evolved for these qualifications have been written to incorporate the knowledge base required to demonstrate competent practice and qualifications and will be available at Level 5, often acknowledged as an entry requirement for a profession. So recognition and professional status are likely to come together. In November 1996 the government issued a position paper on higher level vocational qualifications, putting this more clearly into perspective and suggesting higher level NVQs/SVQs to meet continuing professional development needs (DFEE, 1996).

Counsellors, psychotherapists and counselling psychologists, and their systems of voluntary and self-regulation, have obviously gone a long way towards achieving the recognition so many practitioners want. However there are dangers and threats to keeping and maintaining this position. There is some backlash from other professions. Examples of attack from other professionals include that of Dr Myles Harris who believes that labelling creates a magic to which there is no substance (Harris, 1994) or that of Dr Raj Persaud writing in *Counselling* (1996). Criticism from within, constructive as well as destructive, is detailed by Howard (1996). There is also the live possibility that practitioners will themselves destroy the recognition they have been trying so hard to achieve through dissent within their own professional groupings.

In 1982 the UKCP was set up as an autonomous organization having been nurtured by the BAC. In 1991 the British Confederation of Psychotherapists (BCP) was formed in a manner that could be construed as a reaction by the psychoanalytical psychotherapy schools of thought to the formation of UKCP which includes those practising under a much wider conceptualization of psychotherapy theories and techniques. BCP also has its own register. The BPS established in 1901, created the Charter of Counselling Psychologists in 1992 and BAC helped foster and now holds the UK Register of Counsellors established in 1996. In any search for a coherent system of statutory registration it could be said that such fragmentation of the field leads to the question of what exactly is it that one is being asked to recognize and thus regulate. At some point practitioners, through their associations, need to come together in purposeful debate and find clear joint directives that relate to client and public need as well as practitioner needs and aspirations.

Recognition goes beyond the shores of the UK. Information technology has now put practice into the international arena and more particularly into the infrastructure of the European Union. This is particularly important for those calling themselves 'counsellors' rather than psychotherapists because, unlike other continents such as Australasia and North America, the term counsellor has not been widely used in Europe. First, counsellors need to be able to describe and gain recognition for the service they provide. Second, they need to respond to the wide cultural variations they will become exposed to and the impact this should have on practice. Even within the newly formed European Association for Counselling it is evident that a purely Western or Anglocentric model of counselling is often not appropriate. This is particularly so within countries where ideas of individual liberty and freedom of expression are alien and where poor communication links and geography rule out face-to-face or telephone counselling. On a more practical note, practitioners will have to be informed on what appropriate qualifications, training and equivalencies, both within and between countries, are required before they can take advantage of mobility of labour through the transparent borders of the EU. It is to this end, that is, gaining recognition of counselling and psychotherapy in all its forms, that professional bodies have been setting up registration systems, statutory, self-regulatory or voluntary, which can be recognized in some special way both by their own government and by the EU and its member states.

In summary, recognition and professional status do not necessarily go together. The many moves towards registration are, however, very important in the context of professional recognition because any system of registration which implements the standards set for the occupational grouping with the purpose of informing and protecting the public and users of the service is an important component of any definition of a profession. Practitioners do need to heed the warning that a system which is used or seen to be used for the prime purpose of protecting the practitioner is highly likely to fail in this current climate of deregulation, citizen's rights, charters and contractual relationships (Baron, 1996).

Professional status

There are many and varied definitions of a profession. Definitions are usually based on what are seen to be a profession's essential charac-teristics rather than that which is seen to flow from the label pro-fessional. Yet the aspiring or emerging professions are often accused of being interested in the flow which includes bargaining power, social status, remuneration, international acceptance and mobility of labour. Yet what is wrong with accepting these benefits if the basis for them is true achievement and a valued and effective service for the client?

Here we need to consider the perceived essential characteristics of a profession or professional. Value, effective and good service are dealt with elsewhere. The Monopolies and Mergers Commission (1970) believed the professional should process and offer to some degree: a specialist skill and service; intellectual and practical training in a well-defined area of study; detachment and integrity; a direct personal relationship based on confidence, faith and trust; a collective sense of responsibility for maintaining the competence and integrity of the profession; certain methods of attracting business and an affiliation to a body which tests competence and regulates standards of competence and conduct. Other attributes defining the professional include an allegiance more aligned to the profession than to the setting or employer, a broad theoretical base to the work, higher educational qualifications, proven intellectual skills and discretion in the workplace with the individual able to work autonomously and take on multiple responsibilities. Basic to the work of the professional is a relationship of trust, accountability to the client and society and set standards against which to judge one's work. The characteristic which counselling and psychotherapy does not include, and which is becoming much less evident in established professions such as medicine, is that the practitioner does not exercise personal judgement on behalf of a client (Baron, 1996).

Professional recognition relates to the commitment of the individual practitioner to the rules of the profession and for personal accountability. This is well documented in publications such as BAC's *Code of Ethics and Practice for Counsellors* (1993). This is not a commitment through a third party or a supervisor although the route to such a commitment could be assisted by them in some way such as sponsorship; it is a personal one. The potential practitioner needs to know that they are expected to take this personal responsibility for their work before they embark on the career, just as they will expect their clients to take personal responsibility for their decisions and actions as a result of the contractual counselling or psychotherapeutic relationship.

The list of characteristics and achievements required for a counsellor or psychotherapist is a long and difficult one for the individual to achieve. It is known from experience in the field and the wide background of members of organizations such as BAC and UKCP that not everyone currently designated as a counsellor or psychotherapist aspires to or can achieve all the characteristics such as higher educational qualifications or multiple responsibilities in the workplace. The individual needs to consider how far on the road to professional status they wish to go or are able to go while still valuing themselves and being valued for their personal achievements, ambitions and service to clients. What could now be fundamental is how the entry to the profession is set and that this is understood and accepted by the wider occupational group with respect and not envy.

Will this entry point be at the level of registration for independent practice, or at a point which does not devalue or fail to recognize the many and wide skills now required for the 'corporate' practitioner. These are matters which urgently need to be addressed in order to shape the emerging professional profile. There is no longer a 'tidy professional activity' (Howard, 1996). Practitioners need to consider carefully the options opened up by the ingredients described for Level 5 National Vocational Qualifications (NVQs) (NCVQ, 1995) where skills additional to direct delivery of service are outlined. In many cases NVQs could, for example, also bypass the traditional element of higher educational qualifications for professionals by substituting evidence of competence and expertise.

> Competence which involves the application of a significant range of fundamental principles and complex techniques across a wide and often unpredictable variety of contexts. Very substantial personal autonomy and

often significant responsibility for the work of others and for the allocation of substantial resources features strongly, as do personal accountabilities for analysis and diagnosis, design, planning, execution and evaluation. (NCVQ, 1995: 11)

Yet the government's position paper on higher level vocational qualifications (DFEE, 1996) also acknowledges that for many professions definitions of qualifications by bodies of employers who have no precise knowledge of the requirements of the profession as is implied by the NVQ process is inappropriate. It is suggested that groups of professionals or bodies representing them need to be consulted and joint work in partnership with such bodies and industry-based national training organizations is seen to be a likely way forward for defining professional status. This is further evidence that to achieve such consultation practitioners in the field need to come together in positive partnership to use the opportunity that exists to shape the profession and the benefits which deservedly flow from it.

Summary

In my view the vast majority of people working as counsellors and psychotherapists deserve recognition for their work and the level of this work defined as a professional activity. The public, through their demonstrated interest and understanding of the use of the activities, give that recognition. Exceptional hard work, commitment and willingness to be open to public scrutiny and awareness of the choices on the part of the practitioners are demonstrated in the chapters of this book. Any self-deprecation or unsubstantiated attack on colleagues by the therapist cannot be beneficial to the client. Regular review of competence and quality of performance on the part of the therapist is beneficial to clients. Aspiring to and achieving professional status in the manner and route currently being undertaken is the best guarantee of help for clients. Individual practitioners need to stand up and be counted and come together in association to present, promote and regulate their work. Unresolved differences between competing collegial organizations and between counsellors and psychotherapists assist neither practitioner nor client. They are not needed, deserved or useful.

References

BAC (1993) *Code of Ethics and Practice for Counsellors*. Rugby: British Association for Counselling.

Baron, J.R. (1996) The emergence of counselling as a profession, in R. Bayne, I. Horton and J. Bimrose (eds), *New Directions in Counselling*. London: Routledge.

DFEE (1996) *Higher Level Vocational Qualifications: Government Position Paper*. London: Department for Education and Employment.

Harris, M. (1994) *Magic in the Surgery*. Social Affairs Unit: Bury St Edmunds.

Howard, A. (1996) *Challenges to Counselling and Psychotherapy*. London: Macmillan.

Monopolies and Mergers Commission (1970) *The Supply of Professional Services*. London: Monopolies and Mergers Commission.

NHS Psychotherapy Services in England (1996) *Review of Strategic Policy*. London: Department of Health.

NCVQ (1995) *NVQ Criteria and Guidance*. London: NCVQ. p. 11.

Persaud, R. (1996) The wisest counsel?, *Journal of the British Association for Counselling*, 7 (3): 199–201.

Reddy, M. (ed.) (1993) *EAPs and Counselling Provision in UK Organisations*. Milton Keynes: ICAS.

Value Added Tax Act (1983). Item 1(c) of Group 9 of Schedule 6. London: HMSO.

White, L. (1997) Speaking your mind, *The Sunday Times Magazine*, 5 January: 38.

15

Envy and Gratitude: Attitudes to Collaboration

Cassie Cooper

The philosophy of half and half

If we look at the differences in ideologies which exist in any group of professional psychotherapists and counsellors, not only are there fundamental differences in theory and training, conviction and method but also a stormy sea of rivalry about status, salary scales, types of qualifications, university, college or private training organizations, statutory, voluntary or private practice.

It is an acknowledged problem of this mythical community that there are different theoretical schools of thought in the field which are usually labelled by the names of the school founders. Existing differences in theory and technique arouse deep emotion in psychotherapists and counsellors who are, and this is partly in the nature of their work, defensively over-identified with their specific views. Both will have learned their therapeutic skills in emotional and highly charged student–teacher relationships of long and intensive duration. Different courses in therapy and counselling develop their own allegiances in groups, and more specifically language. Graduates need to reinforce their view of life by expressing contempt for each other. Often they give the impression of being bunkered in a fall-out shelter of their own making with filtrated air, water and, sadly, filtrated ideas which cause a real communication failure.

Psychotherapists and counsellors have been debating since the early 1970s whether and how they could combine within a single recognized profession, with some form of statutory registration. Collaboration with colleagues is often highlighted as the expressed desire of the profession but a perception of the competitive processes inherent in society, of necessity, impinges on the process of psychotherapy and of counselling. However, it is important to stress that the theoretical points of divergence and difficulty which I have stressed have always been equalled by an intense desire within the therapeutic community for peaceful co-existence. We long to be able to function together, we wish we could integrate and be one. We form societies, groups, associations and sections. Witness the consistent emergence of strong parental figures to contain, confine and cajole the opposing factions in an attempt to restrict our divergencies to a subterranean rumble.

However, psychotherapy and counselling are individualized private activities and sharing these experiences can be difficult. They are also emotionally demanding activities which can often leave the therapist or counsellor feeling inadequate, uncertain, frustrated and angry and, when it comes to attempting collaboration, very defensive. It is a unique activity in which practitioners are put on their mettle as instruments of treatment. This instinctive quality, instead of providing the individual with a solid base, seems to be the source of collective shame, unease and guilt. This sets up problems of its own when considering the substantial need inherent in each psychotherapist and counsellor for dependable support and replenishment.

The proliferation of professional institutions is not entirely differentiated by significant stances in approach and theory. A major factor in adhering to a special group seems to stem from the individual's need to find a fully supportive group with which to identify. Powerful peer groups exude a certainty and a sense of being 'right' in their client work. But only very experienced therapists and counsellors know that certainty and rightness are unattainable. Understanding and accepting these concepts is fundamental in tackling the problems of coming together as a profession.

Fission is a natural law and yet as we move towards the year 2000 psychotherapists and counsellors involved in the process of collaboration (both within and between UKCP and BAC and now latterly the British Psychological Society) invariably experience violent antagonisms and intimate alliances as accusations and counter accusations about eligibility and accreditation flow back and forth. The forceful vehemence exhibited at annual general meetings of constituent members seems to furnish satisfactions of its own that collaboration and acknowledgement of orderly and rational differentiations cannot provide.

The multiplication of therapies, theorists and institutions which appear to serve the community from the cradle to the grave obviously serve at this stage to give both psychotherapists and counsellors reassurance about their professional identity.

Feelings of insecurity reinforce the need to cling to one's own professional group and if these groups are to maintain their cohesion, then it may be felt inadvisable to scrutinize possible internal problems and to open themselves to other ideas and ways of working. Yet, it probably is safer to assume sameness and not rock the boat too much, but without debate and without scrutiny it is difficult to give credence to a definition of a professional role. So there exists definition only by exclusion.

Cynicism, folly and camouflage

Clients mobilize anxiety about practitioner inadequacy and lack of further development and training. What better way of dealing with these inadequacies than to populate the therapeutic world with organ-izations that can be seen to offer less competence and rigour, who ignore their own feared deficiencies and ensure that it is more comfortable to project them on to others.

Collaboration is a touchy subject which appears to make many therapists feel guilty. Surely the time has come for us to manage these feelings in a less primitive way? Theories and techniques are important in training but they have only a limited application. If growth is stulti-fied in the therapist, what is the effect on the client?

This chapter seeks to argue that while individualism seems to make some psychotherapists and counsellors feel guilty, individualism can be regarded not necessarily as a constraint on professional development and professional attitudes, but rather as a characteristic which can be taken more positively into account in the collaborative process.

Sigmund Freud, Melanie Klein, Donald Winnacott, John Bowlby, Albert Ellis, Carl Rogers, George Kelly and others did not consider their own theoretical orientations as a close approximation to divinely inspired truth. They entertained the possibility that their students might go beyond them in apprehending the reality of the therapeutic process. Such a sense of tentativeness about our present theorizing might especially lead us to maximize the choice-making behaviour of the therapeutic professions to precipitate them into discovering their own interpretation of the collaborative experience. It is therapists of this ilk who will make the discoveries that will enrich the whole field.

Each psychotherapist and counsellor has in the past tended to see him or herself in one or other of the partisan groups I have mentioned, identification with a specific group being a necessary external represen-tation of a similar need within oneself. But over and above and around the walls of our own small professional communities there exist other caring professions with their own highly developed systems and expectations; the psychiatrist and psychologist who function in a hospital, the social worker in an agency, the academic in an educational institution. Expec-tations differ in each environment which reinforce the filtration necessary to the 'bunker' system by encouraging a hidebound modality which in the end can only produce authority bound attitudes and prejudice.

What happens to therapists who refuse to recognize their narrowing attitudes and skills, their sheer ignorance and the gaps in their knowl-edge which result from denial of their developmental needs which can only be met by co-ordination and collaboration of professional principles through a functional view of our professional community?

In 1912 Freud, addressing himself to the stresses endured by the practising analyst, cautioned that therapeutic ambition, above all, should not be allowed to get in the way of achieving the desired aim to put aside all feelings, all human sympathy, in an effort to concentrate one's mental forces on the single act of working with the transference as skilfully as possible.

In working with their adult clients, psychotherapists and counsellors are brought up sharply and consistently to confront their own fallibility. To understand that weakness and illness, envy, malice and manipulation, passion, sexual desire and shame are not merely the province of their clients. In identifying us as practising therapists we take it upon us to translate the theoretical themes to which we have been introduced in the course of training and, in particular, as Freud predicted, into the behaviour we have learnt, to identify these themes not only in our patients, our clients, our colleagues, but more importantly in ourselves.

We learn the strategies we employ to live our daily lives. Bulging caseloads, missed meals, traffic jams, balanced against the needs of husbands, wives, lovers, children, parents, friends. What overextends our capabilities and our resources? When it is appropriate to offer help to someone in a crisis and how far does one go in taking responsibility for someone else's problems when we live in a world which includes so many unresolved problems of our own? We can deny that such problems exist, often distorting the evidence so that things appear to be satisfactory. We are reassured that psychotherapists and counsellors have regular supervision so they must be on the right track and there is always the possibility of signing on for yet another training course. This is our profession's chosen penance for subsuming uncomfortable feelings which are difficult to acknowledge. Coping, conning, but collaborating – now there's a different thing? As a result many people in the therapeutic profession have become frustrated, disillusioned and anxious about their chosen discipline and their chosen theoretical stance. It may well be that the splintering of the field into several schools of thought and its over-institutionalization have played a part in the declining prestige of our work.

Free enquiry, free thought, free speech

While the conceptualization of the therapeutic encounter in an interpersonal frame of reference can be a major inspiration, its incompleteness, limitations and misdirections can constantly frustrate the therapist. In our violent society the interpersonal theory of therapy has encouraged therapists to look into other disciplines in order to learn something from related fields which may or may not help their adult clients. There is the feeling that they need to stay in close contact with the biological, social and psychological sciences as a complementary frame of reference to their speciality.

Working with adult clients they find themselves constantly fumbling and stumbling over ideological, political and personal barriers. How can this be addressed? Many of our clients show a genuine if confused concern with moral issues, with questions of social justice, violence, sexual and racial discrimination. Most of them have abused ideals.

Therapists and their clients have few illusions about the discrepancies between their own pretensions and performances. They are often acutely conscious of not living up to their own ideals and to the extent to which they may fall short of what they might expect of themselves. In particular, an important concern for many thoughtful people in the field is that in its present form the psychological therapies have not met their social obligation of coping efficiently with major mental disorders.

A haunting theme of our time suggests that the rapid transformation in Western society of social, scientific and institutional orderings is shattering yesterday's assumptions and standards of human belief and action. This transformation is offering little direction that guarantees qualitatively worthwhile human survival. Robert Nisbet (1975) has suggested that the West is in a 'twilight age' and goes on to describe such an age as one in which processes of decline and erosion of institutions are more evident than those of genesis and development, something like a vacuum obtains in the moral order for large numbers of people. He postulates that human loyalties, uprooted from accustomed soil, can be seen tumbling across the landscape with no scheme of larger purpose to fix them and that there is a widely expressed sense of degradation of values and corruption of culture. When the sense of estrangement from community is strong, the need to be seen to be right and in the right has the resultant effect of professional rigidity.

More recently Nathan Field puts it like this:

> It is entirely admirable that we should aim to become better psychotherapists. But where this becomes an obsession with the correctness of therapeutic technique it may prove counter-productive. Too great a striving for perfection on the part of the Therapist does not help the patient it only re-enacts the compulsion to perfection from which the patient himself very likely suffers. Not only is it human to err, error itself and *the capacity to recover from it* can provide both therapist and patient with unique opportunities for insight and personal growth. (Field, 1992: 139)

Into the vacuum of the twilight and the particularities has crept power, centralized in nature, corporate in scope. It is against a background of such an implied assessment that this chapter came to be written.

Perhaps the economic uncertainties of the industrial revolution have led us to become obsessed with work, with achievement and with acquiring knowledge or skills of commercial value. Our youth, however, is rightly protesting against the denials of the power of feelings in human development; and our greater affluence with increasing time to contemplate our lives is also pressing us towards the fuller recognition of what is going on inside ourselves.

A further problem involves more than the need to share the new tasks of the future. The difficulties here are seriously affected by failures in the earlier stages of human development. Individuals who have not developed a secure or strong enough central self, and, indeed, what security they have may be diminished by a threatened rise in the relative strength of their subselves. Such imbalances are most commonly seen in adolescence but they may be precipitated by many later changes. At the other end of the life cycle, we are all familiar with the person who goes to pieces on retirement, or with the loss of a spouse or of some especially valued possession. In the adolescent, it is the drive towards new relationships occasioned by the development of sexuality which evokes profound anxieties leading to massive withdrawals from others or to impulsive, ill-adapted attempts to cope with the new tensions. With older people, we see individuals who have managed to cope with rather immature dependent needs by surrounding themselves with particularly undemanding people or jobs they could safely use. If these generalizations concerning the development of an individual under the duress of modern life in Western society possess any degree of significance, they bear profound implications for counselling and psychotherapy.

It is fundamental to the training of some counsellors and psychotherapists that each participant should have personal therapy. To adhere to such an ideal within the orbit of UKCP or BAC or The British Psychological Society would be to frustrate such a training programme before it could ever get off the ground. The exact setting of the requirements for entrance into specialist psychotherapy and counselling training becomes then an administrative decision based on a judicial, but not opportunistic, consideration of the relevant variables, including both social realities and available training possibilities. This means that with the prerequisites and requirements for embarking on such a career, the question of the varying professional background of those who are taught counselling and psychotherapy becomes very relevant. Trainers share the conviction that the proper practice of therapy and counselling represents a teachable body of skills acquired through a process of learning under supervision, and carry with it the overall assumption that no formal degree of licensure itself guarantees therapeutic skills.

Skill in therapy and counselling is something to be taught in addition to other specific training, whether in psychiatry, psychology, social work or in other clinical professions. But for each such discipline, minimal acceptance standards of admission and performance have been set by the executive group.

Both the UKCP and BAC evolved as voluntary groups, as an opportunity offered to those who had the stated prerequisites such as either a full or part-time commitment to counselling or psychotherapy and preferably a few years of actual experience in some form of therapy. Attendance and adherence to this first group depended on a voluntary decision and as such the then executive chose to take its time. The members chose originally to meet regularly purely as a symbol of identification with the stated purpose and function of a particular group. In this setting and as a measure of the skill with which the group was led, more and more eligible members began to participate. The formula 'you can come if you wish' led to a growing voluntary adherence. By the mid-1990s the groups had acquired a group cohesiveness and some common body of conviction and skill. This brought an interesting development. Yet another debate begun about professionalism. Who is eligible for admittance to the inner group – those who have struggled throughout the years? The original proposition 'you can come if you wish' is followed by a new stance 'you can come only if we allow'.

Viewed from the backbenches this struggle over eligibility for membership could be predicted; a little tardy perhaps, but in professional terms, the beginning of a true group structure. With the community and educational services belt-tightening to a stranglehold, it is not only the professional groups which display a newly developed concern with requirements and prerequisites.

Consideration is given to the fact that counselling and psychotherapy can mobilize a trainee's own anxieties. If these are not dealt with in training then the trainee is unlikely to help clients with difficulties in the same area. Trainees in psychotherapy and counselling, as in other disciplines, learn to some extent by identification with their teachers. It is recognized that such identification may be valuable, but it can be a disadvantage if it is extended to a copying of minor details, such as mannerisms and gestures, and a feeling that any deviation from this identification is in some way necessarily 'wrong'.

Does anyone really believe that these assumptions about competence and self-responsibility for continuous development have been either clearly understood or wholeheartedly accepted? How many new qualified therapists and counsellors, hotfoot from their respective training courses, have had emphasis placed on continuous training as a therapist's ability to perform and take responsibility for developing their capacities still further? Rather, emphasis is placed on the quality and quantity of supervision that such a therapist is expected to receive. This lets everyone off the hook.

Independence, originality and, therefore, dissent

What goes on in training is more frequently meritorious than shocking, but the intrusion of rivalry, paternalism, infantilization, defiance, submission struggles, and just plain ill temper is all too often disquieting. One could shrug off this observation by quoting to the emerging therapist words concerning the virtues and evils of all personal relations and perhaps on a note of cynicism add the remark 'that's life'.

We know that the most effective learning is that which is self-motivated. It is stimulated by normal impulses towards growth and reaches its highest level when associated with self-responsibility for achievement. It is unsound and limiting to have the achievement of education goals largely dependent on supervision as the main medium for learning, even if it does cover up for deficiencies in continued training and later development. New therapists do not entirely accept the fact that they have the ability to perform on the job. Their doubts are revealed in their anxiety to be given 'good' supervision. Nor is this anxiety confined to the person who is seeking a first counselling or therapist appointment. Much of it stems from the wish to be seen to be helpful to people, to be seen to be conscientious, but some of it is related to the inordinate value falsely placed on supervision as a priority means of learning and assuring good service. Psychotherapists or counsellors working in a hospital or university, unlike other functionaries within the same institutions, are alone in deciding the depth of their responsibility for identifying areas of competence, personal and practical ability or of its limitations. This includes identifying the gaps which exist in their theoretical knowledge or in the application of theory to practice or in the knowledge and understanding that they cannot work alone. There are special skills or problems in diagnosis, evaluation or treatment. There exist special abilities or limitations in dealing with various problems or personalities and the acknowledgement of personal reactions that enhance or interfere with client relationships. Making these identifications takes time. It can be accomplished only through a continuous collaborative experience integrating both theory and practice throughout the profession.

What happens to the psychotherapist or counsellor, in many institutions answerable to no one regarding professional development, who refuses to recognize narrowing skills and gaps in knowledge not only in day-to-day work with clients but in forming concepts derived and understood from an examination of groups of cases and other working practices? Regular self-assessment is a necessary basis for acknowledging areas of success and those which need continuous professional development, but does the word accountability ever appear on annual conference programmes? Is accountability satisfied when the therapist appears to be supervised? Who spells out for beginning or experienced practitioners that from the outset of employment in an institution or the private sector they should know that they will be held accountable for their work; for formulating thinking about clients prior to seeking supervisory assistance; for deciding what specific areas of work require consultation and collaboration with other agencies; for examining the trends in therapeutic counselling. Without ongoing training and development, without honing the edge of work, of understanding, all is lost in spite of the frequency with which they may attend meetings of their 'special' group.

In a work situation learning is not a specific goal in itself but is related to increasing one's ability to provide effective service. Personal growth cannot be set as a job requirement. As the therapist identifies developmental needs, it is he or she alone who has the privilege of deciding where and how these needs are to be met; how much reading is needed;

what classes or training events should be attended; when and how to seek supervision; when to seek help from other agencies. But it is only with ongoing training that a therapist, as in any other professional society, can gain assurance and skill in choosing the appropriate resources.

One result of this growth of knowledge and the urge to meet the emerging demands is that the professional workers have devised additional methods of developing their competence. As skills developed, professionals have become more 'professional'. Skills can become a way of helping some, but of not helping other people. If the client does not fit one's skill, one cannot do anything, or one does not want to do anything. Another effect is that as skills get more expert, the work of giving psychological help gets more technical. The professional begins to get absorbed in the technicalities of the work and can lose sight of the fact that the fundamental and basic factor in giving personal help is the concern of one human being for another. Related to the acquisition of more professionalism has been the understandable caution on the part of the groups with more developed skills towards the groups with less skill, and many inter-group rivalries have appeared. Difficulties arise most readily when groups are uncertain of what they are doing. Anybody who is in the psychotherapeutic field, from Samaritans to psychoanalysts, is uncertain or confused some of the time. For free collaboration, the limits of understanding and skills have to be readily acknowledged without any sense of failure. Sometimes professionals and other groups have behaved as though they were going to be put out of business when their limits were exposed. Fortunately, this insecurity is disappearing as the scale of needs is appreciated and as the value of many sources and kinds of personal help are recognized.

Great developments were stimulated in the post-war era when the NHS came into being. Needs became more pressing and psychoanalysts became concerned to share skills with others. More striking was the way in which various groups of non-professionals began to appear to fill the many gaps in the services, a response influenced by the knowledge about human problems that was being transmitted to the public by writers, dramatists and artists, and especially by newspapers, magazines and television. The Marriage Guidance Council had been established before the war, but it began to develop its services rapidly in the post-war era. Student counsellors also appeared in universities and colleges of further and higher education, a few in schools and in a new force of self-help groups, such as Alcoholics Anonymous, Gingerbread, Release, Gay Liberation, Samaritans, Child Line, the Terence Higgins Trust, Drug Concern. Even more recently phone-in radio programmes with their own form of 'agony aunt' have prospered.

Recognition of the scale of needs for personal help and the swell of personal services to meet these have not been without their difficulties. On the medical side, the whole training of a doctor and nurse is to diagnose the problem. The great advances in medical knowledge have enabled them to do this in much of their work. They are interested in identifying illness and the treatment which then follows. This has led medical staff to think of psychological problems and needs in the same way. Along with the almost impossible task of giving people with problems sufficient time to talk about them (still only ten minutes at a time), there is a resultant tendency to treat psychological problems as something best dealt with by a drug or a tranquillizer of some sort. Of course, there is a great pressure from the public for the doctors to take this stance because there are powerful wishes for magical solutions rather than to face the realities that underlie our psychological make-up. There is also the adoption of what might be termed a pseudo-scientific view of human life. In this respect, doctors are not alone, for many psychologists and others also share this outlook. Psychotherapists and counsellors who are involved in a caring relationship with others have found it very difficult to adopt this sort of simplistic approach. When studying isolated areas of human behaviour, the value of a reductive approach is very appealing, but the plain fact is that people are complex, that being a person and operating as a person, functioning on a personal level, requires a conceptual framework that does justice to these immensely complex forces. As a physicist said to one of his psychological friends when he had been watching a child at play, 'My work is child's play compared with the study of child's play.'

The need is vast for the kind of help offered by trained psychotherapists and counsellors and every effort continues to be made to try to meet it. To find ways of doing so requires research into methods which, while being effective, can also be seen to be economical of time and money. An adequate supply of people capable of practising therapy and counselling is also required. Such is the background against which this chapter is written. If we are to accept the need for collaboration between both psychotherapists and counsellors who have been trained in theoretically divergent modalities then we have to strike a balance between conflicting demands.

On the one hand, since flexibility and scope for development are essential components of collaborative practice, it is a mistake to define therapeutic modalities too precisely or to outline training schemes that are too rigid or constricting. On the other hand sound professional standards are established and for this purpose there must be a clear formulation of the therapeutic work that therapists set out to do, and the training that is necessary in order to practise competently.

People who work under the aegis of many differing agencies can be seen to utilize some of the theory and methods of dynamic psychotherapy. However, differences can be made categorically between the use of psychotherapeutic skills and the practice of therapy and counselling used by counsellors and therapists who have qualified and specialized according to the standards and training required by the two main professional organizations which exist in the UK.

A return to common sense

However, counselling (with various shades of interpretation and method) is a basic function in many occupational roles, sometimes playing a major part and at other times a minor one. After all the roots of counselling lie in many fields, in medicine, in law and the teaching professions, as also do the roots of psychotherapy and social work. One could take for a model the idea of a family tree whose roots are in the older professions of psychoanalysis and psychiatry, but whose branches are in counselling, guidance, pastoral care and social work. Dorothy Rowe, who has the reputation for straight talking, suggested that the choice of a label between the so-called 'talking' therapies was a matter of pretension.

> Psychiatrists do psychotherapy so do psychologists, nurses, social workers and occupational therapists. If people feel that psychotherapy is too pretentious a word to apply to what they do, they describe what they do as counselling. (Rowe, 1989: 8)

In training for both psychotherapist and counsellor it is expected that they will have a thorough grounding in one of the major theoretical systems of depth psychology and at least some acquaintance with the others. In the present state of modern psychological knowledge eclecticism is inevitable and welcome. Difficulties arise when this knowledge is the outcome of a superficial acquaintance with a number of theories. Eclecticism should be the result of a broadening in outlook arising from the integration of additional knowledge and concepts into a firmly based theoretical framework.

However the teaching and practice of psychotherapy and counselling have remained relatively static. Throughout the many years of development of the profession it has somehow failed to supersede certain illusory aspects of the original blueprint as to how the profession could and should be, and of its latter-day modifications. Neither compliance nor defiance in regard to standard therapeutic prescriptions has liberated us from our thraldom to long-standing verbal and social misperceptions. There is considerable evidence that the psychotherapeutic approach has lost ground as well as prestige in recent years. Perhaps this was to be expected to some degree in view of unrealistic expectations which had been fostered by both lay people and by professionals. Therapists talking among themselves bemoan a distinct reduction in the number of suitable clients. This is not something that we can exclusively trace to the growing number of qualified and unqualified practising counsellors. There are strong indications in the media that many people have become discouraged with the thought of a prolonged and expensive therapeutic involvement without the assurance of favourable results. In addition there is even uncertainty about some of the favourable results reported by the so-called 'successfully' treated patients.

Our differences run far deeper than the profession dares to admit. Clients often assume that all counsellors are basically talking about the same phenomena but attaching difference words to them in regard to therapeutic, non-therapeutic or anti-therapeutic procedures. Clients can experience a major jolt when they find that this assumption is clearly not true. One counsellor's concept of helping a client may well turn out to be another therapist's concept of damaging the client. We are no longer justified in the reassuring assumption that all experienced psychotherapists and counsellors merely speak in different tongues, while basically performing the same therapeutic operations. The differences are real and they exist both in content and in process. They manifest themselves at UKCP and BAC annual conferences in terms of role confusion and role conflict as well as in terms of misdirections in the informational and emotional flow. Our critics have grown more articulate and more mature.

Some of the criticism and disenchantment with counselling and related fields is by no means confined to the public and the media. Many counsellors have become frustrated and disillusioned with their chosen discipline and tried to expose it as if it were a perceptual distortion. Others have become strongly anti-analytic without any or much awareness of this having occurred. We can usually observe two extremes among this disenchanted group. Group One has become rigidly orthodox and/or super-biological while Group Two has gone in an opposite direction, displacing psychoanalytic theories and injecting a note of militant hopelessness with a blend of emotional mysticism. Both of these groups are undermining the true foundations of our discipline, good practice and a continuous process of collaborative learning and sharing with each other.

It may well be that the splintering of the field into many schools of thought and its over-institutionalization have played a part in the declining prestige of the talking therapies. Other disciplines do not share our personal cultism. Physicists do not distinguish between Newtonians, Plankians, Einsteinians, etc. This attitude is peculiar to psychotherapists, counsellors and religious sects. We also have the problems of professional role definition, the vagueness pertaining to technique and to the verification of treatment results as well as unrealistic expectations on both sides.

While some counsellors and psychotherapists in practice may well find the conceptualization of the therapeutic encounter in an interpersonal frame of reference to be a major inspiration, others may say that its incompleteness, limitations and misdirections can frustrate them greatly. The interpersonal theory of therapy should however encourage both psychotherapists and counsellors to look to other disciplines and to learn something from related fields.

It is folly within certain sections of the psychotherapeutic sphere to ignore the fact that Freudian analysis has made scientific progress regardless of the rigidity of a few diehard partisans. Likewise the practice of counselling has not stood still in spite of a tendency toward inbuilt conservatism. If some therapists regard themselves as secessionists, it is wrong to isolate themselves from a major body of knowledge and certainly wrong to deride or invalidate other therapeutic methods because they happen to be classical or orthodox in origin.

Let us consider the aspect of interpersonal postulates. This relates to the concept of collaboration and integration. It is thought that interpersonal processes not only exist but have force, which manifests itself in the tendency toward integration in an interpersonal situation. Integrating tendencies can be defined in terms of their goals which might be said to be reflected in all those situations in which two or more people tend to understand each other better in order to come to a clearer grasp of their particular little differences of views and impulses. These goals are to seek intimacy – a highly desirable interpersonal state.

In therapeutic terms it is assumed that the barrier to experiencing intimacy is a client's low self-esteem. The task of the therapist is then, by means of participant observation, to impinge on the parataxic field or self-esteem so that the client can gain a greater measure of satisfaction and feel more secure among people.

The achievement of ends

How then are practitioners going to achieve their therapeutic goals without having a workable frame of reference which makes allowances for the necessary adaptation required of therapist and client in the therapeutic process? How can intimacy be achieved unless the respective expectations of both participants come to the fore? We have to assume that the evolution of reciprocal attitudes between clients and their therapist is an essential factor before a meaningful shift in the client can take place.

There are several other considerations, however, in debating the way things stand in current psychodynamic and counselling practice and teaching.

In the natural process of living all human beings remain basically the same, while we all recognizably change externally and internally. We move on to different roles at different times and in different phases of the life cycle. These roles reflect the position in the life situation in which therapists are integrated. Life situations which may be relatively rigid or potentially flexible can reflect the possibility of the therapist's ability to create more effective, expressive and progressive roles in their personal lives, but also in their working roles.

If counsellors and psychotherapists are able to accept this concept of identity, that it is best conceptualized as a dynamic system or process, perhaps then they can surely move on from what increasingly appears to be a static entity, a preoccupation with the quest for peer group identity, alienation from the true self and a place of safety in which they lurk, contented by others who share similar, sometimes vague goals.

A sense of identity is reinforced by accepting a pattern of inter-dependence between theories, between the sharing of unique experiences, between the use of the therapist's own potentially unique endowment or equipment, and their interpersonal transactions within the existing socio-cultural matrix of schools of psychotherapy and counselling.

In this chapter I am appealing or strengthening, advancing and revitalizing the practice and teaching of the therapies, utilizing the concept of psychotherapists and counsellors working within a collabora-tive field. A thoughtful and sensitive application of dilation in breaking the present stalemate, where instead of entrenching oneself in theory the emphasis is placed on clarification of the expressive role of client and practitioner over and above the instrumental role. Again, an effort could be made to point to the necessity of grasping the significance of mental health as a focal consideration of organized human behaviour. This would lead to an acceptance of the dual function of any therapeutic approach: first, to use process and theory more effectively in the fight against mental illness and attitudes to mental illness; second, to use psychotherapy and counselling as a tool in promoting person-to-person intimacy. Finally, there is the necessity of sharing what we are taught and how we practise and to practise not dissimilarly to the way in which we teach.

As a profession counsellors and psychotherapists have not success-fully exploited the richness of possibilities connected with the analytic process. They have adhered too long to unworkable blueprints and they have also rebelliously ignored some of the more useful procedures, while getting bunkered down in their respective defensive shelters.

In the post-war years between 1950 and 1970 psychotherapists and counsellors started out with the potential for an interdisciplinary heritage which would have given an unprecedented opportunity, with combined effort, to make a major contribution to society. For this goal, however, they had to be relatively free of parochialism and to have clarity and pride in their respective professional roles. Instead, insistence on dissimilar traditions, defensive and deviating experiences, cover ups and neglect in training programmes have led to the evolution of divergent professional roles.

The creative potential remains dormant. While many counsellors and psychotherapists have contributions to make within a common frame of reference, they have been strangely fearful of studying their own functioning as a group. Opportunism hides behind professed loyalty to the ideas of famous figures or powerful people in the training hierarchy. What gets said or does not get said at association meetings is skewed towards pleasing the hierarchy with a view to later personal success. Members who make themselves useful and serve narcissistic as well as defensive needs for those in power are frequently elected to positions which might otherwise be allocated on different and more objective criteria. Thus the psychopathology of institutes whether orthodox or eclectic in a similar manner perpetuates a favourable climate for those who adhere to the 'good child' model. Those who can be seen to enter into covert alliances with their parental figures do so because they do not wish to separate and individuate.

As in any organization, and perhaps especially in BAC and UKCP, the pressure upwards comes with much distortion, displacement of feeling and a kind of psychopathic acting out. This is a fact that professionals do not like to face – and I include myself. Professionals see themselves predominantly as 'givers of service' by virtue of the so-called expertise they have gained. In human interaction, however, process is no respector of idealized virtue and group dynamics apply to elite professional groups of therapists as well as to the less prestigious business organizations. It seems to me that what we want to be is sadly lacking in human dignity and subject too much to our own indulgence and capitulation to bureaucratic and narcissistic needs. Our aims so often are puerile. As professionals, we have each settled into our own little enclave for minimum growth and maximum comfort, forgetting that how we act with each other, colleagues and clients is more important than status or knowledge. Bureaucratic climates traditionally foster the ossification of growth and do not facilitate the kind of process either in collaborative exchanges, interpersonal relationships or a treatment which makes for growth, lending itself rather to perpetuating inhibiting and unoriginal ideas and a degradation of the therapeutic process itself.

Society looks to us as counsellors and psychotherapists and here we stand in danger of becoming anachronisms by making a mockery of what we allegedly stand for. We risk becoming extinct unless we can adapt and make room for each other.

As a psychotherapist, I believe that in spite of a seemingly hostile press there has been some lessening in the phobic anxiety which occurs when mistakes are made in therapy. However, the overwhelming majority of currently published papers in reputable journals aim to demonstrate therapists' success, but rarely to expose any weakness. This is another loss to our profession; we learn as much from each other's mistakes as we do from our successes. In sharing our imperfections and our doubts, we will more easily come to understand them and hopefully, in time, to work more effectively. But again, if we place too much emphasis on correctness of boundaries or interpretations it will obscure the creative potential of our mistakes and the way we can recover from them. There is a professional collusion among our splintered associations which puts a heavy taboo on any concept of rethink or revision. There remains instead a collective anal obsession that places enormous strain on any one of us who is required to toe the line and to cope alone with self-doubt and challenging interpretations.

Klein (1957) suggests that 'the best interpretations serve to bring out the strongest envy'.

The 'good' professional member tends to be idealized and seen to be 'perfect' and 'trustworthy', but there is also an army of psychotherapists and counsellors who neither teach, publish or shine in supervision but who still provide help to their clients on a very wide range of presenting problems. The bunkered culture of exclusivity invalidates the quality of these quiet and undramatic practitioners who are deeply committed to their work, but do not wish to seek out, identify or feel at ease with rigid forums where they could pass on their approaches, attitudes and feelings.

> When differences are viewed as claims to position within a hierarchy of therapeutic tribes, divisiveness may overpower any potential for collaboration and mutual enhancement of standards. Divisiveness between the talking therapies diminishes our credibility as having a contribution to resolving the problems of modern society. A professional group which avoids replicating the divisiveness of modern society is much more attractive as a source of help for personal and social problems than professions which merely reflect the commonplace social divisions of the market place. In order to achieve such collaboration, it is important that we listen to each other and work together at local or national levels. (Bond, 1996: 33)

Crisis and change should produce a challenge for psychotherapists and counsellors. In meeting change head on they should recall that the adaptive growth needed by the personality to cope with stress situations is often best met by sharing and collaboration.

References

Bond, T. (1996) Competition or collaboration within the talking therapies, in I. James and S. Palmer (eds), *Professional Therapeutic Titles, Myths and Realities*. London: British Psychological Society, Division of Counselling Psychology Occasional Papers.

Field, N. (1992) The way of imperfection, *British Journal of Psychotherapy*, 9 (2).

Klein, M. (1957) *Envy and Gratitude*. London: Tavistock.

Nisbet, R. (1975) *Twilight of Authority*. New York: Oxford University Press.

Rowe, D. (1989) Foreword, in J. Masson, *Against Therapy*. London: Collins.

Index

Universities Psychotherapy Association
   (UPA), 110, 115

values, 13, 88
vocation, sense of, 207

welfare, of clients, 141–3
welfare capitalism, 43
Wheeler, S., 8, 96, 109, 120–33, 168,
   172

White, M., 161
Winter, R., 10, 12, 13, 14
working conditions, 184–5
writing, 8, 65, 152, 153–4, 162–4
   and professional identity, 156–8
   as a therapeutic intervention, 160–2
   as therapy for counsellors and therapists,
      183, 189–92

Zohar, D., 61